CEOE 074

OGET

Oklahoma General Education Test

Teacher Certification Exam

By: Sharon Wynne, M.S.

XAMonline, INC.

Boston

XAMonline, Inc.
25 First Street, Suite 106
Cambridge, MA 02141
Toll Free 1-800-509-4128
Email: info@xamonline.com
Web www.xamonline.com
Fax: 1-617-583-5552

Library of Congress Cataloging-in-Publication Data

Wynne, Sharon A.
      CEOE: OGET Oklahoma General Education Test 074 Teacher Certification / Sharon A. Wynne.
      ISBN:978-1-58197-798-1
      1. CEOE: OGET Oklahoma General Education Test 074   2. Study Guides.
      3. CEOE   4. Teachers' Certification & Licensure.   5. Careers

Disclaimer:
The opinions expressed in this publication are the sole works of XAMonline and were created independently from the National Education Association, Educational Testing Service, or any State Department of Education, National Evaluation Systems or other testing affiliates.

Between the time of publication and printing, state specific standards as well as testing formats and website information may change that is not included in part or in whole within this product. Sample test questions are developed by XAMonline and reflect similar content as on real tests; however, they are not former tests. XAMonline assembles content that aligns with state standards but makes no claims nor guarantees teacher candidates a passing score. Numerical scores are determined by testing companies such as NES or ETS and then are compared with individual state standards. A passing score varies from state to state.

Printed in the United States of America   œ-1

CEOE: OGET Oklahoma General Education Test 074
ISBN: 978-1-58197-798-1

Table of Contents

SUBAREA VI.   WRITING

Great Study and Testing Tips!

What to study in order to prepare for the subject assessments is the focus of this study guide but equally important is *how* you study.

You can increase your chances of truly mastering the information by taking some simple, but effective steps.

Study Tips:

1. **Some foods aid the learning process.** Foods such as milk, nuts, seeds, rice, and oats help your study efforts by releasing natural memory enhancers called CCKs (*cholecystokinin*) composed of *tryptophan*, *choline*, and *phenylalanine*. All of these chemicals enhance the neurotransmitters associated with memory. Before studying, try a light, protein-rich meal of eggs, turkey, and fish. All of these foods release the memory enhancing chemicals. The better the connections, the more you comprehend.

Likewise, before you take a test, stick to a light snack of energy boosting and relaxing foods. A glass of milk, a piece of fruit, or some peanuts all release various memory-boosting chemicals and help you to relax and focus on the subject at hand.

2. **Learn to take great notes.** A by-product of our modern culture is that we have grown accustomed to getting our information in short doses (i.e. TV news sound bites or USA Today style newspaper articles.)

Consequently, we've subconsciously trained ourselves to assimilate information better in neat little packages. If your notes are scrawled all over the paper, it fragments the flow of the information. Strive for clarity. Newspapers use a standard format to achieve clarity. Your notes can be much clearer through use of proper formatting. A very effective format is called the *"Cornell Method."*

> Take a sheet of loose-leaf lined notebook paper and draw a line all the way down the paper about 1-2" from the left-hand edge.

> Draw another line across the width of the paper about 1-2" up from the bottom. Repeat this process on the reverse side of the page.

Look at the highly effective result. You have ample room for notes, a left hand margin for special emphasis items or inserting supplementary data from the textbook, a large area at the bottom for a brief summary, and a little rectangular space for just about anything you want.

3. Get the concept then the details. Too often we focus on the details and don't gather an understanding of the concept. However, if you simply memorize only dates, places, or names, you may well miss the whole point of the subject.

A key way to understand things is to put them in your own words. If you are working from a textbook, automatically summarize each paragraph in your mind. If you are outlining text, don't simply copy the author's words.

Rephrase them in your own words. You remember your own thoughts and words much better than someone else's, and subconsciously tend to associate the important details to the core concepts.

4. Ask Why? Pull apart written material paragraph by paragraph and don't forget the captions under the illustrations.

Example: If the heading is "Stream Erosion", flip it around to read "Why do streams erode?" Then answer the questions.

If you train your mind to think in a series of questions and answers, not only will you learn more, but it also helps to lessen the test anxiety because you are used to answering questions.

5. Read for reinforcement and future needs. Even if you only have 10 minutes, put your notes or a book in your hand. Your mind is similar to a computer; you have to input data in order to have it processed. *By reading, you are creating the neural connections for future retrieval.* The more times you read something, the more you reinforce the learning of ideas.

Even if you don't fully understand something on the first pass, *your mind stores much of the material for later recall.*

6. Relax to learn so go into exile. Our bodies respond to an inner clock called biorhythms. Burning the midnight oil works well for some people, but not everyone.

If possible, set aside a particular place to study that is free of distractions. Shut off the television, cell phone, pager and exile your friends and family during your study period.

If you really are bothered by silence, try background music. Light classical music at a low volume has been shown to aid in concentration over other types. Music that evokes pleasant emotions without lyrics are highly suggested. Try just about anything by Mozart. It relaxes you.

7. **Use arrows not highlighters.** At best, it's difficult to read a page full of yellow, pink, blue, and green streaks. Try staring at a neon sign for a while and you'll soon see that the horde of colors obscure the message.

A quick note, a brief dash of color, an underline, and an arrow pointing to a particular passage is much clearer than a horde of highlighted words.

8. **Budget your study time.** Although you shouldn't ignore any of the material, *allocate your available study time in the same ratio that topics may appear on the test.*

Testing Tips:

1. **Get smart, play dumb.** **Don't read anything into the question.** Don't make an assumption that the test writer is looking for something else than what is asked. Stick to the question as written and don't read extra things into it.

2. **Read the question and all the choices _twice_ before answering the question.** You may miss something by not carefully reading, and then re-reading both the question and the answers.

If you really don't have a clue as to the right answer, leave it blank on the first time through. Go on to the other questions, as they may provide a clue as to how to answer the skipped questions.

If later on, you still can't answer the skipped ones . . . **_Guess._** The only penalty for guessing is that you _might_ get it wrong. Only one thing is certain; if you don't put anything down, you will get it wrong!

3. **Turn the question into a statement.** Look at the way the questions are worded. The syntax of the question usually provides a clue. Does it seem more familiar as a statement rather than as a question? Does it sound strange?

By turning a question into a statement, you may be able to spot if an answer sounds right, and it may also trigger memories of material you have read.

4. **Look for hidden clues.** It's actually very difficult to compose multiple-foil (choice) questions without giving away part of the answer in the options presented.

In most multiple-choice questions you can often readily eliminate one or two of the potential answers. This leaves you with only two real possibilities and automatically your odds go to Fifty-Fifty for very little work.

5. **Trust your instincts.** For every fact that you have read, you subconsciously retain something of that knowledge. On questions that you aren't really certain about, go with your basic instincts. **Your first impression on how to answer a question is usually correct.**

6. **Mark your answers directly on the test booklet.** Don't bother trying to fill in the optical scan sheet on the first pass through the test.

7. **Watch the clock!** You have a set amount of time to answer the questions. Don't get bogged down trying to answer a single question at the expense of 10 questions you can more readily answer.

COMPETENCY 1.0   IDENTIFY A WRITER'S POINT OF VIEW AND INTENDED MEANING.

Skill 1.1   Identify the statement that best expresses the main idea of a paragraph or passage.

The main idea of a passage or paragraph is the basic message, idea, point concept, or meaning that the author wants to convey to you, the reader. Understanding the main idea of a passage or paragraph is the key to understanding the more subtle components of the author's message. The main idea is what is being said about a topic or subject. Once you have identified the basic message, you will have an easier time answering other questions that test critical skills.

Main ideas are either *stated* or *implied*. A *stated main idea* is explicit: it is directly expressed in a sentence or two in the paragraph or passage. An *implied main idea* is suggested by the overall reading selection. In the first case, you need not pull information from various points in the paragraph or passage in order to form the main idea because it is already stated by the author. If a main idea is implied, however, you must formulate, in your own words, a main idea statement by condensing the overall message contained in the material itself.

Practice Question: Read the following passage, and select an answer.

Sometimes too much of a good thing can become a very bad thing indeed. In an earnest attempt to consume a healthy diet, dietary supplement enthusiasts have been known to overdose. Vitamin C, for example, long thought to help people ward off cold viruses, is currently being studied for its possible role in warding off cancer and other diseases that cause tissue degeneration. Unfortunately, an overdose of vitamin C – more than 10,000 mg – on a daily basis can cause nausea and diarrhea. Calcium supplements, commonly taken by women, are helpful in warding off osteoporosis. More than just a few grams a day, however, can lead to stomach upset and even kidney and bladder stones. Niacin, proven useful in reducing cholesterol levels, can be dangerous in large doses to those who suffer from heart problems, asthma, or ulcers.

The main idea expressed in this paragraph is:

    A.   Supplements taken in excess can be a bad thing indeed.
    B.   Dietary supplement enthusiasts have been known to overdose.
    C.   Vitamins can cause nausea, diarrhea, and kidney or bladder stones.
    D.   People who take supplements are preoccupied with their health.

Answer: Answer A is a paraphrase of the first sentence and provides a general framework for the rest of the paragraph: excess supplement intake is bad. The rest of the paragraph discusses the consequences of taking too many vitamins. Options B and C refer to major details, and Option D introduces the idea of preoccupation, which is not included in this paragraph.

Skill 1.2   Recognize ideas that support, illustrate, or elaborate the main idea of a paragraph or passage.

Supporting details are examples, facts, ideas, illustrations, cases, and anecdotes used by a writer to explain, expand on, and develop the more general main idea. A writer's choice of supporting materials is determined by the nature of the topic being covered. Supporting details are specifics that relate directly to the main idea. Writers select and shape material according to their purposes. An advertisement writer seeking to persuade the reader to buy a particular running shoe, for instance, will emphasize only the positive characteristics of the shoe for advertisement copy. A columnist for a running magazine, on the other hand, might list the good and bad points about the same shoe in an article recommending appropriate shoes for different kinds of runners. Both major details (those that directly support the main idea) and minor details (those that provide interesting, but not always essential, information) help create a well-written and fluid passage.

In the following paragraph, the sentences in **bold print** provide a skeleton of a paragraph on the benefits of recycling. The sentences in bold are generalizations that by themselves do not explain the need to recycle. The sentences in *italics* add details to SHOW the general points in bold. Notice how the supporting details help you understand the necessity for recycling.

While one day recycling may become mandatory in all states, right now it is voluntary in many communities. *Those of us who participate in recycling are amazed by how much material is recycled.* **For many communities, the blue-box recycling program has had an immediate effect.** *By just recycling glass, aluminum cans, and plastic bottles, we have reduced the volume of disposable trash by one third, thus extending the useful life of local landfills by over a decade. Imagine the difference if those dramatic results were achieved nationwide.* **The amount of reusable items we thoughtlessly dispose of is staggering.** *For example, Americans dispose of enough steel everyday to supply Detroit car manufacturers for three months. Additionally, we dispose of enough aluminum annually to rebuild the nation's air fleet. These statistics, available from the Environmental Protection Agency (EPA), should encourage all of us to watch what we throw away.* **Clearly, recycling in our homes and in our communities directly improves the environment.**

Notice how the author's supporting examples enhance the message of the paragraph and relate to the author's thesis noted above. If you only read the sentences in bold, you have a glimpse at the topic. This paragraph of illustration, however, is developed through numerous details creating specific images: *reduced the volume of disposable trash by one-third; extended the useful life of local landfills by over a decade; enough steel everyday to supply Detroit car manufacturers for three months; enough aluminum to rebuild the nation's air fleet.* If the writer had merely written a few general sentences, as those shown in bold face, you would not fully understand the vast amount of trash involved in recycling or the positive results of current recycling efforts.

Skill 1.3   Use the content, word choice, and phrasing of a passage to determine a writer's opinions or point of view (e.g., belief, position on an issue).

The **tone** of a written passage is the author's attitude toward the subject matter. The tone (mood, feeling) is revealed through the qualities of the writing itself and is a direct product of such stylistic elements as language and sentence structure. The tone of the written passage is much like a speaker's voice; instead of being spoken, however, it is the product of words on a page.

Often, writers have an emotional stake in the subject, and their purpose, either explicitly or implicitly, is to convey those feelings to the reader. In such cases, the writing is generally subjective: that is, it stems from opinions, judgments, values, ideas, and feelings. Both sentence structure (syntax) and word choice (diction) are instrumental tools in creating tone.

Tone may be thought of generally as positive, negative, or neutral. Below is a statement about snakes that demonstrates this.

> *Many species of snakes live in Florida. Some of those species, both poisonous and non-poisonous, have habitats that coincide with those of human residents of the state.*

The voice of the writer in this statement is neutral. The sentences are declarative (not exclamations or fragments or questions). The adjectives are few and nondescript—*many, some, poisonous* (balanced with *non -poisonous*). Nothing much in this brief paragraph would alert the reader to the feelings of the writer about snakes. The paragraph has a neutral, objective, detached, impartial tone.

Then again, if the writer's attitude toward snakes involves admiration or even affection, the tone would generally be positive:

> *Florida's snakes are a tenacious bunch. When they find their habitats invaded by humans, they cling to their home territories as long as they can, as if vainly attempting to fight off the onslaught of the human hordes.*

An additional message emerges in this paragraph: The writer quite clearly favors snakes over people. The writer uses adjectives like *tenacious* to describe his/her feelings about snakes. The writer also humanizes the reptiles, making them brave, beleaguered creatures. Obviously, the writer is more sympathetic to snakes than to people in this paragraph.

If the writer's attitude toward snakes involves active dislike and fear, then the tone would also reflect that attitude by being negative:

> *Countless species of snakes, some more dangerous than others, still lurk on the urban fringes of Florida's towns and cities. They will often invade domestic spaces, terrorizing people and their pets.*

Here, obviously, the snakes are the villains. They *lurk,* they *invade,* and they *terrorize.* The tone of this paragraph might be said to be distressed about snakes.

In the same manner, a writer can use language to portray characters as good or bad. A writer uses positive and negative adjectives, as seen above, to convey the manner of a character.

COMPETENCY 2.0   ANALYZE THE RELATIONSHIP AMONG IDEAS IN WRITTEN MATERIAL

Skill 2.1   Identify the sequence of events or steps presented in technical, scientific, or research material.

The ability to organize events or steps provided in a passage (especially when presented in random order) serves a useful purpose, and it encourages the development of logical thinking and the processes of analysis and evaluation.

Working through and discussing with your students examples like the one below helps students to gain valuable practice in sequencing events.

Practice Question: Identify the proper order of events or steps.

1. Matt had tied a knot in his shoelace.
2. Matt put on his green socks because they were clean and complimented the brown slacks he was wearing.
3. Matt took a bath and trimmed his toenails.
4. Matt put on his brown slacks.

Answer: The proper order of events is: 3, 4, 2, and 1

Skill 2.2   Identify cause-effect relationships from information in a passage.

A cause is the necessary source of a particular outcome. If a writer were addressing the question, "How will the new tax laws affect small businesses?" or "Why has there been such political unrest in Somalia?" he or she would use cause and effect as an organizational pattern to structure his or her response. In the first case, the writer would emphasize effects of the tax legislation as they apply to owners of small businesses. In the second, he or she would focus on the causes of the current political situation in Somalia.

Some word clues that identify a cause-effect passage are: accordingly, as a result, therefore, because, consequently, hence, in short, thus, then, due to, and so on.

Sample passage:

Simply put, inflation is an increase in price levels. It happens when a government prints more currency than is already in circulation, and there is, consequently, additional money available for the same amount of goods or services. There might be multiple reasons for a government to crank up the printing presses. A war, for instance, could cause an immediate need for steel. A national disaster might create a sudden need for social services. To get the money it needs, a government can raise taxes, borrow, or print more currency. However, raising taxes and borrowing are not always plausible options.

Analysis: The paragraph starts with a definition and proceeds to examine a causal chain. The words *consequently*, *reasons*, and *cause* provide the clues.

Explicit Cause and Effect

General Hooker failed to anticipate General Lee's bold flanking maneuver. As a result, Hooker's army was nearly routed by a smaller force.

Mindy forgot to bring the lunch her father had packed for her. Consequently, she had to borrow money from her friends at school during lunch period.

Implicit Cause and Effect

The engine in Lisa's airplane began to sputter. She quickly looked below for a field in which to land.

Luther ate the creamed shrimp that had been sitting in the sun for hours. Later that night, he was so sick he had to be rushed to the hospital.

Skill 2.3   Analyze relationships between ideas in opposition (e.g., pro and con).

Whenever there are two ideas in opposition, there is the ghost of an "either/or" conceptual basis lurking invisibly in the background of the "pro/con" setting.

For example, one person may argue that automobiles are a safer mode of transportation than are motorcycles and support that contention with statistics showing that fatalities are more frequent per accident in motorcycle crashes than in car crashes.

The opposition to this argument may counter that while fatalities are more frequent per accident in motorcycle accidents, it is erroneous to over generalize from that statistic that motorcycles are "therefore more dangerous."

Thus, each participant in the argument has assumed a position of "either or," that is to say, the automobile is "either" safer than the motorcycle, or it is not (or the motorcycle is "either" safer than the automobile or it is not). With the argument thus formulated, a conclusion acceptable to both sides is not likely to happen.

Here is a short essay showing how to avoid this deadlock.

Which is safer? The car or the motorcycle?

Most experienced drivers would agree that while it is more exhilarating to ride a motorcycle than to drive an automobile, it is illogical to therefore conclude that this exhilaration leads to careless driving and, therefore, more accidents, deaths, and injuries to motorcycle riders than car drivers. The critical concept to be understood here is not exhilaration, which is a given, but how the exhilaration comes about and is a cause of serious injury and death of motorcycle riders.

There is safe and unsafe thrill seeking. "Exhilaration" is defined as the "state of being stimulated, refreshed, or elated". An example of safe exhilaration is the excitement of sledding downhill, which results in the sled rider feeling stimulated, refreshed, and/or elated.

Unsafe exhilaration, which is usually the consequence of reckless thrill seeking, is therefore a state of being over-stimulated, frightened, and depressed by terror.

Which then causes more dangerous exhilaration, the car or the motorcycle? The answer is that the two forms of exhilaration are the consequents not of the motorcycle or the automobile, per se, but of the operation of the respective vehicles. Without an operator, both vehicles are metal entities, sitting in space, neither threatening nor harmful to anyone.

Therefore, neither the motorcycle nor the car is more or less dangerous than one another: it is the attitude of their operators that creates the danger, death, and dismemberment resultant from accidents.

Notice how the writer has avoided the logical trap of the "either/or" construction built into the "pro/con" argument by defining the key term "exhilaration" to clarify the issue (and shift the focus to the operator) and to resolve the either/or dilemma by arguing that it is the operators of the vehicles who are responsible for negative consequences, not the vehicles themselves.

Skill 2.4   Identify a solution to a problem presented in a passage.

Within the assessment of reading, working with more than one selection is important in deciding if students can make generalizations. Utilizing the information read to find the answer to a situation presented is the skill. Sometimes this may involve problems specifically identified within what was read. For example, the characters in the story may be having a specific problem, such as a lack of money. Then, as you continue to read the passage, the characters in the story were hired for a new job, which allowed them to earn more money. Using the information read, identify the problem (a lack of money) and the solution (a new job).

In other cases, generalizations will need to be made across multiple selections. In those cases, selecting problems and solutions may be more evasive. Problems and solutions across texts will require broader thinking. The problems and solutions will not be as clearly spelled out in the text. It will involve you thinking on a different level about how the two passages relate. Connecting texts to other texts and finding common elements within them allows you to then draw out the common problems and solutions. Working through multiple selections requires more complex thinking skills and thinking of problems and solutions sometimes in other terms. Perhaps thinking of the challenge or issue that was faced and how that issue was overcome would help to broaden the scope and understanding of identifying the common problem and therefore the solution.

Skill 2.5   Draw conclusions inductively and deductively from information stated or implied in a passage.

An **inference** is sometimes called an "educated guess" because it requires that you go beyond the strictly obvious to create additional meaning by taking the text one logical step further. Inferences and conclusions are based on the content of the passage – that is, on what the passage says or how the writer says it – and are derived by reasoning.

Inference is an essential and automatic component of most reading. For example, readers make educated guesses about the meaning of unknown words, the author's main idea, or whether he or she is writing with a bias. Such is the essence of inference: you use your own ability to reason in order to figure out what the writer implies. As a reader, then, you must often logically extend meaning that is only implied.

Consider the following example. Assume you are an employer, and you are reading over the letters of reference submitted by a prospective employee for the position of clerk/typist in your real estate office. The position requires the applicant to be neat, careful, trustworthy, and punctual. You come across this letter of reference submitted by an applicant:

To Whom It May Concern:

Todd Finley has asked me to write a letter of reference for him. I am well qualified to do so because he worked for me for three months last year. His duties included answering the phone, greeting the public, and producing some simple memos and notices on the computer. Although Todd initially had few computer skills and little knowledge of telephone etiquette, he did acquire some during his stay with us. Todd's manner of speaking, both on the telephone and with the clients who came to my establishment, could be described as casual. He was particularly effective when communicating with peers. Please contact me by telephone if you wish to have further information about my experience with Todd.

Here, the writer implies, rather than openly states, the main idea. This letter calls attention to itself because there's a problem with its tone. A truly positive letter would say something like, "I have the distinct honor of recommending Todd Finley." Here, however, the letter simply verifies that Todd worked in the office. Second, the praise is obviously lukewarm. For example, the writer says that Todd "was particularly effective when communicating with peers." An educated guess translates that statement into a nice way of saying Todd was not serious about his communication with clients.

COMPETENCY 3.0   USE CRITICAL REASONING SKILLS TO EVALUATE WRITTEN MATERIAL.

Skill 3.1   Draw valid conclusions using information from written communications.

In order to draw **inferences** and make **conclusions**, a reader must use prior knowledge and apply it to the current situation. A conclusion or inference is never stated. You must rely on your common sense.

Practice Questions: Read the following passages and select an answer.

1.   The Smith family waited patiently around carousel number 7 for their luggage to arrive. They were exhausted after their 5-hour trip and were anxious to get to their hotel. After about an hour, they realized that they no longer recognized any of the other passengers' faces. Mrs. Smith asked the person who appeared to be in charge if they were at the right carousel. The man replied, "Yes, this is it, but we finished unloading that baggage almost half an hour ago."

From the man's response we can infer that:

(A) The Smiths were ready to go to their hotel.
(B) The Smith's luggage was lost.
(C) The man had their luggage.
(D) They were at the wrong carousel.

2.   Tim Sullivan had just turned 15. As a birthday present, his parents had given him a guitar and a certificate for 10 guitar lessons. He had always shown a love of music and a desire to learn an instrument. Tim began his lessons, and before long, he was making up his own songs. At the music studio, Tim met Josh, who played the piano, and Roger, whose instrument was the saxophone. They all shared the same dream, to start a band, and each was praised by his teacher as having real talent.

From this passage one can infer that:

(A) Tim, Roger, and Josh are going to start their own band.
(B) Tim is going to give up his guitar lessons.
(C) Tim, Josh, and Roger will no longer be friends.
(D) Josh and Roger are going to start their own band.

Answers:

1. Since the Smiths were still waiting for their luggage, we know that they were not yet ready to go to their hotel. From the man's response, we know that they were not at the wrong carousel and that he did not have their luggage. Therefore, though not directly stated, it appears that their luggage was lost. Choice (B) is the correct answer.

2. (A) is the correct choice. Given the facts that Tim wanted to be a musician and start his own band, after meeting others who shared the same dreams, we can infer that they joined together in an attempt to make their dreams become a reality.

Skill 3.2   Evaluate the stated or implied assumptions on which the validity of a writer's argument depends.

On the test, the terms **valid** and **invalid** have special meaning. If an argument is valid, it is reasonable. It is objective (not biased) and can be supported by evidence. If an argument is invalid, it is not reasonable. It is not objective. In other words, one can find evidence of bias.

Practice Questions: Read the following passages, and select an answer.

1.   Most dentists agree that Bright Smile Toothpaste is the best for fighting cavities. It tastes good and leaves your mouth minty fresh.

        Is this a valid or invalid argument?

        (A) valid
        (B) invalid

2.   It is difficult to decide who will make the best presidential candidate, Senator Johnson or Senator Keeley. They have both been involved in scandals and have both gone through messy divorces while in office.

        Is this argument valid or invalid?

        (A) valid
        (B) invalid

Answers:

1. It is invalid B. It mentions that "most" dentists agree. What about those who do not agree? The author is clearly exhibiting bias in leaving those who disagree out.

2. A. is the correct choice. The author appears to be listing facts. He does not seem to favor one candidate over the other.

Skill 3.3   Determine the relevance or importance of particular facts, examples, or graphic data to a writer's argument.

It is important to continually assess whether or not a sentence contributes to the overall task of supporting the main idea. When a sentence is deemed irrelevant, it is best to either omit it from the passage or to make it relevant by one of the following strategies:

1. Adding detail – Sometimes a sentence can seem out of place if it does not contain enough information to link it to the topic. Adding specific information can show how the sentence is related to the main idea.

2. Adding an example – This is especially important in passages in which information is being argued or compared or contrasted. Examples can support the main idea and give the document overall credibility.

3. Using diction effectively – It is important to understand connotation, avoid ambiguity, and steer clear of too much repetition when selecting words.

4. Adding transitions – Transitions are extremely helpful for making sentences relevant because they are specifically designed to connect one idea to another. They can also reduce a paragraph's choppiness.

Skill 3.4 Use inductive and deductive reasoning to recognize fallacies in the logic of a writer's argument.

An argument is a generalization that is proven or supported with facts. If the facts are not accurate, the generalization remains unproven. Using inaccurate "facts" to support an argument is called a *fallacy* in reasoning. Some factors to consider in judging whether the facts used to support an argument are accurate are as follow:

1. Are the facts current or are they out of date? For example, if the proposition, "Birth defects in babies born to drug-using mothers are increasing," then the data must include the latest that is available.
2. Another important factor to consider in judging the accuracy of a fact is its source. Where was the data obtained, and is that source reliable?
3. The calculations on which the facts are based may be unreliable. It's a good idea to run one's own calculations before using a piece of derived information.

Even facts that are true and have a sharp impact on the argument may not be relevant to the case at hand.

1. Health statistics from an entire state may have no relevance, or little relevance, to a particular county or zip code. Statistics from an entire country cannot be used to prove very much about a particular state or county.
2. An analogy can be useful in making a point, but the comparison must match up in all characteristics, or it will not be relevant. Analogy should be used very carefully. It is often just as likely to destroy an argument as it is to strengthen it.

The importance or significance of a fact may not be sufficient to strengthen an argument. For example, of the millions of immigrants in the U.S., using a single family to support a solution to the immigration problem will not make much difference overall even though those single-example arguments are often used to support one approach or another. They may achieve a positive reaction, but they will not prove that one solution is better than another. If enough cases were cited from a variety of geographical locations, the information might be significant.

How much is enough? Generally speaking, three strong supporting facts are sufficient to establish the thesis of an argument. For example:

Conclusion: All green apples are sour.

- When I was a child, I bit into a green apple from my grandfather's orchard, and it was sour.
- I once bought green apples from a roadside vendor, and when I bit into one, it was sour.
- My grocery store had a sale on green Granny Smith apples last week, and I bought several, only to find that they were sour when I bit into one.

The fallacy in the above argument is that the sample was insufficient. A more exhaustive search of literature, etc., will probably turn up some green apples that are not sour.

Sometimes more than three arguments are too many. On the other hand, it's not unusual to hear public speakers, particularly politicians, who will cite a long litany of facts to support their positions.

A very good example of the omission of facts in an argument is the résumé of an applicant for a job. The applicant is arguing that he/she should be chosen to be awarded a particular job. The application form will ask for information about past employment, and unfavorable dismissals from jobs in the past may just be omitted. Employers are usually suspicious of periods of time when the applicant has not listed an employer.

A writer makes choices about which facts will be used and which will be discarded in developing an argument. Those choices may exclude anything that is not supportive of the point of view the arguer is taking. It's always a good idea for the reader to do some research to spot the omissions and to ask whether they have an impact on the acceptance of the point of view presented in the argument.

No judgment is either black or white. If the argument seems too neat or too compelling, there are probably facts that might be relevant that have not been included.

Skill 3.5   Evaluate the validity of analogies used in written material.

An argument by analogy states that if two things have one thing in common, they probably have other things in common. For example, peaches and plums are both fruits that have chemicals good for people to eat. Both peaches and plums are circular in shape; thus, it could be argued by analogy that "because" something is circular in shape, it is fruit and something good for people to eat. However, this analogical deduction is not logical (For example, a baseball is circular in shape but hardly good to eat.).

An analogy is a comparison of the likenesses of two things. The danger of arguing by analogy rests in a failure to correctly perceive the limitations of the likenesses between the two things compared. Because something is like something else does not make it the same as the compared object or, for that matter, put it in the same class as the original object.

For example, a false argument based on analogical thinking could go like this: "Blake and Blunder are both democrats. Both are married. Both have three children, a dog, and a kitten at home. Therefore, it is likely they will both vote the same way about the school mileage proposal because of their similarities."

This is a false argument by analogy; while the likenesses cited are somewhat striking, these are only likenesses coincidental in nature, and not compelling causative roots predictive of behaviors.

However, perceiving the analogical relationship between two things or phenomena is often also the starting point for scientific investigations of reality, and such perceptions are the subjects of a host of scientific theories (i.e., the work of Charles Darwin) and investigations (i.e., "wave/particle" theories in quantum physics). Such analogical relations require austere scrutiny and analysis, and without such, are essentially meaningless or the stuff of poetic comparisons ("To see the world in a grain of sand"-William Blake).

Thinking in analogies is the way we all began as children to perceive the world and to sort it into categories of "good and bad" (e.g., "Water is a liquid that is good for me; hot oil is a liquid that is bad for me."). Mature writers and thinkers discriminate carefully between all elements of an argument by analogy.

Skill 3.6   Distinguish between fact and opinion in written material.

Facts are statements that are verifiable. Opinions are statements that must be supported in order to be accepted, such as beliefs, values, judgments, or feelings. Facts are objective statements used to support subjective opinions. For example, "Jane is a bad girl" is an opinion. However, "Jane hit her sister with a baseball bat" is a *fact* upon which the opinion is based. Judgments are opinions—decisions or declarations based on observation or reasoning that express approval or disapproval. Facts report what has happened or exists and come from observation, measurement, or calculation. Facts can be tested and verified, whereas opinions and judgments cannot. They can only be supported with facts.

Most statements cannot be so clearly distinguished. "I believe that Jane is a bad girl" is a fact. The speaker knows what he/she believes. However, it obviously includes a judgment that could be disputed by another person who might believe otherwise. Judgments are not usually so firm. They are, rather, plausible opinions that provoke thought or lead to factual development.

Joe DiMaggio, a Yankees' center-fielder, was replaced by Mickey Mantle in 1952.

This is a fact. If necessary, evidence can be produced to support this.

First year players are more ambitious than seasoned players.

This is an opinion. There is no proof to support that everyone feels this way

Practice Questions: Decide if the statement is fact or opinion.

1. The Inca were a group of Indians who ruled an empire in South America.

   (A) fact
   (B) opinion

2. The Inca were clever.

   (A) fact
   (B) opinion

3. The Inca built very complex systems of bridges.

   (A) fact
   (B) opinion

Answers:

1. A. is the correct answer. Research can prove this to be true.
2. B. is the correct answer. It is doubtful that all people who have studied the Inca agree with this statement. Therefore, no proof is available.
3. A. is the correct answer. As with question number one, research can prove this to be true.

Skill 3.7   Assess the credibility, objectivity, or bias of the writer or source of written material.

Bias is defined as an opinion, feeling, or influence that strongly favors one side in an argument. A statement or passage is biased if an author attempts to convince a reader of something.

Is there evidence of bias in the following statement?

> *Using a calculator cannot help a student understand the process of graphing, so its use is a waste of time.*

Since the author makes it perfectly clear that he does not favor the use of the calculator in graphing problems, the answer is yes, there is evidence of bias. He has included his opinion in this statement.

Practice Question: Read the following paragraph, and select an answer.

> There are teachers who feel that computer programs are quite helpful in helping students grasp certain math concepts. There are also those who disagree with this feeling. It is up to each individual math teacher to decide if computer programs benefit her particular group of students.
>
> Is there evidence of bias in this paragraph?
>
> (A) yes
> (B) no

Answer:

B. is the correct answer. The author seems to state both sides of the argument without favoring a particular side.

The sky is blue," and "The sky looks like rain," one a fact and the other an opinion. This is because one is **readily provable by objective empirical data**, while the other is a **subjective evaluation based upon personal bias**. This means that facts are things that can be proved by the usual means of study and experimentation. We can look and see the color of the sky. Since the shade we are observing is expressed as the color blue and is an accepted norm, the observation that the sky is blue is therefore a fact. (Of course, this depends on other external factors such as time and weather conditions).

This brings us to our next idea: that it looks like rain. This is a subjective observation, in that an individual's perception will differ from another. What looks like rain to one person will not necessarily look like that to another person. The question thus remains as to how to differentiate fact from opinion. The best and only way is to ask oneself if what is being stated can be proved from other sources, by other methods, or by the simple process of **reasoning**.

Primary and secondary sources

The resources used to support a piece of writing can be divided into two major groups: primary sources and secondary sources.

Primary sources are works, records, etc. that were created during the period being studied or immediately after it. Secondary sources are works written significantly after the period being studied and based upon primary sources. Primary sources are the basic materials that provide raw data and information. Secondary sources are the works that contain the explications of, and judgments on, this primary material.

Primary sources include the following kinds of materials:

- Documents that reflect the immediate, everyday concerns of people: memoranda, bills, deeds, charters, newspaper reports, pamphlets, graffiti, popular writings, journals or diaries, records of decision-making bodies, letters, receipts, snapshots, etc.
- Theoretical writings which reflect care and consideration in composition and an attempt to convince or persuade. The topic will generally be deeper and more pervasive than is the case with "immediate" documents. These may include newspaper or magazine editorials, sermons, political speeches, philosophical writings, etc.
- Narrative accounts of events, ideas, trends, etc. written with intentionality by someone contemporary with the events described.
- Statistical data, although statistics may be misleading.
- Literature and nonverbal materials, novels, stories, poetry and essays from the period, as well as coins, archaeological artifacts, and art produced during the period.

Secondary sources include the following kinds of materials:

- Books written on the basis of primary materials about the period of time.
- Books written on the basis of primary materials about persons who played a major role in the events under consideration.
- Books and articles written on the basis of primary materials about the culture, the social norms, the language, and the values of the period.
- Quotations from primary sources.
- Statistical data on the period.
- The conclusions and inferences of other historians.
- Multiple interpretations of the ethos of the time.

Guidelines for the use of secondary sources:

1. Do not rely upon only a single secondary source.
2. Check facts and interpretations against primary sources whenever possible.
3. Do not accept the conclusions of other historians uncritically.
4. Place greatest reliance on secondary sources created by the best and most respected scholars.
5. Do not use the inferences of other scholars as if they were facts.
6. Ensure that you recognize any bias the writer brings to his/her interpretation of history.
7. Understand the primary point of the book as a basis for evaluating the value of the material presented in it to your questions.

COMPETENCY 4.0   RECOGNIZE THE ROLES OF PURPOSE AND AUDIENCE IN WRITTEN COMMUNICATION.

Skill 4.1   Recognize a writer's stated or implied purpose for writing (e.g., to persuade, to describe).

An essay is an extended discussion of a writer's point of view about a particular topic. This point of view may be supported by using such writing modes as examples, argument and persuasion, analysis, or comparison/contrast. In any case, a good essay is clear, coherent, well organized, and fully developed.

When an author sets out to write a passage, he/she usually has a purpose for doing so. That purpose may be to simply give information that might be interesting or useful to some reader or other; it may be to persuade the reader to a point of view or to move the reader to act in a particular way; it may be to tell a story; or it may be to describe something in such a way that an experience becomes available to the reader through one of the five senses. Following are the primary devices for expressing a particular purpose in a piece of writing:

- **Basic expository writing** simply gives information not previously known about a topic or is used to explain or define one. Facts, examples, statistics, cause and effect, direct tone, objective rather than subjective delivery, and non-emotional information are presented in a formal manner.

- **Descriptive writing** centers on a person, place, or object, using concrete and sensory words to create a mood or impression and arranging details in a chronological or spatial sequence.

- **Narrative writing** is developed using an incident or anecdote or related series of events. Chronology, the 5 W's, topic sentence, and conclusion are essential ingredients.

- **Persuasive writing** implies the writer's ability to select vocabulary and arrange facts and opinions in such a way as to direct the actions of the listener/reader. Persuasive writing may incorporate exposition and narration as they illustrate the main idea.

- **Journalistic writing** is theoretically free of author bias. It is essential when relaying information about an event, person, or thing that it be factual and objective. Provide students with an opportunity to examine newspapers and create their own. Many newspapers have educational programs that are offered free to schools.

Skill 4.2   Evaluate the appropriateness of written material for a specific purpose or audience.

Tailoring language for a particular **audience** is an important skill. Writing to be read by a business associate will surely sound different from writing to be read by a younger sibling. Not only are the vocabularies different, but the formality/informality of the discourse will also need to be adjusted.

Determining what the language should be for a particular audience, then, hinges on two things: **word choice** and **formality/informality**. The most formal language does not use contractions or slang. The most informal language will probably feature a more casual use of common sayings and anecdotes. Formal language will use longer sentences and will not sound like a conversation. The most informal language will use shorter sentences—not necessarily simple sentences—but shorter constructions and may sound like a conversation.

In both formal and informal writing, there exists a **tone**, the writer's attitude toward the material and/or readers. Tone may be playful, formal, intimate, angry, serious, ironic, outraged, baffled, tender, serene, depressed, etc. The overall tone of a piece of writing is dictated by both the subject matter and the audience. Tone is also related to the actual words that make up the document, as we attach affective meanings to words, called **connotations**. Gaining this conscious control over language makes it possible to use language appropriately in various situations and to evaluate its uses in literature and other forms of communication. By evoking the proper responses from readers/listeners, we can prompt them to take action.

The following questions are an excellent way to assess the audience and tone of a given piece of writing.

1. Who is your audience? (friend, teacher, business person, someone else)
2. How much does this person know about you and/or your topic?
3. What is your purpose? (to prove an argument, to persuade, to amuse, to register a complaint, to ask for a raise, etc.)
4. What emotions do you have about the topic? (nervous, happy, confident, angry, sad, no feelings at all)
5. What emotions do you want to register with your audience? (anger, nervousness, happiness, boredom, interest)
6. What persona do you need to create in order to achieve your purpose?
7. What choice of language is best suited to achieving your purpose with your particular subject? (slang, friendly but respectful, formal)
8. What emotional quality do you want to transmit to achieve your purpose (matter of fact, informative, authoritative, inquisitive, sympathetic, angry) And to what degree do you want to express this tone?

Skill 4.3   **Recognize the likely effect on an audience of a writer's choice of a particular word or words (e.g., to evoke sympathy, to undermine an opposing point of view).**

See Skill 4.2.

COMPETENCY 5.0   RECOGNIZE UNITY, FOCUS, AND DEVELOPMENT IN WRITING.

Skill 5.1   Recognize unnecessary shifts in point of view (e.g., shifts from first to third person) or distracting details that impair the development of the main idea in a piece of writing.

Point of view defines the focus a writer assumes in relation to a given topic. It is extremely important to maintain a consistent point of view in order to create coherent paragraphs. Point of view is related to matters of person, tense, tone, and number.

Person – A shift in the form that indicates whether a person is speaking (first), is being spoken to (second), or is being spoken about (third) can disrupt continuity of a passage. In your essay, it is recommended that you write in the third person, as it is often considered to be the most formal of the modes of person. If you do decide to use the more informal first or second person (I, you, we) in your essay, be careful not to shift between first, second, and third persons from sentence to sentence or paragraph to paragraph.

Tense – Verb tenses indicate the time of an action or state of being – the past, present, or future. It is important to largely stick to a selected tense, though this may not always be the case. For instance, in an essay about the history of environmental protection, it might be necessary to include a paragraph about the future benefits or consequences of protecting the earth.

Tone – The tone of an essay varies greatly with the purpose, subject, and audience. It is best to assume a formal tone for this essay. (See Domain II, Skill 2.3.)

Number – Words change when their meanings are singular or plural. Make sure that you do not shift number needlessly; if a meaning is singular in one sentence, do not make it plural in the subsequent sentence.

Skill 5.2   Recognize revisions that improve the unity and focus of a piece of writing.

Most students want to write one draft of their writing and then be finished with it. It takes years of practice to reinforce the idea that they need to revise the writing by elaborating on the words to bring clarity to the topic. Elaboration is the detail or description that brings the characters, places, and events in the writing to life. Students need instruction and modeling on how they can add words, reorder sentences or phrases, make good transitions from one paragraph to the next, and take out unnecessary information.

One of the best ways to model this craft of good writing is to read from descriptive books and point out how the author uses words that help the readers see what the author wants them to see. Students also need exemplars of good writing for comparison with their own writing. This gives them models to go by as they craft their own pieces.

Transition words and phrases help deliver clear connections between the sentences so that the writing flows smoothly. Teachers can introduce this in a mini-lesson and then follow up by working with small groups of students who need extra help. A poster displaying a list of transition words in the classroom gives the students a reference they can use when revising their writing. Common transition words and phrases include:

- Besides
- Furthermore
- Therefore
- In addition to
- As a result
- First
- Next
- Moreover
- In order to
- However
- Although
- Meanwhile

Early writers often overuse the word "then" and use it to start every paragraph. Another problem that early writers have is that they connect every sentence with the word "and" so that each paragraph consists of one long sentence. Teachers should use models of poor writing to demonstrate how students can improve their writing.

A list of ways students can include elaboration in their writing is:

- Add details about a person, place, or event
- Use vocabulary to paint a picture
- Tell how something feels, tastes, smells, sounds or looks
- Make a comparison between two things
- Use the exact words of a character

Writers need to see the difference between vague and specific writing. A good way of describing vague writing is comparing it to the bones of a skeleton. When writers add details or specific word choices, then they add meat to the bones. By reading two separate pieces of writing to students – one that is vague and one that is specific – students can determine which piece was best. The teacher can then dissect each one to show how the revision helped improve the writing.

Skill 5.3   Recognize examples of well-developed writing.

Sample Prompt and Well-Written Response:

Written on July 15, 1944, three weeks before the Frank family was arrested by the Nazis, Anne's diary entry explains her worldview and future hopes.

It's difficult in times like these: ideals, dreams, and cherished hopes rise within us, only to be crushed by grim reality. It's a wonder I haven't abandoned all my ideals; they seem so absurd and impractical. Yet I cling to them because I still believe, in spite of everything, that people are truly good at heart.

It's utterly impossible for me to build my life on a foundation of chaos, suffering, and death. I see the world being slowly transformed into a wilderness, I hear the approaching thunder that, one day, will destroy us too, I feel the suffering of millions, and yet, when I look up at the sky, I somehow feel that everything will change for the better, that this cruelty too shall end, that peace and tranquility will return once more. In the meantime, I must hold on to my ideals. Perhaps the day will come when I will be able to realize them!

Using your knowledge of literature, write a response in which you:

- Compare and contrast Anne's ideals with her awareness of the conditions in which she lives; and
- Discuss how the structure of Anne's writing—her sentences and paragraphs—emphasize the above contrast.

Sample Response

This excerpt from The Diary of Anne Frank reveals the inner strength of a young girl who refuses, despite the wartime violence and danger surrounding her, to let her idealism be overcome by hatred and mass killing. This idealism is reflected, in part, by her emphases on universal human hopes, such as peace, tranquility, and goodwill. But Anne Frank is no dreamy Pollyanna. Reflecting on her idealism in the context of the war raging around her, she matter-of-factly writes: "My dreams, they seem so absurd and impractical."

This indicates Anne Frank's awareness of not only her own predicament, but of human miseries that extend beyond the immediate circumstances of her life. For elsewhere, she writes in a similar vein, "In times like these... I see the world being slowly transformed into a wilderness;" despite her own suffering, she can "feel the suffering of millions."

And yet Anne Frank believes, "In spite of everything, that people are truly good at heart." This statement epitomizes the stark existential contrast of her worldview with the wartime reality that ultimately claimed her life.

The statement also exemplifies how Anne's literary form—her syntax and diction—mirror thematic content and contrasts. "In spite of everything," she still believes in people. She can "hear the approaching thunder...yet, when I look up at the sky, I somehow feel that everything will change for the better." At numerous points in this diary entry, first-hand knowledge of violent tragedy stands side-by-side with belief in humanity and human progress.

"I must hold on to my ideals," Anne concludes. "Perhaps the day will come when I'll be able to realize them!" In her diary, she has done so, and more.

COMPETENCY 6.0   RECOGNIZE EFFECTIVE ORGANIZATION IN WRITING

Skill 6.1   Recognize methods of paragraph organization.

The **organization** of a written work includes two factors: the order in which the writer has chosen to present the different parts of the discussion or argument and the relationships he or she constructs between these parts.

Written ideas need to be presented in a **logical order** so that a reader can follow the information easily and quickly. There are many different ways to order a series of ideas, but they all share one thing in common: to lead the reader along a desired path, while avoiding backtracking and skipping around, in order to give a clear, strong presentation of the writer's main idea. The following are *some* of the ways in which a paragraph may be organized:

Sequence of events – In this type of organization, the details are presented in the order in which they have occurred. Paragraphs that describe a process or procedure, give directions, or outline a given period of time (such as a day or a month) are often arranged chronologically.

Statement support – In this type of organization, the main idea is stated, and the rest of the paragraph explains or proves it. This is also referred to as relative importance. There are four ways in which this type of order is organized: most to least, least to most, most-least-most, and least-most-least.

Comparison-Contrast – The compare-contrast pattern is used when a paragraph describes the differences or similarities of two or more ideas, actions, events, or things. Usually, the topic sentence describes the basic relationship between the ideas or items, and the rest of the paragraph explains this relationship.

Classification – In this type of organization, the paragraph presents grouped information about a topic. The topic sentence usually states the general category, and the rest of the sentences show how various elements of the category have a common base and also how they differ from the common base.

Cause and Effect – This pattern describes how two or more events are connected. The main sentence usually states the primary cause(s) and the primary effect(s) and how they are basically connected. The rest of the sentences explain the connection – how one event caused the next.

Spatial/Place – In this type of organization, certain descriptions are organized according to the location of items in relation to each other and to a larger context. The orderly arrangement guides the reader's eye as he or she mentally envisions the scene or place being described.

Skill 6.2   Reorganize sentences to improve cohesion and the effective sequence of ideas.

The following passage has several irrelevant sentences that are highlighted in bold:

The New City Planning Committee is proposing a new capitol building to represent the multicultural face of New City. **The current mayor is a Democrat.** The new capitol building will be on 10th street across from the grocery store and next to the Recreational Center. It will be within walking distance to the subway and bus depot, as the designers want to emphasize the importance of public transportation. Aesthetically, the building will have a contemporary design, featuring a brushed-steel exterior and large, floor-to-ceiling windows. **It is important for employees to have a connection with the outside world even when they are in their offices.** Inside the building, the walls will be moveable. This will not only facilitate a multitude of creative floor plans, but it will also create a focus on open communication and flow of information. **It sounds a bit gimmicky to me.** Finally, the capitol will feature a large outdoor courtyard full of lush greenery and serene fountains. **Work will now seem like Club Med to those who work at the New City capitol!**

Skill 6.3   Recognize the appropriate use of transitional words or phrases to convey text structure (e.g., however, therefore).

Even if the sentences that make up a given paragraph or passage are arranged in logical order, the document as a whole can still seem choppy, the various ideas disconnected. **Transitions**, words that signal relationships between ideas, can help improve the flow of a document. Transitions can help achieve clear and effective presentation of information by establishing connections between sentences, paragraphs, and sections of a document. With transitions, each sentence builds on the ideas in the last, and each paragraph has clear links to the preceding one. As a result, the reader receives clear directions on how to piece together the writer's ideas in a logically coherent argument. By signaling how to organize, interpret, and react to information, transitions allow a writer to effectively and elegantly explain his or her ideas.

Logical Relationship	Transitional Expression
Similarity	also, in the same way, just as ... so too, likewise, similarly
Exception/Contrast	but, however, in spite of, on the one hand ... on the other hand, nevertheless, nonetheless, notwithstanding, in contrast, on the contrary, still, yet
Sequence/Order	first, second, third, ... next, then, finally
Time	after, afterward, at last, before, currently, during, earlier, immediately, later, meanwhile, now, recently, simultaneously, subsequently, then
Example	for example, for instance, namely, specifically, to illustrate
Emphasis	even, indeed, in fact, of course, truly
Place/Position	above, adjacent, below, beyond, here, in front, in back, nearby, there
Cause and Effect	accordingly, consequently, hence, so, therefore, thus
Additional Support or Evidence	additionally, again, also, and, as well, besides, equally important, further, furthermore, in addition, moreover, then
Conclusion/Summary	finally, in a word, in brief, in conclusion, in the end, in the final analysis, on the whole, thus, to conclude, to summarize, in sum, in summary

The following example shows good logical order and transitions, with the transition words being highlighted:

No one really knows how Valentine's Day started. There are several legends, **however**, which are often told. The **first** attributes Valentine's Day to a Christian priest who lived in Rome during the third century, under the rule of Emperor Claudius. Rome was at war, and **apparently** Claudius felt that married men didn't fight as well as bachelors. **Consequently**, Claudius banned marriage for the duration of the war. **But** Valentinus, the priest, risked his life to secretly marry couples in violation of Claudius' law. The **second** legend is **even more** romantic. **In this story**, Valentinus is a prisoner, having been condemned to death for refusing to worship pagan deities. **While** in jail, he fell in love with his jailer's daughter, who happened to be blind. Daily, he prayed for her sight to return, and miraculously it did. On February 14, the day that he was condemned to die, he was allowed to write the young woman a note. **In this farewell letter**, he promised eternal love, and signed at the bottom of the page the now famous words, "Your Valentine."

COMPETENCY 7.0 RECOGNIZE SENTENCES THAT EFFECTIVELY COMMUNICATE INTENDED MESSAGES.

Skill 7.1 Recognize ineffective repetition and inefficiency in sentence construction.

Wordiness

These items occur in passages of 45 words or less with five underlined choices. The passages contain irrelevant, repetitive, and/or wordy expressions. This section requires you to choose the word or word group that is unnecessary to the context without affecting the overall meaning of the passage. The other word options all serve a function in the passages. Choose the underlined portion that is unnecessary within the context of the passage.

1) Some children decide to <u>actively</u> participate in <u>extracurricular</u> activities, like after-school sports and <u>various</u> clubs. Many teachers and administrators <u>willingly</u> volunteer to supervise the children during their <u>spare</u> time.

    A) actively
    B) extracurricular
    C) various
    D) willingly
    E) spare

2) Our high-school reunion, which was being held for the first time at the <u>swanky</u> Boca Hilton, is known for its elegance and <u>glamour</u>. We arrived in a <u>long</u> stretch limo and prepared to dance and have a good time <u>reminiscing</u> with our <u>dear</u> friends.

    A) swanky
    B) glamour
    C) long
    D) reminiscing
    E) dear

3) Once we reached <u>the top of</u> the mountain, a <u>powerful</u> storm came from <u>out of</u> nowhere, bringing rain and <u>large</u> hailstones from the dark <u>black</u> skies above.

    A) the top of
    B) powerful
    C) out of
    D) large
    E) black

4) Policemen often undergo a rigorous <u>harsh</u> training period to <u>adequately</u> prepare them for the <u>intense</u> dangers and stresses of the job. <u>Only</u> the most physically fit candidates are capable of handling the challenges of dealing with the <u>criminal</u> elements of our society.

A) harsh
B) adequately
C) intense
D) Only
E) criminal

5) The <u>early morning</u> hurricane struck at dawn, knocking out power lines and <u>ripping the roofs</u> from buildings <u>all</u> throughout Broward County. <u>Massive</u> winds and rain wreaked havoc, as terrified residents ran <u>madly</u> for shelter and safety.

A) early morning
B) ripping the roofs from
C) all
D) Massive
E) madly

6) Alan's alcoholism affected the entire family <u>very deeply</u>. When his father asked <u>him to</u> stop drinking, he <u>refused and</u> drove off in his sister's car, which crashed into a utility pole. <u>Fortunately</u>, Alan miraculously survived and now is undergoing intensive treatment in a top-notch facility <u>that is well-regarded</u>.

A) very deeply
B) him to
C) refused and
D) Fortunately
E) that is well-regarded

7) Soap operas are popular among <u>many</u> television viewers because of their ability to <u>blend</u> real issues like drug abuse, infidelity, and AIDS, <u>with melodramatic plots</u> concerning lust, greed, vanity, and revenge. <u>These shows</u> often have very devoted followings among viewers, who watch them <u>faithfully</u> every day.

A) many
B) blend
C) with melodramatic plots
D) These
E) faithfully

8) Walt Disney World <u>is one of</u> the most visited tourist attractions in the United States. Its success <u>and prosperity</u> can be attributed to the <u>blend of</u> childhood fantasy and adult imagination. The park features rides and <u>attractions</u> that hold considerable appeal for <u>both</u> children and adults.

A) is one of
B) and prosperity
C) blend of
D) attractions
E) both

9) Jason was the best <u>baseball</u> player on the Delray Beach High School baseball team; in fact, he was known as the star <u>of the team</u>. He could play several positions on the field <u>with enthusiasm and skill</u>, but his strength was hitting balls <u>out of the park</u>. When Jason was at the plate, the coach expected him to score a home run <u>every time</u>.

A) baseball
B) of the team
C) with enthusiasm and skill
D) out of the park
E) every time

10) Many of the major cities in the United States are grappling with <u>a variety of</u> problems, such as crime, crumbling roadways, a shortage of <u>funding for</u> schools and health care, and a lack of jobs. There are <u>no easy</u> solutions to these problems, but mayors who have <u>strong</u> leadership abilities <u>work to</u> create good ideas to deal with them.

A) a variety of
B) funding for
C) no easy
D) strong
E) work to

ANSWERS: 1) D, 2) A, 3)E, 4) A, 5) A, 6) E, 7) E, 8) B, 9) A, 10) E

Sentence structure

Recognize simple, compound, complex, and compound-complex sentences. Use dependent (subordinate) and independent clauses correctly to create these sentence structures.

Simple – Consists of one independent clause.
> Joyce wrote a letter.

Compound – Consists of two or more independent clauses. The two clauses are usually connected by a coordinating conjunction (and, but, or, nor, for, so, yet). Compound sentences are sometimes connected by semicolons.
> Joyce wrote a letter, and Dot drew a picture.

Complex – Consists of an independent clause plus one or more dependent clauses. The dependent clause may precede the independent clause or follow it.
> While Joyce wrote a letter, Dot drew a picture.

Compound/Complex – Consists of one or more dependent clauses plus two or more independent clauses.
> When Mother asked the girls to demonstrate their newfound skills, Joyce wrote a letter, and Dot drew a picture.

Note: Do **not** confuse compound sentence elements with compound sentences.

> Simple sentences with compound subjects:
> <u>Joyce</u> and <u>Dot</u> wrote letters.
> The <u>girl</u> in row three and the <u>boy</u> next to her were passing notes across the aisle.

> Simple sentences with compound predicates:
> Joyce <u>wrote letters</u> and <u>drew pictures</u>.
> The captain of the high school debate team <u>graduated with honors</u> and <u>studied broadcast journalism in college</u>.

> Simple sentence with compound object of preposition:
> Coleen graded the students' essays for <u>style</u> and <u>mechanical accuracy</u>.

Types of Clauses

Clauses are connected word groups that are composed of *at least* one subject and one verb. (A subject is the doer of an action or the element that is being joined. A verb conveys either the action or the link.)

Students are waiting for the start of the assembly.
(Subject)   (Verb)

At the end of the play, students wait for the curtain to come down.
                    (Subject) (Verb)

Clauses can be independent or dependent.

Independent clauses can stand alone or can be joined to other clauses.

Independent clause	for	
	and	
	nor	
Independent clause,	but	Independent clause
	or	
	yet	
	so	
Independent clause	;	Independent clause
Dependent clause	,	Independent clause
Independent clause		Dependent clause

Dependent clauses, by definition, contain at least one subject and one verb. However, they cannot stand alone as a complete sentence. They are structurally dependent on the main clause.

There are two types of dependent clauses: (1) those with a subordinating conjunction and (2) those with a relative pronoun.

Sample subordinating conjunctions:

Although
When
If
Unless
Because

Unless a cure is discovered, many more people will die of the disease.
      (Dependent clause   +   Independent clause)

Sample relative pronouns:

Who
Whom
Which
That

The White House has an official website, which contains press releases, news updates, and biographies of the President and Vice-President.
(Independent clause + relative pronoun + relative dependent clause)

Skill 7.2 **Identify effective placement of modifiers, parallel structure, and use of negatives in sentence formation.**

Correct use of adjectives and adverbs

Adjectives are words that modify or describe nouns or pronouns. Adjectives usually precede the words they modify, but not always; for example, an adjective occurs after a linking verb.

Adverbs are words that modify verbs, adjectives, or other adverbs. They cannot modify nouns. Adverbs answer such questions as how, why, when, where, how much, or how often something is done. Many adverbs are formed by adding -ly.

Error: The birthday cake tasted sweetly.

Problem: *Tasted* is a linking verb; the modifier that follows should be an adjective, not an adverb.

Correction: *The birthday cake tasted sweet.*

Error: You have done good with this project.

Problem: *Good* is an adjective and cannot be used to modify a verb phrase such as *have done.*

Correction: *You have done well with this project.*

Error: The coach was positive happy about the team's chance of winning.

Problem: The adjective *positive* cannot be used to modify another adjective, *happy.* An adverb is needed instead.

Correction: *The coach was positively happy about the team's chance of winning.*

Error: The fireman acted quick and brave to save the child from the burning building.

Problem: *Quick and brave* are adjectives and cannot be used to describe a verb. Adverbs are needed instead.

Correction: *The fireman acted quickly and bravely to save the child from the burning building.*

PRACTICE EXERCISE – ADJECTIVES AND ADVERBS

Choose the option that corrects an error in the underlined portion(s).
If no error exists, choose "No change is necessary."

1)   Moving <u>quick</u> throughout the house, the burglar <u>removed</u> several priceless antiques before <u>carelessly</u> dropping his wallet.

      A) quickly
      B) remove
      C) careless
      D) No change is necessary.

2)   The car <u>crashed loudly</u> into the retaining wall before spinning <u>wildly</u> on the sidewalk.

      A) crashes
      B) loudly
      C) wild
      D) No change is necessary.

3)   The airplane <u>landed</u> <u>safe</u> on the runway after <u>nearly</u> colliding with a helicopter.

      A) land
      B) safely
      C) near
      D) No change is necessary.

4)   The <u>horribly</u> <u>bad</u> special effects in the movie disappointed us <u>great</u>.

      A) horrible
      B) badly
      C) greatly
      D) No change is necessary.

5)   The man promised to <u>faithfully</u> obey the rules of the social club.

      A) faithful
      B) faithfulness
      C) faith
      D) No change is necessary.

ANSWER KEY: PRACTICE EXERCISE FOR ADJECTIVES AND ADVERBS

1) A   The adverb *quickly* is needed to modify *moving*. Option B is incorrect because it uses the wrong form of the verb. Option C is incorrect because the adverb *carelessly* is needed before the verb *dropping,* not the adjective *careless*.

2) D   The sentence is correct as it is written. Adverbs *loudly* and *wildly* are needed to modify *crashed* and *spinning*. Option A incorrectly uses the verb *crashes* instead of the participle *crashing*, which acts as an adjective.

3) B   The adverb *safely* is needed to modify the verb *landed*. Option A is incorrect because *land* is a noun. Option C is incorrect because *near* is an adjective, not an adverb.

4) C   The adverb *greatly* is needed to modify the verb *disappointed.* Option A is incorrect because *horrible* is an adjective, not an adverb. Option B is incorrect because *bad* needs to modify the adverb *horribly*.

5) D   The adverb *faithfully* is the correct modifier of the verb *promised.* Option A is an adjective used to modify nouns. Neither Option B nor Option C, which are both nouns, is a modifier.

Faulty parallelism

Two or more elements stated in a single clause should be expressed with the same (or parallel) structure (e.g., all adjectives, all verb forms, or all nouns).

Error: She needed to be beautiful, successful, and have fame.

Problem: The phrase *to be* is followed by two different structures: *beautiful* and *successful* are adjectives, and *have fame* is a verb phrase.

Correction: *She needed to be <u>beautiful</u>, <u>successful</u>, and <u>famous</u>.*
       (adjective) (adjective)   (adjective)
                 OR
She needed <u>beauty</u>, <u>success</u>, and <u>fame</u>.
      (noun) (noun)   (noun)

Error: I plan either to sell my car during the spring or during the summer.

Problem: Paired conjunctions (also called correlative conjunctions, such as either-or, both-and, neither-nor, not only-but also) need to be followed with similar structures. In the sentence above, *either* is followed by *to sell my car during the spring*, while *or* is followed only by the phrase *during the summer*.

Correction: *I plan to sell my car during either the spring or the summer.*

Error: The President pledged to lower taxes and that he would cut spending to lower the national debt.

Problem: Since the phrase *to lower taxes* follows the verb *pledged*, a similar structure of *to* is needed with the phrase *cut spending*.

Correction: *The President pledged to lower taxes and to cut spending to lower the national debt.*
                 OR
The President pledged that he would lower taxes and cut spending to lower the national debt.

PRACTICE EXERCISE – PARALLELISM

Choose the sentence that expresses the thought most clearly and effectively and that has no error in structure.

1. A. Andy found the family tree, researches the Irish descendents, and he was compiling a book for everyone to read.

    B. Andy found the family tree, researched the Irish descendents, and compiled a book for everyone to read.

    C. Andy finds the family tree, researched the Irish descendents, and compiled a book for everyone to read.

2. A. In the last ten years, computer technology has advanced so quickly that workers have had difficulty keeping up with the new equipment and the increased amount of functions.

    B. Computer technology has advanced so quickly in the last ten years that workers have had difficulty to keep up with the new equipment and by increasing amount of functions.

    C. In the last ten years, computer technology has advanced so quickly that workers have had difficulty keeping up with the new equipment and the amount of functions are increasing.

3. A. The Florida State History Museum contains exhibits honoring famous residents, a video presentation about the state's history, an art gallery featuring paintings and sculptures, and they even display a replica of the Florida Statehouse.

    B. The Florida State History Museum contains exhibits honoring famous residents, a video presentation about the state's history, an art gallery featuring paintings and sculptures, and even a replica of the Florida Statehouse.

    C. The Florida State History Museum contains exhibits honoring famous residents, a video presentation about the state's history, an art gallery featuring paintings and sculptures, and there is even a replica of the Florida Statehouse.

4.   A.   Either the criminal justice students had too much practical experience and limited academic preparation or too much academic preparation and little practical experience.

     B.   The criminal justice students either had too much practical experience and limited academic preparation or too much academic preparation and little practical experience.

     C.   The criminal justice students either had too much practical experience and limited academic preparation or had too much academic preparation and little practical experience.

5.   A.   Filmmaking is an arduous process in which the producer hires the cast and crew, chooses locations for filming, supervises the actual production, and guides the editing.

     B.   Because it is an arduous process, filmmaking requires the producer to hire a cast and crew and choose locations, supervise the actual production, and guides the editing.

     C.   Filmmaking is an arduous process in which the producer hires the cast and crew, chooses locations for filming, supervises the actual production, and guided the editing.

ANSWER KEY: PRACTICE EXERCISE FOR PARALLELISM

1. B   Option B uses parallelism by presenting a series of past tense verbs: *found, researched*, and *compiled*. Option A interrupts the parallel structure of past tense verbs: *found, researches*, and *he was compiling*. Option C uses present tense verbs and then shifts to past tense: *finds, researched*, and *compiled*.

2. A   Option A uses parallel structure at the end of the sentence: *the new equipment and the increased amount of functions*. Option B creates a faulty structure with *to keep up with the new equipment and by increasing amount of functions*. Option C creates faulty parallelism with *the amount of functions are increasing*.

3. B   Option B uses parallelism by presenting a series of noun phrases acting as objects of the verb *contains*. Option A interrupts that parallelism by inserting *they even display*, and Option C interrupts the parallelism with the addition of *there is*.

4. C   In the either-or parallel construction, look for a balance on both sides. Option C creates that balanced parallel structure: *either had...or had*. Options A and B do not create the balance. In Option A, the structure is *Either the students...or too much*. In Option B, the structure is *either had...or too much*.

5. A   Option A uses parallelism by presenting a series of verbs with objects: *hires the cast and crew, chooses locations for filming, supervises the actual production, and guides the editing*. The structure of Option B incorrectly suggests that filmmaking chooses locations, supervises the actual production, and guides the editing. Option C interrupts the series of present tense verbs by inserting the participle *guided*, instead of the present tense *guides*.

Negation

Positive	Negative

To Be

I <u>am</u> afraid of the dark.	I <u>am not</u> afraid of the dark. (I'm not)
You are going to the store.	You <u>are not</u> going to the store (you're not / aren't)
They <u>were</u> pretty flowers.	They <u>were not</u> pretty flowers. (weren't)
I <u>was</u> enjoying my day off.	I <u>was not</u> enjoying my day off (wasn't)

Conditionals

Charlotte <u>will</u> arrive at 8.	Charlotte <u>will not</u> arrive at 8. (won't arrive)
Robert <u>can</u> run 26 miles.	Robert <u>cannot</u> run 26 miles (can't run)
I <u>could have</u> been great!	I <u>could not</u> have been great. (couldn't have)

Present simple

I <u>want</u> to go home.	I <u>do not</u> want to go home (don't)
Veronica <u>walks</u> too slow.	Veronica <u>does not</u> walk too slow. (doesn't)

Past Simple

I <u>skipped</u> rope daily.	I <u>did not</u> skip rope daily. (didn't)

Present Perfect

My mom <u>has</u> made my costume.	My mom <u>has not</u> made my costume. (hasn't)
The Thompsons <u>have</u> just bought a dog.	The Thompsons <u>have not</u> just bought a dog. (haven't)

Have Versus Have Got

I <u>have</u> 2 sisters.	I <u>don't</u> have two sisters.
I <u>have</u> got 2 sisters.	I <u>haven't</u> got two sisters.
Jeremy <u>has</u> school tomorrow.	Jeremy <u>doesn't</u> have school tomorrow.
Jeremy <u>has</u> got school tomorrow.	Jeremy <u>hasn't</u> got school tomorrow.

Common negative words include:
no, not, none, nothing, nowhere, neither, nobody, no one, hardly, scarcely, barely.

A **double negative** occurs when two forms of negation are used in the same sentence. In order to correct a double negative, one of the negative words should be removed.

Error: I haven't got nothing.

Correction: I haven't got anything.
                        OR
                I have nothing.

Error: Don't nobody leave until 7 o'clock.

Correction: Do not leave until 7 o'clock.
                        OR
                Nobody leave until 7 o'clock.

It is also incorrect to combine a negative with an adverb, such as "barely," "scarcely," or "hardly."

Error: I can't barely stand it.

Correction: I can't stand it.
                        OR
                I can barely stand it.

Skill 7.3   Recognize imprecise and inappropriate word choices.

Students frequently encounter problems with **homonyms**—words that are spelled and pronounced the same as another but that have different meanings, such as mean, a verb, "to intend;" mean an adjective, "unkind;" and mean a noun or adjective, "average." These words are actually both homonyms and homographs (written the same way).

A similar phenomenon that causes trouble is heteronyms (also sometimes called heterophones), words that are spelled the same but have different pronunciations and meanings (in other words, they are homographs that differ in pronunciation or, technically, homographs that are not homophones). For example, the homographs desert (abandon) and desert (arid region) are heteronyms (pronounced differently); but mean (intend) and mean (average) are not. They are pronounced the same, or are homonyms.

Another similar occurrence in English is the capitonym, a word that is spelled the same but has different meanings when it is capitalized and may or may not have different pronunciations. Example: polish (to make shiny) and Polish (from Poland).

Some of the most troubling homonyms are those that are spelled differently but sound the same. Examples: its (3rd person singular neuter pronoun) and it's ("it is"); there, their (3rd person plural pronoun), and they're ("they are"); and to, too, and two.

Some homonyms/homographs are particularly complicated and troubling. Fluke, for instance is a fish, a flatworm, the end parts of an anchor, the fins on a whale's tail, and a stroke of luck.

Common misused words:

Accept is a verb meaning to receive or to tolerate. **Except** is usually a preposition meaning excluding. Except is also a verb meaning to exclude.

Advice is a noun meaning recommendation. **Advise** is a verb meaning to recommend.

Affect is usually a verb meaning to influence. **Effect** is usually a noun meaning result. Effect can also be a verb meaning to bring about.

An **allusion** is an indirect reference. An **illusion** is a misconception or false impression.

Add is a verb meaning to put together. **Ad** is a noun that is the abbreviation for the word advertisement.

Ain't is a common nonstandard contraction for the contraction **aren't**.

Allot is a verb meaning to distribute. **A lot** can be an adverb that means often or to a great degree. It can also mean a large quantity.

Allowed is used here as an adjective that means permitted. **Aloud** is an adverb that means audibly.

Bare is an adjective that means naked or exposed. It can also indicate a minimum. As a noun, **bear** is a large mammal. As a verb, bear means to carry a heavy burden.

Capital refers to a city, **capitol** to a building where lawmakers meet. **Capital** also refers to wealth or resources.

A **chord** is a noun that refers to a group of musical notes. **Cord** is a noun meaning rope or a long electrical line.

Compliment is a noun meaning a praising or flattering remark. **Complement** is a noun that means something that completes or makes perfect.

Climactic is derived from climax, the point of greatest intensity in a series or progression of events. **Climatic** is derived from climate; it refers to meteorological conditions.

Discreet is an adjective that means tactful or diplomatic; **discrete** is an adjective that means separate or distinct.

Dye is a noun or verb used to indicate artificially coloring something. **Die** is a verb that means to pass away. **Die** is also a noun that means a cube-shaped game piece.

Effect is a noun that means outcome. **Affect** is a verb that means to act or produce an effect on.

Elicit is a verb meaning to bring out or to evoke. **Illicit** is an adjective meaning unlawful.

Emigrate means to leave one country or region to settle in another. **Immigrate** means to enter another country and reside there.

Lead is a verb that means to guide or serve as the head of. It is also a noun that is a type of metal.

Medal is a noun that means an award that is strung round the neck. **Meddle** is a verb that means to involve oneself in a matter without right or invitation. **Metal** is an element such as silver or gold. **Mettle** is a noun meaning toughness or guts.

Morning is a noun indicating the time between midnight and midday. **Mourning** is a verb or noun pertaining to the period of grieving after a death.

Past is a noun meaning a time before now (past, present, and future). **Passed** is the past tense of the verb "to pass."

Piece is a noun meaning portion. **Peace** is a noun meaning the opposite of war.

Peak is a noun meaning the tip or height to reach the highest point. **Peek** is a verb that means to take a brief look. **Pique** is a verb meaning to incite or raise interest.

Principal is a noun meaning the head of a school or an organization or a sum of money. **Principle** is a noun meaning a basic truth or law.

Rite is a noun meaning a special ceremony. **Right** is an adjective meaning correct or direction. **Write** is a verb meaning to compose in writing.

Than is a conjunction used in comparisons; **then** is an adverb denoting time. That pizza is more <u>than</u> I can eat. Tom laughed, and <u>then</u> we recognized him. **Than** is used to compare; both words have the letter a in them. **Then** tells when; both are spelled the same, except for the first letter.

There is an adverb specifying place; it is also an expletive. Adverb: Sylvia is lying <u>there</u> unconscious. Expletive: <u>There</u> are two plums left. **Their** is a possessive pronoun. **They're** is a contraction of they are. Fred and Jane finally washed <u>their</u> car. <u>They're</u> later than usual today.

To is a preposition; **too** is an adverb; **two** is a number.

Your is a possessive pronoun; **you're** is a contraction of you are.

Other confusing words

Lie is an intransitive verb meaning to recline or rest on a surface. Its principal parts are lie, lay, lain. **Lay** is a transitive verb meaning to put or place. Its principal parts are lay, laid.

> Birds lay eggs.
> I lie down for bed around 10 PM.

Set is a transitive verb meaning to put or to place. Its principal parts are set, set, set. **Sit** is an intransitive verb meaning to be seated. Its principal parts are sit, sat, sat.

> I set my backpack down near the front door.
> They sat in the park until the sun went down.

Among is a preposition to be used with three or more items. **Between** is to be used with two items.

> Between you and me, I cannot tell the difference among those three Johnson sisters.

Choose the most effective word or phrase within the context suggested by the sentences.

1)   The defendant was accused of_____money from his employer.

A) stealing
B) embezzling
C) robbing

2)   O.J. Simpson's angry disposition_____ his ex-wife Nicole.

A) mortified
B) intimidated
C) frightened

3)   Many tourists are attracted to Florida because of its_____climate.

A) friendly
B) peaceful
C) balmy

4)   The woman was angry because the tomato juice left an_____stain on her brand new carpet.

A) unsightly
B) ugly
C) unpleasant

5)   After disobeying orders, the army private was_____by his superior officer.

A) degraded
B) attacked
C) reprimanded

6)   Sharon's critical evaluation of the student's book report left him feeling _____ , which caused him to want to quit school.

A) surprised
B) depressed
C) discouraged

7) The life-saving medication created by the scientist had a very_____ impact on further developments in the treatment of cancer.

A) beneficial
B) fortunate
C) miraculous

8) *Phantom of The Opera* is one of Andrew Lloyd Webber's most successful musicals, largely because of its_____themes.

A) romantic
B) melodramatic
C) imaginary

9) The massive Fourth of July fireworks display_____the partygoers with lots of sound and colored light.

A) disgusted
B) captivated
C) captured

10) Many of the residents of Grand Forks, North Dakota were forced to _____their homes because of the flood.

A) escape
B) evacuate
C) exit

ANSWERS : 1.A., 2.C., 3.C., 4.A. ,5.C., 6.C., 7.A., 8.A., 9.B., 10.B.

Choose the sentence that expresses the thought most clearly and most effectively and is structurally correct in grammar and syntax.

1)   A. The movie was three hours in length, featuring interesting characters, and moved at a fast pace.

       B. The movie was three hours long, featured interesting characters, and moved at a fast pace.

       C. Moving at a fast pace, the movie was three hours long and featured interesting characters.

2)   A. We were so offended by the waiter's demeanor that we left the restaurant without paying the check.

       B. The waiter's demeanor offended us so much that without paying the check, we left the restaurant.

       C. We left the restaurant without paying the check because we were offended by the waiter's demeanor.

3)   A. In today's society, information about our lives is provided to us by computers.

       B. We rely on computers in today's society to provide us information about our lives.

       C. In today's society, we rely on computers to provide us with information about our lives.

4)   A. Folding the sides of the tent carefully, Jack made sure to be quiet so none of the other campers would be woken up.

       B. So none of the other campers would be woken up, Jack made sure to be quiet by folding the sides of the tent carefully.

       C. Folding the sides of the tent carefully, so none of the other campers would wake up, Jack made sure to be quiet.

ANSWER KEY

1) B.
2) A.
3) C.
4) A.

Choose the most effective word or phrase within the context suggested by the sentence(s).

1)   The six hundred employees of General Electric were_____by the company due to budgetary cutbacks.

   A) released
   B) terminated
   C) downsized

2)   The force of the tornado_____the many residents of the town of Russell, Kansas.

   A) intimidated
   B) repulsed
   C) frightened

3)   Even though his new car was a lot easier to drive, Fred_____to walk to work every day because he liked the exercise.

   A) needed
   B) preferred
   C) considered

4)   June's parents were very upset over the school board's decision to suspend her from Adams High for a week. Before they filed a lawsuit against the board, they_____with a lawyer to help them make a decision.

   A) consulted
   B) debated
   C) conversed

5)   The race car driver's_____in handling the automobile was a key factor in his victory.

   A) patience
   B) precision
   C) determination

6)   After impressing the judges with her talent and charm, the beauty contestant_____more popularity by singing an aria from *La Boheme*.

   A) captured
   B) scored
   C) gained

7) The stained glass window was_____after a large brick flew through it during the riot.

A) damaged
B) cracked
C) shattered

8) The class didn't know what happened to the professor until it was_____ by the principal why he dropped out of school.

A) informed
B) discovered
C) explained

9) The giant penthouse on the top of the building allows the billionaire industrialist_____the citizens on the street.

A) to view from above
B) the chance to see
C) to glance at

10) Sally's parents_____her to attend the dance after she promised to return by midnight.

A) prohibited
B) permitted
C) asked

ANSWERS: 1) C., 2) C., 3) B., 4) A., 5) B., 6) C., 7) C., 8) C., 9) C., 10) B

COMPETENCY 8.0   RECOGNIZE STANDARD CONVENTIONS OF FORMAL WRITTEN ENGLISH USAGE IN THE UNITED STATES.

Skill 8.1   Recognize the standard use of verb forms.

Standard verb forms

Past tense and past participles
Both regular and irregular verbs must appear in their standard forms for each tense. Note: the -ed or -d ending is added to regular verbs in the past tense and for past participles.

Infinitive	Past Tense	Past Participle
Bake	Baked	Baked

Irregular Verb Forms

Infinitive	Past Tense	Past Participle
Be	Was, were	Been
Become	Became	Become
Break	Broke	Broken
Bring	Brought	Brought
Choose	Chose	Chosen
Come	Came	Come
Do	Did	Done
Draw	Drew	Drawn
Eat	Ate	Eaten
Fall	Fell	Fallen
Forget	Forgot	Forgotten
Freeze	Froze	Frozen
Give	Gave	Given
Go	Went	Gone
Grow	Grew	Grown
Have/has	Had	Had
Hide	Hid	Hidden
Know	Knew	Known
Lay	Laid	Laid
Lie	Lay	Lain
Ride	Rode	Ridden
Rise	Rose	Risen
Run	Ran	Run
See	Saw	Seen
Steal	Stole	Stolen
Take	Took	Taken
Tell	Told	Told
Throw	Threw	Thrown
Wear	Wore	Worn
Write	Wrote	Written

Error: She should have went to her doctor's appointment at the scheduled time.

Problem: The past participle of the verb *to go* is *gone. Went* expresses the simple past tense.

Correction: *She should have gone to her doctor's appointment at the scheduled time.*

Error: My train is suppose to arrive before two o'clock.

Problem: The verb following *train* is a present tense passive construction which requires the present tense verb *to be* and the past participle.

Correction: *My train is supposed to arrive before two o'clock.*

Error: Linda should of known that the car wouldn't start after leaving it out in the cold all night.

Problem: *Should of* is a nonstandard expression. *Of is* not a verb.

Correction: *Linda should have known that the car wouldn't start after leaving it out in the cold all night.*

PRACTICE EXERCISE – STANDARD VERB FORMS

Choose the option that corrects an error in the underlined portion(s). If no error exists, choose "No change is necessary."

1)   My professor <u>had knew</u> all along that we would pass his course.

    A. know
    B. had known
    C. knowing
    D. No change is necessary.

2)   Kevin was asked to erase the vulgar words he <u>had wrote</u>.

    A. writes
    B. has write
    C. had written
    D. No change is necessary.

3)   Melanie <u>had forget</u> to tell her parents that she left the cat in the closet.

    A. had forgotten
    B. forgot
    C. forget
    D. No change is necessary.

4)   Craig always <u>leave</u> the house a mess when his parents aren't there.

    A. left
    B. leaves
    C. leaving
    D. No change is necessary.

5)   The store manager accused Kathy of <u>having stole</u> more than five hundred dollars from the safe.

    A. has stolen
    B. having stolen
    C. stole
    D. No change is necessary.

ANSWER KEY : PRACTICE EXERCISE FOR STANDARD VERB FORMS

1. B   Option B is correct because the past participle needs the helping verb *had*. Option A is incorrect because *it* is in the infinitive tense. Option C incorrectly uses the present participle.

2. C   Option C is correct because the past participle follows the helping verb *had*. Option A uses the verb in the present tense. Option B is an incorrect use of the verb.

3. A   Option A is correct because the past participle uses the helping verb *had*. Option B uses the wrong form of the verb. Option C uses the wrong form of the verb.

4. B   Option B correctly uses the past tense of the verb. Option A uses the verb in an incorrect way. Option C uses the verb without a helping verb like *is*.

5. B   Option B is correct because it is the past participle. Option A and C use the verb incorrectly.

Inappropriate shifts in verb tense

Verb tenses must refer to the same time period consistently, unless a change in time is required.

Error: Despite the increased amount of students in the school this year, overall attendance is higher last year at the sporting events.

Problem: The verb *is* represents an inconsistent shift to the present tense when the action refers to a past occurrence.

Correction: *Despite the increased amount of students in the school this year, overall attendance was higher last year at sporting events.*

Error: My friend Lou, who just competed in the marathon, ran since he was twelve years old.

Problem: Because Lou continues to run, the present perfect tense is needed.

Correction: *My friend Lou, who just competed in the marathon, has ran since he was twelve years old.*

Error: The Mayor congratulated Wallace Mangham, who renovates the city hall last year.

Problem: Although the speaker is talking in the present, the action of renovating the city hall was in the past.

Correction: *The Mayor congratulated Wallace Mangham, who renovated the city hall last year.*

PRACTICE EXERCISE – SHIFTS IN TENSE

Choose the option that corrects an error in the underlined portion(s).
If no error exists, choose "No change is necessary."

1)   After we <u>washed</u> the fruit that had <u>growing</u> in the garden, we knew
        there <u>was</u> a store that would buy them.

        A) washing
        B) grown
        C) is
        D) No change is necessary.

2)   The tourists <u>used</u> to visit the Atlantic City boardwalk whenever they
        <u>vacationed</u> during the summer. Unfortunately, their numbers have
        <u>diminished</u> every year.

        A) use
        B) vacation
        C) diminish
        D) No change is necessary.

3)   When the temperature <u>drops</u> to below thirty-two degrees Fahrenheit,
        the water on the lake <u>freezes</u>, which <u>allowed</u> children to skate across it.

        A) dropped
        B) froze
        C) allows
        D) No change is necessary.

4)   The artists were <u>hired</u> to <u>create</u> a monument that would pay tribute to
        the men who were <u>killed</u> in World War Two.

        A) hiring
        B) created
        C) killing
        D) No change is necessary.

5)   Emergency medical personnel rushed to the scene of the shooting,
        where many injured people <u>waiting</u> for treatment.

        A) wait
        B) waited
        C) waits
        D) No change is necessary.

ANSWER KEY : PRACTICE EXERCISE FOR SHIFTS IN TENSE

1) B   The past participle *grown* is needed instead of *growing*, which is the progressive tense. Option A is incorrect because the past participle *washed* takes the *-ed*. Option C incorrectly replaces the past participle *was* with the present tense *is*.

2) D   Option A is incorrect because *use* is the present tense. Option B incorrectly uses the noun *vacation*. Option C incorrectly uses the present tense *diminish* instead of the past tense *diminished*.

3) C   The present tense *allows* is necessary in the context of the sentence. Option A is incorrect because *dropped* is a past participle. Option B is incorrect because *froze* is also a past participle.

4) D   Option A is incorrect because *hiring* is the present tense. Option B is incorrect because *created* is a past participle. In Option C, *killing* doesn't fit into the context of the sentence.

5) B   In Option B, *waited* corresponds with the past tense *rushed*. In Option A, *wait* is incorrect because it is present tense. In Option C, *waits* is incorrect because the noun *people* is plural and requires the singular form of the verb.

Skill 8.2   Recognize the standard use of pronouns.

Rules for clear pronoun references

Make sure that the antecedent reference is clear and cannot refer to something else.

A "distant relative" is a relative pronoun or a relative clause that has been placed too far away from the antecedent to which it refers. It is a common error to place a verb between the relative pronoun and its antecedent.

Error: Return the books to the library that are overdue.
Problem: The relative clause "that are overdue" refers to the "books" and should be placed immediately after the antecedent.
Correction: Return the books that are overdue to the library. -OR- Return the overdue books to the library.

A pronoun should not refer to adjectives or possessive nouns.

Adjectives, nouns, or possessive pronouns should not be used as antecedents. This will create ambiguity in sentences.

Error: In Todd's letter, he told his mom he'd broken the priceless vase.
Problem: In this sentence, the pronoun "he" seems to refer to the noun phrase "Todd's letter," though it was probably meant to refer to the possessive noun "Todd's."
Correction: In his letter, Todd told his mom that he had broken the priceless vase.

A pronoun should not refer to an implied idea.

A pronoun must refer to a specific antecedent rather than an implied antecedent. When an antecedent is not stated specifically, the reader has to guess or assume the meaning of a sentence. Pronouns that do not have antecedents are called expletives. "It" and "there" are the most common expletives, though other pronouns can also become expletives as well. In informal conversation, expletives allow for the casual presentation of ideas without supporting evidence; however, in more formal writing, it is best to be more precise.

Error: She said that it is important to floss every day.
Problem: The pronoun "it" refers to an implied idea.
Correction: She said that flossing every day is important.

Error: They returned the book because there were missing pages.
Problem: The pronouns "they" and "there" do not refer to the antecedent.
Correction: The customer returned the book with missing pages.

Using Who, That, and Which

Who, whom and **whose** refer to human beings and can either introduce essential or nonessential clauses. **That** refers to things other than humans and is used to introduce essential clauses. **Which** refers to things other than humans and is used to introduce nonessential clauses.

Error: The doctor that performed the surgery said the man would be fully recovered.
Problem: Since the relative pronoun is referring to a human, *who* should be used.
Correction: The doctor who performed the surgery said the man would be fully recovered.

Error: That ice cream cone that you just ate looked really delicious.
Problem: That has already been used, so you must use *which* to introduce the next clause, whether it is essential or nonessential.
Correction: That ice cream cone, which you just ate, looked really delicious.

Proper Case Forms

Pronouns, unlike nouns, change case forms. Pronouns must be in the subjective, objective, or possessive form according to their function in the sentence.

Personal Pronouns

	Subjective (Nominative)		Possessive		Objective	
	Singular	Plural	Singular	Plural	Singular	Plural
1st person	I	We	My	Our	Me	Us
2nd person	You	You	Your	Your	You	You
3rd person	He She It	They	His Her Its	Their	Him Her It	them

Relative Pronouns

Who	Subjective/Nominative
Whom	Objective
Whose	Possessive

Error: Tom and me have reserved seats for next week's baseball game.

Problem: The pronoun *me* is the subject of the verb *have reserved* and should be in the subjective form.

Correction: *Tom and I have reserved seats for next week's baseball game.*

Error: Mr. Green showed all of we students how to make paper hats.

Problem: The pronoun *we* is the object of the preposition *of*. It should be in the objective form, *us*.

Correction: *Mr. Green showed all of us students how to make paper hats.*

Error: Who's coat is this?

Problem: The interrogative possessive pronoun is *whose*; *who's* is the contraction for who is.

Correction: *Whose coat is this?*

Error: The voters will choose the candidate whom has the best qualifications for the job.

Problem: The case of the relative pronoun *who* or *whom* is determined by the pronoun's function in the clause in which it appears. The word *who* is in the subjective case, and *whom* is in the objective. Analyze how the pronoun is being used within the sentence.

Correction: *The voters will choose the candidate who has the best qualifications for the job.*

PRACTICE EXERCISE – PRONOUN CASE

Choose the option that corrects an error in the underlined portion(s).
If no error exists, choose "No change is necessary".

1) Even though Sheila and <u>he</u> had planned to be alone at the diner, <u>they</u> were joined by three friends of <u>their's</u> instead.

   A) him
   B) him and her
   C) theirs
   D) No change is necessary.

2) Uncle Walter promised to give his car to <u>whomever</u> will guarantee to drive it safely.

   A) whom
   B) whoever
   C) them
   D) No change is necessary.

3) Eddie and <u>him</u> gently laid <u>the body</u> on the ground next to <u>the sign</u>.

   A) he
   B) them
   C) it
   D) No change is necessary.

4) Mary, <u>who</u> is competing in the chess tournament, is a better player than <u>me</u>.

   A) whose
   B) whom
   C) I
   D) No change is necessary.

5) <u>We, ourselves,</u> have decided not to buy property in that development; however, our friends have already bought <u>themselves</u> some land.

   A) We, ourself,
   B) their selves
   C) their self
   D) No change is necessary.

ANSWER KEY : PRACTICE EXERCISE FOR PRONOUN CASE

1) C   The possessive pronoun *theirs* doesn't need an apostrophe. Option A is incorrect because the subjective pronoun *he* is needed in this sentence. Option B is incorrect because the subjective pronoun *they*, not the objective pronouns *him* and *her*, is needed.

2) B   The subjective case *whoever*--not the objective case *whomever* --is the subject of the relative clause *whoever will guarantee to drive it safely*. Option A is incorrect because *whom* is an objective pronoun. Option C is incorrect because *car* is singular and takes the pronoun *it*.

3) A   The subjective pronoun *he* is needed as the subject of the verb *laid*. Option B is incorrect because *them* is vague; the noun *body* is needed to clarify *it*. Option C is incorrect because *it* is vague, and the noun *sign* is necessary for clarification.

4) C   The subjective pronoun *I* is needed because the comparison is understood. Option A incorrectly uses the possessive *whose*. Option B is incorrect because the subjective pronoun *who*, and not the objective *whom*, is needed.

5) D   The reflexive pronoun *themselves* refers to the plural *friends*. Option A is incorrect because the plural *we* requires the reflexive *ourselves*. Option C is incorrect because the possessive pronoun *their* is never joined with either *self* or *selves*.

Agreements between pronoun and antecedent

A pronoun must correspond to its antecedent in number (singular or plural), person (first, second, or third person) and gender (male, female, or neutral). A pronoun must refer clearly to a single word, not to a complete idea.

A **pronoun shift** is a grammatical error in which the author starts a sentence, paragraph, or section of a paper using one particular type of pronoun and then suddenly shifts to another. This often confuses the reader.

Error: A teacher should treat all their students fairly.

Problem: Since *A teacher* is singular, the pronoun referring to it must also be singular. Otherwise, the noun has to be made plural.

Correction: *Teachers should treat all their students fairly.*

Error: When an actor is rehearsing for a play, it often helps if you can memorize the lines in advance.

Problem: *Actor* is a third-person word; that is, the writer is talking about the subject. The pronoun *you* is in the second person, which means the writer is talking to the subject.

Correction: *When actors are rehearsing for plays, it helps if they can memorize the lines in advance.*

Error: The workers in the factory were upset when his or her paychecks didn't arrive on time.

Problem: *Workers* is a plural form, while *his or her* refers to one person.

Correction: *The workers in the factory were upset when their paychecks didn't arrive on time.*

Error: The charity auction was highly successful, which pleased everyone.

Problem: In this sentence, the pronoun *which* refers to the idea of the auction's success. In fact, *which* has no antecedent in the sentence; the word *success* is not stated.

Correction: *Everyone was pleased at the success of the auction.*

PRACTICE EXERCISE – PRONOUN/ANTECEDENT AGREEMENT

Choose the option that corrects an error in the underlined portion(s).
If no error exists, choose "No change is necessary."

1) <u>You</u> can get to Martha's Vineyard by driving from Boston to Woods Hole. Once there, you can travel over on a ship, but <u>you</u> may find traveling by <u>airplane</u> to be an exciting experience.
   A. They
   B. visitors
   C. it
   D. No change is necessary.

2) Both the city leader and the <u>journalist</u> are worried about the new interstate; <u>she fears</u> <u>the new roadway</u> will destroy precious farmland.
   A. journalist herself
   B. they fear
   C. it
   D. No change is necessary.

3) When <u>hunters</u> are looking for deer in <u>the woods, you</u> must remain quiet for long periods of time.
   A. they
   B. it
   C. we
   D. No change is necessary.

4) Florida's strong economy is based on the importance of the citrus industry. <u>Producing</u> orange juice for most of the country.
   A. They produce
   B. Who produce
   C. Farmers there produce
   D. No change is necessary.

5) Dr. Kennedy told Paul Elliot, <u>his</u> assistant, that <u>he</u> would have to finish grading the tests before going home, no matter how long <u>it</u> took.
   A. their
   B. he, Paul
   C. they
   D. No change is necessary.

ANSWER KEY: PRACTICE EXERCISE FOR PRONOUN AGREEMENT

1) D   Pronouns must be consistent. As *you* is used throughout the sentence, the shift to *visitors* is incorrect. Option A, *They*, is vague and unclear. Option C, *it*, is also unclear.

2) B   The plural pronoun *they* is necessary to agree with the two nouns *leader* and *journalist*. There is no need for the reflexive pronoun *herself* in Option A. In Option C, *it* is vague.

3) A   The shift to *you* is unnecessary. The plural pronoun *they* is necessary to agree with the noun *hunters*. The word *we* in Option C is vague; the reader does not know who the word *we* might refer to. In Option B, *it* has no antecedent.

4) C   The noun *farmers* is needed for clarification because *producing* is vague. Option A is incorrect because *they produce* is vague. Option B is incorrect because *who* has no antecedent and creates a fragment.

5) B   The repetition of the name *Paul* is necessary to clarify who the pronoun *he* is referring to. (It could be Dr. Kennedy.) Option A is incorrect because the singular pronoun *his* is needed, not the plural pronoun *their*. Option C is incorrect because the pronoun *it* refers to the plural noun *tests*.

Skill 8.3 **Recognize the standard formation and use of adverbs, adjectives, comparatives and superlatives, and plural and possessive forms of nouns.**

Correct use of adjectives and adverbs

See Skill 7.2.

Appropriate comparative and superlative degree forms

When comparisons are made, the correct form of the adjective or adverb must be used. The comparative form is used for two items. The superlative form is used for more than two.

	Comparative	Superlative
slow	slower	slowest
young	younger	youngest
tall	taller	tallest

With some words, *more* and *most* are used to make comparisons instead of -er and -est.

quiet	more quiet	most quiet
energetic	more energetic	most energetic
quick	more quickly	most quickly

Comparisons must be made between similar structures or items. In the sentence, "My house is similar in color to Steve's," one house is being compared to another house, as understood by the use of the possessive Steve's.

On the other hand, if the sentence reads, "My house is similar in color to Steve," the comparison would be faulty because it would be comparing the house to Steve, not to Steve's house.

Error: Last year's rides at the carnival were bigger than this year.

Problem: In the sentence as it is worded above, the rides at the carnival are being compared to this year, not to this year's rides.

Correction: *Last year's rides at the carnival were bigger than this year's.*

PRACTICE EXERCISE – LOGICAL COMPARISONS

Choose the sentence that logically and correctly expresses the comparison.

1) A. This year's standards are higher than last year.

    B. This year's standards are more high than last year.

    C. This year's standards are higher than last year's.

2) A. Tom's attitudes are very different from his father's.

    B. Toms attitudes are very different from his father.

    C. Tom's attitudes are very different from his father.

3) A. John is the stronger member of the gymnastics team.

    B. John is the strongest member of the gymnastics team.

    C. John is the most strong member of the gymnastics team.

4) A. Tracy's book report was longer than Tony's.

    B. Tracy's book report was more long than Tony's.

    C. Tracy's book report was longer than Tony.

5) A. Becoming a lawyer is as difficult as, if not more difficult than, becoming a doctor.

    B. Becoming a lawyer is as difficult, if not more difficult than, becoming a doctor.

    C. Becoming a lawyer is difficult, if not more difficult than, becoming a doctor.

6) A. Better than any movie of the modern era, Schindler's List portrays the destructiveness of hate.

    B. More better than any movie of the modern era, Schindler's List portrays the destructiveness of hate.

    C. Better than any other movie of the modern era, Schindler's List portrays the destructiveness of hate.

ANSWER KEY: PRACTICE EXERCISE FOR LOGICAL COMPARISONS

1) C   Option C is correct because the comparison is between this year's standards and last year's. [Standards is understood.] Option A compares the standards to last year. In Option B, the faulty comparative *more high* should be higher.

2) A   Option A is incorrect because Tom's attitudes are compared to his father's. [Attitudes is understood.] Option B deletes the necessary apostrophe to show possession (Tom's), and the comparison is faulty with *attitudes* compared to *father*. While Option C uses the correct possessive, it retains the faulty comparison shown in Option B.

3) B   In Option B, John is correctly the strongest member of a team that consists of more than two people. Option A uses the comparative *stronger* (comparison of two items), rather than the superlative *strongest* (comparison of more than two). Option C uses a faulty superlative, *most strong*.

4) A   Option A is correct because the comparison is between Tracy's book report and Tony's (book report). Option B uses the faulty comparative *more long* instead of *longer*. Option C wrongly compares Tracy's book report to Tony.

5) A   In Option A, the dual comparison is correctly stated: *as difficult as*, *if not more difficult than*. Remember to test the dual comparison by taking out the intervening comparison. Option B deletes the necessary *as* after the first *difficult*. Option C deletes the *as* before and after the first *difficult*.

6) C   Option C includes the necessary word *other* in the comparison *better than any other movie*. The comparison in Option A is not complete, and Option B uses a faulty comparative *more better*.

Plural nouns

The multiplicity and complexity of spelling rules based on phonics, letter doubling, and exceptions to rules - not mastered by adulthood - should be replaced by a good dictionary. As spelling mastery is also difficult for adolescents, our recommendation is the same. Learning to use a dictionary and thesaurus will be a more rewarding use of time.

Most plurals of nouns that end in hard consonants or hard consonant sounds followed by a silent *e* are made by adding *s*. Some words ending in vowels only add *s*.

fingers, numerals, banks, bugs, riots, homes, gates, radios, bananas

Nouns that end in soft consonant sounds *s, j, x, z, ch,* and *sh,* add *es*. Some nouns ending in *o* add es.

dresses, waxes, churches, brushes, tomatoes

Nouns ending in *y* preceded by a vowel just add *s*.

boys, alleys

Nouns ending in *y* preceded by a consonant change the *y* to *i* and add *es*.

babies, corollaries, frugalities, poppies

Some nouns' plurals are formed irregularly or remain the same.

sheep, deer, children, leaves, oxen

Some nouns derived from foreign words, especially Latin, may make their plurals in two different ways—one of them Anglicized. Sometimes, the meanings are the same; other times, the two plurals are used in slightly different contexts. It is always wise to consult the dictionary.

appendices, appendixes   criterion, criteria
indexes, indices   crisis, crises

Make the plurals of closed (solid) compound words in the usual way, except for words ending in *ful,* which make their plurals on the root word.

timelines, hairpins

Make the plurals of open or hyphenated compounds by adding the change in inflection to the word that changes in number.

>   fathers-in-law, courts-martial, masters of art, doctors of medicine

Make the plurals of letters, numbers, and abbreviations by adding *s*.

>   fives and tens, IBMs, 1990s, *p*s and *q*s (Note that letters are italicized.)

Possessive nouns

Make the possessives of singular nouns by adding an apostrophe followed by the letter *s* (*'s*).

>   baby's bottle, father's job, elephant's eye, teacher's desk, sympathizer's protests, week's postponement

Make the possessive of singular nouns ending in *s* by adding either an apostrophe or an (*'s*), depending upon common usage or sound. When making the possessive causes difficulty, use a prepositional phrase instead. Even with the sibilant ending, with a few exceptions, it is advisable to use the (*'s*) construction.

>   dress's color, species' characteristics or characteristics of the species, James' hat or James's hat, Delores's shirt

Make the possessive of plural nouns ending in *s* by adding the apostrophe after the *s*.

>   horses' coats, jockeys' times, four days' time

Make possessives of plural nouns that do not end in *s* the same as singular nouns by adding *'s*.

>   children's shoes, deer's antlers, cattle's horns

Make possessives of compound nouns by adding the inflection at the end of the word or phrase.

>   the mayor of Los Angeles' campaign, the mailman's new truck, the mailmen's new trucks, my father-in-law's first wife, the keepsakes' values, several daughters-in-law's husbands

Skill 8.4   Recognize standard punctuation.

Commas

Commas indicate a brief pause. They are used to set off dependent clauses and long introductory word groups, to separate words in a series, to set off unimportant material that interrupts the flow of the sentence, and to separate independent clauses joined by conjunctions.

Error: After I finish my master's thesis I plan to work in Chicago.

Problem: A comma is needed after an introductory dependent word-group containing a subject and verb.

Correction: *After I finish my master's thesis, I plan to work in Chicago.*

Error: I washed waxed and vacuumed my car today.

Problem: Nouns, phrases, or clauses in a list, as well as two or more coordinate adjectives that modify one word, should be separated by commas. Although the word *and* is sometimes considered optional, it is often necessary to clarify the meaning.

Correction: *I washed, waxed, and vacuumed my car today.*

Error: She was a talented dancer but she is mostly remembered for her singing ability.

Problem: A comma is needed before a conjunction that joins two independent clauses (complete sentences).

Correction: *She was a talented dancer, but she is mostly remembered for her singing ability.*

Error: This incident is I think typical of what can happen when the community remains so divided.

Problem: Commas are needed between nonessential words or words that interrupt the main clause.

Correction: *This incident is, I think, typical of what can happen when the community remains so divided.*

TEACHER CERTIFICATION STUDY GUIDE

Semicolons and colons

Semicolons are needed to separate two or more closely related independent clauses when the second clause is introduced by a transitional adverb. (These clauses may also be written as separate sentences, preferably by placing the adverb within the second sentence). **Colons** are used to introduce lists and to emphasize what follows.

Error: I climbed to the top of the mountain, it took me three hours.

Problem: A comma alone cannot separate two independent clauses. Instead, a semicolon is needed to separate two related sentences.

Correction: *I climbed to the top of the mountain; it took me three hours.*

Error: In the movie, asteroids destroyed Dallas, Texas, Kansas City, Missouri, and Boston, Massachusetts.

Problem: Semicolons are needed to separate items in a series that already contain internal punctuation.

Correction: *In the movie, asteroids destroyed Dallas, Texas; Kansas City, Missouri; and Boston, Massachusetts.*

Error: Essays will receive the following grades, A for excellent, B for good, C for average, and D for unsatisfactory.

Problem: A colon is needed to emphasize the information or list that follows.

Correction: *Essays will receive the following grades: A for excellent, B for good, C for average, and D for unsatisfactory.*

Error: The school carnival included: amusement rides, clowns, food booths, and a variety of games.

Problem: The material preceding the colon and the list that follows is not a complete sentence. Do not separate a verb (or preposition) from the object.

Correction: *The school carnival included amusement rides, clowns, food booths, and a variety of games.*

Apostrophes

Apostrophes are used to show either contractions or possession.

Error: She shouldnt be permitted to smoke cigarettes in the building.

Problem: An apostrophe is needed in a contraction in place of the missing letter.

Correction: *She shouldn't be permitted to smoke cigarettes in the building.*

Error: My cousins motorcycle was stolen from his driveway.

Problem: An apostrophe is needed to show possession.

Correction: *My cousin's motorcycle was stolen from his driveway.* (Note: The use of the apostrophe before the letter "s" means that there is just one cousin. The plural form would read the following way: My cousins' motorcycle was stolen from their driveway.)

Error: The childrens new kindergarten teacher was also a singer..

Problem: An apostrophe is needed to show possession.

Correction: *The childrens' new kindergarten teacher was also a singer.* (Note: The apostrophe after the "s" indicates that there is more than one child).

Error: Children screams could be heard for miles.

Problem: An apostrophe and the letter "s" are needed in the sentence to show whose screams it is.

Correction: *Children's screams could he heard for miles.* (Note: Because the word children is already plural, the apostrophe and *s* must be added afterward to show ownership.)

Quotation marks

In a quoted statement that is either declarative or imperative, place the period inside the closing quotation marks.

"The airplane crashed on the runway during takeoff."

If the quotation is followed by other words in the sentence, place a comma inside the closing quotations marks and a period at the end of the sentence.

"The airplane crashed on the runway during takeoff," said the announcer.

In most instances in which a quoted title or expression occurs at the end of a sentence, the period is placed before either the single or double quotation marks.

"The middle school readers were unprepared to understand Bryant's poem 'Thanatopsis.'"

Early book-length adventure stories like *Don Quixote* and *The Three Musketeers* were known as "picaresque novels."

There is an instance in which the final quotation mark would precede the period—if the content of the sentence were about a speech or quote so that the understanding of the meaning would be confused by the placement of the period.

The first thing out of his mouth was, "Hi, I'm home."
                              -but-
The first line of his speech began, "I arrived home to an empty house".

In sentences that are interrogatory or exclamatory, the question mark or exclamation point should be positioned outside the closing quotation marks if the quote itself is a statement or command or cited title.

Who decided to lead us in the recitation of the "Pledge of Allegiance"?

Why was Tillie shaking as she began her recitation, "Once upon a midnight dreary..."?

I was embarrassed when Mrs. White said, "Your slip is showing"!

In sentences that are declarative, but the quotation is a question or an exclamation, place the question mark or exclamation point inside the quotation marks.

> The hall monitor yelled, "Fire! Fire!"

> "Fire! Fire!" yelled the hall monitor.

> Cory shrieked, "Is there a mouse in the room?" (In this instance, the question supersedes the exclamation.)

Quotations - whether words, phrases, or clauses - should be punctuated according to the rules of the grammatical function they serve in the sentence.

> The works of Shakespeare, "the bard of Avon," have been contested as originating with other authors.

> "You'll get my money," the old man warned, "when 'Hell freezes over'."

> Sheila cited the passage that began "Four score and seven years ago...." (Note the ellipsis followed by an enclosed period.)

> "Old Ironsides" inspired the preservation of the U.S.S. Constitution.

Use quotation marks to enclose the titles of shorter works: songs, short poems, short stories, essays, and chapters of books. (See "Using Italics" for punctuating longer titles.)

> "The Tell-Tale Heart"   "Casey at the Bat"   "America the Beautiful"

Dashes and Italics

Place **dashes** to denote sudden breaks in thought.

> Some periods in literature - the Romantic Age, for example -
> spanned different time periods in different countries.

Use dashes instead of commas if commas are already used elsewhere in the sentence for amplification or explanation.

> The Fireside Poets included three Brahmans - James Russell
> Lowell, Henry David Wadsworth, Oliver Wendell Holmes -
> and John Greenleaf Whittier.

Use **italics** to punctuate the titles of long works of literature, names of periodical publications, musical scores, works of art and motion picture television, and radio programs. (When unable to write in italics, students should be instructed to underline in their own writing where italics would be appropriate.)

The Idylls of the King	*Hiawatha*	*The Sound and the Fury*
Mary Poppins	*Newsweek*	*The Nutcracker Suite*

Capitalization

Capitalize all proper names of persons (including specific organizations or agencies of government); places (countries, states, cities, parks, and specific geographical areas); and things (political parties, structures, historical and cultural terms, and calendar and time designations); and religious terms (any deity, revered person or group, sacred writings).

> Percy Bysshe Shelley, Argentina, Mount Rainier National Park,
> Grand Canyon, League of Nations, the Sears Tower, Birmingham,
> Lyric Theater, Americans, Midwesterners, Democrats, Renaissance,
> Boy Scouts of America, Easter, God, Bible, Dead Sea Scrolls, Koran

Capitalize proper adjectives and titles used with proper names.

California gold rush, President John Adams, French fries, Homeric epic, Romanesque architecture, Senator John Glenn

Note: Some words that represent titles and offices are not capitalized unless used with a proper name.

Capitalized	Not Capitalized
Congressman McKay	the congressman from Florida
Commander Alger	commander of the Pacific Fleet
Queen Elizabeth	the queen of England

Capitalize all main words in titles of works of literature, art, and music.

Error: Emma went to Dr. Peters for treatment since her own Doctor was on vacation.

Problem: The use of capital letters with Emma and Dr .Peters is correct since they are specific (proper) names; the title Dr. is also capitalized. However, the word doctor is not a specific name and should not be capitalized.

Correction: *Emma went to Dr. Peters for treatment since her own doctor was on vacation.*

Error: Our Winter Break does not start until next wednesday.

Problem: Days of the week are capitalized, but seasons are not capitalized.

Correction: *Our winter break does not start until next Wednesday.*

Error: The exchange student from israel, who came to study Biochemistry, spoke spanish very well.

Problem: Languages and the names of countries are always capitalized. Courses are also capitalized when they refer to a specific course; they are not capitalized when they refer to courses in general.

Correction: *The exchange student from Israel, who came to study Biochemistry, spoke Spanish very well.*

Skill 8.5 **Identify sentence fragments and run-on sentences (e.g., fused sentences, comma splices).**

Fragments occur (1) if word groups standing alone are missing either a subject or a verb, and (2) if word groups containing a subject and verb and standing alone are actually made dependent because of the use of subordinating conjunctions or relative pronouns.

Error: The teacher waiting for the class to complete the assignment.

Problem: This sentence is not complete because an -ing word alone does not function as a verb. When a helping verb is added (for example, was waiting), it will become a sentence.

Correction: *The teacher was waiting for the class to complete the assignment.*

Error: Until the last toy was removed from the floor.

Problem: Words such as until, because, although, when, and if make a clause dependent and thus incapable of standing alone. An independent clause must be added to make the sentence complete.

Correction: *Until the last toy was removed from the floor, the kids could not go outside to play.*

Error: The city will close the public library. Because of a shortage of funds.

Problem: The problem is the same as above. The dependent clause must be joined to the independent clause.

Correction: *The city will close the public library because of a shortage of funds.*

Error: Anyone planning to go on the trip should bring the necessary items. Such as a backpack, boots, a canteen, and bug spray.

Problem: The second word group is a phrase and cannot stand alone because there is neither a subject nor a verb. The fragment can be corrected by adding the phrase to the sentence.

Correction: *Anyone planning to go on the trip should bring the necessary items, such as a backpack, boots, a canteen, and bug spray.*

PRACTICE EXERCISE – FRAGMENTS

Choose the option that corrects the underlined portion(s) of the sentence.
If no error exists, choose "No change is necessary."

1) Despite the lack of funds in the <u>budget it</u> was necessary to rebuild the roads that were damaged from the recent floods.

    A) budget: it
    B) budget, it
    C) budget; it
    D) No change is necessary.

2) After determining that the fire was caused by faulty <u>wiring, the</u> building inspector said the construction company should be fined.

    A) wiring. The
    B) wiring the
    C) wiring; the
    D) No change is necessary.

3) Many years after buying a grand <u>piano Henry</u> decided he'd rather play the violin instead.

    A) piano: Henry
    B) piano, Henry
    C) piano; Henry
    D) No change is necessary.

4) Computers are being used more and more <u>frequently. because</u> of their capacity to store information.

    A) frequently because
    B) frequently, because
    C) frequently; because
    D) No change is necessary.

5) Doug washed the floors <u>every day. to</u> keep them clean for the guests.

    A) every day to
    B) every day,
    C) every day;
    D) No change is necessary.

ANSWER KEY: PRACTICE EXERCISE FOR FRAGMENTS

1. B   The clause that begins with *despite* is independent and must be separated with the clause that follows by a comma. Option A is incorrect because a colon is used to set off a list or to emphasize what follows. In Option B, a comma incorrectly suggests that the two clauses are dependent.

2. D   In the test item, a comma correctly separates the dependent clause *After...wiring* at the beginning of the sentence from the independent clause that follows. Option A incorrectly breaks the two clauses into separate sentences, while Option B omits the comma, and Option C incorrectly suggests that the phrase is an independent clause.

3. B   The phrase *Henry decided...instead* must be joined to the independent clause. Option A incorrectly puts a colon before *Henry decided*, and Option C incorrectly separates the phrase as if it were an independent clause.

4. A   The second clause *because...information* is dependent and must be joined to the first independent clause. Option B is incorrect because as the dependent clause comes at the end of the sentence, rather than at the beginning, a comma is not necessary. In Option C, a semi-colon incorrectly suggests that the two clauses are independent.

5. A   The second clause *to keep...guests* is dependent and must be joined to the first independent clause. Option B is incorrect because as the dependent clause comes at the end of the sentence, rather than at the beginning, a comma is not necessary. In Option C, a semi-colon incorrectly suggests that the two clauses are independent.

Run-on sentences and comma splices

Comma splices appear when two sentences are joined by only a comma. Fused sentences appear when two sentences are run together with no punctuation at all.

Error: Dr. Sanders is a brilliant scientist, his research on genetic disorders won him a Nobel Prize.

Problem: A comma alone cannot join two independent clauses (complete sentences). The two clauses can be joined by a semi-colon, or they can be separated by a period.

Correction: *Dr. Sanders is a brilliant scientist; his research on genetic disorders won him a Nobel Prize.*
                                    -OR-
Dr. Sanders is a brilliant scientist. His research on genetic disorders won him a Nobel Prize.

Error: Florida is noted for its beaches they are long, sandy, and beautiful.

Problem: The first sentence ends with the word beaches, and the second sentence cannot be joined with the first. The fused sentence error can be corrected in several ways: (1) one clause may be made dependent on another with a subordinating conjunction or a relative pronoun; (2) a semi-colon may be used to combine two equally important ideas; (3) the two independent clauses may be separated by a period.

Correction: *Florida is noted for its beaches, which are long, sandy, and beautiful.*
                                    -OR-
Florida is noted for its beaches; they are long, sandy, and beautiful.
                                    -OR-
Florida is noted for its beaches. They are long, sandy, and beautiful.

Error: The number of hotels has increased, however, the number of visitors has grown also.

Problem: The first sentence ends with the word increased, and a comma is not strong enough to connect it to the second sentence. The adverbial transition however does not function the same way as a coordinating conjunction and cannot be used with commas to link two sentences. Several different corrections are available.

Correction: *The number of hotels has increased; however, the number of visitors has grown also.*
[Two separate but closely related sentences are created with the use of the semicolon.]

-OR-

The number of hotels has increased. However, the number of visitors has grown also.
[Two separate sentences are created.]

-OR-

Although the number of hotels has increased, the number of visitors has grown also.
[One idea is made subordinate to the other and separated with a comma.]

-OR-

The number of hotels has increased, but the number of visitors has grown also.
[The comma before the coordinating conjunction *but* is appropriate. The adverbial transition however does not function the same way as the coordinating conjunction but does.]

PRACTICE EXERCISE – FUSED SENTENCES AND COMMA SPLICES

Choose the option that corrects an error in the underlined portion(s). If no error exists, choose "No change is necessary."

1) Scientists are excited at the ability to clone a <u>sheep however,</u> it is not yet known if the same can be done to humans.

    A) sheep, however,
    B) sheep. However,
    C) sheep, however;
    D) No change is necessary.

2) Because of the rising cost of college <u>tuition the</u> federal government now offers special financial assistance, <u>such as loans,</u> to students.

    A) tuition, the
    B) tuition; the
    C) such as loans
    D) No change is necessary.

3) As the number of homeless people continues to <u>rise, the major cities</u> like <u>New York and Chicago,</u> are now investing millions of dollars in low-income housing.

    A) rise. The major cities
    B) rise; the major cities
    C) New York and Chicago
    D) No change is necessary.

4) Unlike in <u>the 1950's, most</u> households find the husband and wife working full-time to make <u>ends meet in many</u> different career fields.

    A) the 1950's; most
    B) the 1950's most
    C) ends meet, in many
    D) No change is necessary.

ANSWER KEY : PRACTICE EXERCISE FOR COMMA SPLICES AND FUSED SENTENCES

1) B   Option B correctly separates two independent clauses. The comma in Option A after the word sheep creates a run-on sentence. The semi-colon in Option C does not separate the two clauses but occurs at an inappropriate point.

2) A   The comma in Option A correctly separates the independent clause and the dependent clause. The semi-colon in Option B is incorrect because one of the clauses is independent. Option C requires a comma to prevent a run-on sentence.

3) C   Option C is correct because a comma creates a run-on. Option A is incorrect because the first clause is dependent. The semi-colon in Option B incorrectly divides the dependent clause from the independent clause.

4) D   Option D correctly separates the two clauses with a comma. Option A incorrectly uses a semi-colon to divide the clauses. The lack of a comma in Option B creates a run-on sentence. Option C puts a comma in an inappropriate place.

Skill 8.6   Identify standard subject-verb agreement.

A verb must correspond in the singular or plural form with the simple subject; it is not affected by any interfering elements. Note: A simple subject is never found in a prepositional phrase (a phrase beginning with a word such as of, by, over, through, until).

Present Tense Verb Form

	Singular	Plural
1st person (talking about oneself)	I do	We do
2nd person (talking to another)	You do	You do
3rd person (talking about someone or something)	He She does It	They do

Error: Sally, as well as her sister, plan to go into nursing.

Problem: The subject in the sentence is *Sally* alone, not the word *sister*. Therefore, the verb must be singular.

Correction: *Sally, as well as her sister, plans to go into nursing.*

Error: There has been many car accidents lately on that street.

Problem: The subject *accidents* in this sentence is plural; the verb must be plural also—even though it comes before the subject.

Correction: *There have been many car accidents lately on that street.*

Error: Every one of us have a reason to attend the school musical.

Problem: The simple subject is *every one*, not the *us* in the prepositional phrase. Therefore, the verb must be singular also.

Correction: *Every one of us has a reason to attend the school musical.*

Error: Either the police captain or his officers is going to the convention.

Problem: In either/or and neither/nor constructions, the verb agrees with the subject closer to it.

Correction: *Either the police captain or his officers are going to the convention.*

PRACTICE EXERCISE – SUBJECT-VERB AGREEMENT

Choose the option that corrects an error in the underlined portion(s).
If no error exists, choose "No change is necessary."

1)   Every year, the store <u>stays</u> open late, when shoppers desperately <u>try</u> to purchase Christmas presents as they <u>prepare</u> for the holiday.

        A. stay
        B. tries
        C. prepared
        D. No change is necessary.

2)   Paul McCartney, together with George Harrison and Ringo Starr, <u>sing</u> classic Beatles songs on a special greatest-hits CD.

        A. singing
        B. sings
        C. sung
        D. No change is necessary.

3)   My friend's cocker spaniel, while <u>chasing</u> cats across the street, always <u>manages</u> to <u>knock</u> over the trash cans.

        A. chased
        B. manage
        C. knocks
        D. No change is necessary.

4)   Some of the ice on the driveway <u>have melted.</u>

        A. having melted.
        B. has melted.
        C. has melt.
        D. No change is necessary.

5)   Neither the criminal forensics expert nor the DNA blood evidence <u>provide</u> enough support for that verdict.

        A. provides
        B. were providing
        C. are providing
        D. No change is necessary.

ANSWER KEY: PRACTICE EXERCISE FOR SUBJECT-VERB AGREEMENT

1) D   Option D is correct because *store* is third person singular and requires the third person singular verbs *stays*. Option B is incorrect because the plural noun *shoppers* requires a plural verb *try*. In Option C, there is no reason to shift to the past tense *prepared*.

2) B   Option B is correct because the subject, *Paul McCartney,* is singular and requires the singular verb *sings*. Option A is incorrect because the present participle *singing* does not stand alone as a verb. Option C is incorrect because the past participle *sung* alone cannot function as the verb in this sentence.

3) D   Option D is the correct answer because the subject *cocker spaniel* is singular and requires the singular verb *manages*. Options A, B, and C do not work structurally with the sentence.

4) B   The subject of the sentence is *some*, which requires a third person singular verb, *has melted*. Option A incorrectly uses the present participle *having*, which does not act as a helping verb. Option C does not work structurally with the sentence.

5) A   In Option A, the singular subject *evidence* is closer to the verb and thus requires the singular in the neither/nor construction. Both Options B and C are plural forms with the helping verb and the present participle.

Sample Test: Reading

Read the passages, and answer the questions that follow.

This writer has often been asked to tutor hospitalized children with cystic fibrosis. While undergoing all the precautionary measures to see these children (i.e., scrubbing thoroughly and donning sterilized protective gear- for the child's protection), she has often wondered why their parents subject these children to the pressures of schooling and trying to catch up on what they have missed because of hospitalization, which is a normal part of cystic fibrosis patients' lives. These children undergo so many tortuous treatments a day that it seems cruel to expect them to learn as normal children do, especially with their life expectancies being as short as they are.

1. **What is meant by the word "precautionary" in the second sentence?**

   A. Careful
   B. Protective
   C. Medical
   D. Sterilizing

2. **What is the author's tone?**

   A. Sympathetic
   B. Cruel
   C. Disbelieving
   D. Cheerful

3. **What is the main idea of this passage?**

   A. There is a lot of preparation involved in visiting a patient with cystic fibrosis.
   B. Children with cystic fibrosis are incapable of living normal lives.
   C. Certain concessions should be made for children with cystic fibrosis.
   D. Children with cystic fibrosis die young.

4. **How is the author so familiar with the procedures used when visiting a child with cystic fibrosis?**

   A. She has read about it.
   B. She works in a hospital.
   C. She is the parent of one.
   D. She often tutors them.

5. **What is the author's purpose?**

   A. To inform
   B. To entertain
   C. To describe
   D. To narrate

6. **What type of organizational pattern is the author using?**

    A. Classification
    B. Explanation
    C. Comparison and contrast
    D. Cause and effect

7. **The author states that it is "cruel" to expect children with cystic fibrosis to learn as "normal" children do. Is this a fact or an opinion?**

    A. Fact
    B. Opinion

8. **Is there evidence of bias in this paragraph?**

    A. Yes
    B. No

9. **What kind of relationship is found within the last sentence, which starts with "These children undergo..." and ends with "...as short as they are"?**

    A. Addition
    B. Explanation
    C. Generalization
    D. Classification

10. **Does the author present an argument that is valid or invalid concerning the schooling of children with cystic fibrosis?**

    A. Valid
    B. Invalid

Disciplinary practices have been found to affect diverse areas of child development, such as the acquisition of moral values, obedience to authority, and performance at school. Even though the dictionary has a specific definition of the word "discipline," it is still open to interpretation by people of different cultures.

There are four types of disciplinary styles: assertion of power, withdrawal of love, reasoning, and permissiveness. Assertion of power involves the use of force to discourage unwanted behavior. Withdrawal of love involves making the love of a parent conditional on a child's good behavior. Reasoning involves persuading the child to behave one way rather than another. Permissiveness involves allowing the child to do as he or she pleases and face the consequences of his/her actions.

11. **What is the meaning of the word "diverse" in the first sentence?**

   A. Many
   B. Related to children
   C. Disciplinary
   D. Moral

12. **What organizational structure is used in the first sentence of the second paragraph?**

   A. Addition
   B. Explanation
   C. Definition
   D. Simple listing

13. **Name the four types of disciplinary styles.**

   A. Reasoning, power assertion, morality, and permissiveness.
   B. Morality, reasoning, permissiveness, and withdrawal of love.
   C. Withdrawal of love, permissiveness, assertion of power, and reasoning.
   D. Permissiveness, morality, reasoning, and power assertion.

14. **What is the main idea of this passage?**

   A. Different people have different ideas of what discipline is.
   B. Permissiveness is the most widely-used disciplinary style.
   C. Most people agree on their definition of discipline.
   D. There are four disciplinary styles.

15. **What is the author's purpose in writing this?**

    A. To describe
    B. To narrate
    C. To entertain
    D. To inform

16. **Is this passage biased?**

    A. Yes
    B. No

17. **What is the author's tone?**

    A. Disbelieving
    B. Angry
    C. Informative
    D. Optimistic

18. **What is the overall organizational pattern of this passage?**

    A. Generalization
    B. Cause and effect
    C. Addition
    D. Summary

19. **The author states that "assertion of power involves the use of force to discourage unwanted behavior." Is this a fact or an opinion?**

    A. Fact
    B. Opinion

20. **From reading this passage, we can conclude that**

    A. The author is a teacher.
    B. The author has many children.
    C. The author has written a book about discipline.
    D. The author has done a lot of research on discipline.

21. **What does the technique of reasoning involve?**

    A. Persuading the child to behave in a certain way.
    B. Allowing the child to do as he/she pleases.
    C. Using force to discourage unwanted behavior.
    D. Making love conditional on good behavior.

One of the most difficult problems plaguing American education is the assessment of teachers. No one denies that teachers ought to be answerable for what they do, but what exactly does that mean? The Oxford American Dictionary defines accountability as: the obligation to give a reckoning or explanation for one's actions.

Does a student have to learn for teaching to have taken place? Historically, teaching has not been defined in this restrictive manner; the teacher was thought to be responsible for the quantity and quality of material covered and the way in which it was presented. However, some definitions of teaching now imply that students must learn in order for teaching to have taken place.

As a teacher who tries my best to keep current on all the latest teaching strategies, I believe that those teachers who do not bother even to pick up an educational journal every once in a while should be kept under close watch. There are many teachers out there who have been teaching for decades and who refuse to change their ways even if research has proven that their methods are outdated and ineffective. There is no place in the profession of teaching for these types of individuals. It is time that the American educational system clean house, for the sake of our children.

22. **What is the meaning of the word "reckoning" in the third sentence?**

    A. Thought
    B. Answer
    C. Obligation
    D. Explanation

23. **What is the organizational pattern of the second paragraph?**

    A. Cause and effect
    B. Classification
    C. Addition
    D. Explanation

24. **What is the main idea of the passage?**

    A. Teachers should not be answerable for what they do.
    B. Teachers who do not do their job should be fired.
    C. The author is a good teacher.
    D. Assessment of teachers is a serious problem in society today.

25. **Is this a valid argument?**

    A. Yes
    B. No

26. From the passage, one can infer that

A. The author considers herself a good teacher.
B. Poor teachers will be fired.
C. Students have to learn for teaching to take place.
D. The author will be fired.

27. Teachers who do not keep current on educational trends should be fired. Is this a fact or an opinion?

A. Fact
B. Opinion

28. The author states that teacher assessment is a problem for

A. Elementary schools
B. Secondary schools
C. American education
D. Families

29. What is the author's purpose in writing this?

A. To entertain
B. To narrate
C. To describe
D. To persuade

30. Is there evidence of bias in this passage?

A. Yes
B. No

31. What is the author's overall organizational pattern?

A. Classification
B. Cause and effect
C. Definition
D. Comparison and contrast

32. The author's tone is one of

A. Disbelief
B. Excitement
C. Support
D. Concern

33. What is meant by the word "plaguing" in the first sentence?

A. Causing problems
B. Causing illness
C. Causing anger
D. Causing failure

34. Where does the author get her definition of "accountability"?

A. Webster's Dictionary
B. Encyclopedia Britannica
C. Oxford Dictionary
D. World Book Encyclopedia

Mr. Smith gave instructions for the painting to be hung on the wall. And then, it leaped forth before his eyes: the little cottages on the river, the white clouds floating over the valley, and the green of the towering mountain ranges that were seen in the distance. The painting was so vivid that it seemed almost real. Mr. Smith was now absolutely certain that the painting had been worth money.

35. **What does the author mean by the expression "it leaped forth before his eyes"?**

    A. The painting fell off the wall.
    B. The painting appeared so real it was almost three-dimensional.
    C. The painting struck Mr. Smith in the face.
    D. Mr. Smith was hallucinating.

36. **From the last sentence, one can infer that**

    A. The painting was expensive.
    B. The painting was cheap.
    C. Mr. Smith was considering purchasing the painting.
    D. Mr. Smith thought the painting was too expensive and decided not to purchase it.

37. **What is the main idea of this passage?**

    A. The painting that Mr. Smith purchased is expensive.
    B. Mr. Smith purchased a painting.
    C. Mr. Smith was pleased with the quality of the painting he had purchased.
    D. The painting depicted cottages and valleys.

38. **The author's purpose is to**

    A. Inform
    B. Entertain
    C. Persuade
    D. Narrate

39. **What is the meaning of the word "vivid" in the third sentence?**

    A. Lifelike
    B. Dark
    C. Expensive
    D. Big

40. **Is this passage biased?**

    A. Yes
    B. No

Answer Key: Reading

1.   B.
2.   A.
3.   C.
4.   D.
5.   C.
6.   B.
7.   B.
8.   A.
9.   B.
10. B.
11. A.
12. D.
13. C.
14. A.
15. D.
16. B.
17. C.
18. C.
19. A.
20. D.
21. A.
22. D.
23. D.
24. D.
25. B.
26. A.
27. B.
28. C.
29. D.
30. A.
31. C.
32. D.
33. A.
34. C.
35. B.
36. A.
37. C.
38. D.
39. A.
40. B.

Answers with Rationale: Reading

1. B. The writer uses expressions such as "protective gear" and "child's protection" to emphasize this.

2. A. The author states that "it seems cruel to expect them to learn as normal children do," thereby indicating that she feels sorry for them.

3. C. The author states that she wonders "why parents subject these children to the pressures of schooling" and that "it seems cruel to expect them to learn as normal children do." In making these statements, she appears to be expressing the belief that these children should not have to do what "normal" children do. They have enough to deal with – their illness itself.

4. D. The writer states this fact in the opening sentence.

5. C. The author is simply describing her experience in working with children with cystic fibrosis.

6. B. The author mentions tutoring children with cystic fibrosis in her opening sentence and goes on to "explain" some of these issues that are involved with her job.

7. B. The fact that she states that it "seems" cruel indicates there is no evidence to support this belief.

8. A. The writer clearly feels sorry for these children and gears her writing in that direction.

9. B. In mentioning that their life expectancies are short, she is explaining by giving one reason why it is cruel to expect them to learn as normal children do.

10. B. Even though, to most readers, the writer's argument makes good sense, it is biased and lacks real evidence.

11. A. Any of the other choices would be redundant in this sentence.

12. D. The author simply states the types of disciplinary styles.

13. C. This is directly stated in the second paragraph.

14. A. Choice C is not true; the opposite is stated in the passage. Choice B could be true, but we have no evidence of this. Choice D is just one of the many facts listed in the passage.

15. D. The author is providing the reader with information about disciplinary practices.

16. B. If the reader were so inclined, he could research discipline and find this information.

17. C. The author appears to simply be stating the facts.

18. C. The author has taken a subject, in this case discipline, and developed it point by point.

19. A. The author appears to have done extensive research on this subject.

20. D. Given all the facts mentioned in the passage, this is the only inference one can make.

21. A. This fact is directly stated in the second paragraph.

22. D. The meaning of this word is directly stated in the same sentence.

23. D. The author goes on to further explain what she meant by "...what exactly does that mean?" in the first paragraph.

24. D. Most of the passage is dedicated to elaborating on why teacher assessment is such a problem.

25. B. In the third paragraph, the author appears to be resentful of lazy teachers.

26. A. The first sentence of the third paragraph alludes to this.

27. B. There may be those who feel they can be good teachers by using old methods.

28. C. This fact is directly stated in the first paragraph.

29. D. The author does some describing, but the majority of her statements seem to be geared towards convincing the reader that teachers who are lazy or who do not keep current should be fired.

30. A. The entire third paragraph is the author's opinion on the matter.

31. C. The author identifies teacher assessment as a problem and spends the rest of the passage defining why it is considered a problem.

32. D. The author appears concerned with the future of education.

33. A. The first paragraph makes this definition clear.

34. C. This is directly stated in the third sentence of the first paragraph.

35. B. This is almost directly stated in the third sentence.

36. A. Choice B is incorrect because, had the painting been cheap, chances are that Mr. Smith would no have considered his purchase. Choices C and D are ruled out by the fact that the painting had already been purchased. The author makes this clear when she says, "...the painting had been worth the money."

37. C. Every sentence in the paragraph alludes to this fact.

38. D. The author is simply narrating or telling the story of Mr. Smith and his painting.

39. A. This is reinforced by the second half of the same sentence.

40. B. The author appears to just be telling what happened when Mr. Smith had his new painting hung on the wall.

Sample Test: Communication Skills

DIRECTIONS: *The passage below contains many errors. Read the passage. Then, answer each test item by choosing the option that corrects an error in the underlined portion(s). No more than one underlined error will appear in each item. If no error exists, choose "No change is necessary."*

Climbing to the top of Mount Everest is an adventure. One which everyone--whether physically fit or not--seems eager to try. The trail stretches for miles, the cold temperatures are usually frigid and brutal.

Climbers must endure severel barriers on the way, including other hikers, steep jagged rocks, and lots of snow. Plus, climbers often find the most grueling part of the trip is their climb back down, just when they are feeling greatly exhausted. Climbers who take precautions are likely to find the ascent less arduous than the unprepared. By donning heavy flannel shirts, gloves, and hats, climbers prevented hypothermia, as well as simple frostbite. A pair of rugged boots is also one of the necesities. If climbers are to avoid becoming dehydrated, there is beverages available for them to transport as well.

Once climbers are completely ready to begin their lengthy journey, they can comfortable enjoy the wonderful scenery. Wide rock formations dazzle the observers eyes with shades of gray and white, while the peak forms a triangle that seems to touch the sky. Each of the climbers are reminded of the splendor and magnificence of God's great Earth.

1. **Climbing to the top of Mount Everest is an <u>adventure. One</u> which everyone —<u>whether</u> physically fit or not—<u>seems</u> eager to try.**

    A. adventure, one
    B. people, whether
    C. seem
    D. No change is necessary.

2. **The <u>trail</u> stretches for <u>miles,</u> the cold temperatures are <u>usually</u> frigid and brutal.**

    A. trails
    B. miles;
    C. usual
    D. No change is necessary.

3. **Climbers must endure <u>severel</u> barriers <u>on the way,</u> <u>including</u> other <u>hikers,</u> steep jagged rocks, and lots of snow.**

    A. several
    B. on the way: including
    C. hikers'
    D. No change is necessary.

4. Plus, climbers often find the most grueling part of the trip is **their** climb back **down, just** when they **are** feeling greatly exhausted.

   A. his
   B. down; just
   C. were
   D. No change is necessary.

5. **Climbers who** take precautions are likely to find the ascent **less difficult** **than** the unprepared.

   A. Climbers, who
   B. least difficult
   C. then
   D. No change is necessary.

6. By donning heavy flannel shirts, boots, and **hats, climbers** **prevented** hypothermia, as well as simple frostbite.

   A. hats climbers
   B. can prevent
   C. hypothermia;
   D. No change is necessary.

7. A pair of rugged boots **is also** **one** of the **necesities**.

   A. are
   B. also, one
   C. necessities
   D. No change is necessary.

8. If climbers are to avoid **becoming** dehydrated, there **is** beverages available for **them** to transport as well.

   A. becomming
   B. are
   C. him
   D. No change is necessary.

9. Once climbers are completely prepared for **their** lengthy **journey, they** can **comfortable** enjoy the wonderful scenery.

   A. they're
   B. journey; they
   C. comfortably
   D. No change is necessary.

10. Wide rock formations dazzle the **observers eyes** with shades of gray and **white, while** the peak **forms** a triangle that seems to touch the sky.

    A. observers' eyes
    B. white; while
    C. formed
    D. No change is necessary.

11. Each of the climbers **are** reminded of the splendor and **magnificence** of **God's** great Earth.

    A. is
    B. magnifisence
    C. Gods
    D. No change is necessary.

DIRECTIONS: *The passage below contains several errors. Read the passage. Then, answer each test item by choosing the option that corrects an error in the underlined portion(s). No more than one underlined error will appear in each item. If no error exists, choose "No change is necessary."*

Every job places different kinds of demands on their employees. For example, whereas such jobs as accounting and bookkeeping require mathematical ability; graphic design requires creative/artistic ability.

Doing good at one job does not usually guarantee success at another. However, one of the elements crucial to all jobs are especially notable: the chance to accomplish a goal.

The accomplishment of the employees varies according to the job. In many jobs, the employees become accustom to the accomplishment provided by the work they do every day.

In medicine, for example, every doctor tests him self by treating badly-injured or critically-ill people. In the operating room, a team of Surgeons, is responsible for operating on many of these patients. In addition to the feeling of accomplishment that the workers achieve, some jobs also give a sense of identity to the employees'. Profesions like law, education, and sales offer huge financial and emotional rewards. Politicians are public servants: who work for the federal and state governments. President bush is basically employed by the American people to make laws and run the country.

Finally; the contributions that employees make to their companies and to the world cannot be taken for granted. Through their work, employees are performing a service for their employers and are contributing something to the world.

12. **Every job places different kinds of demands on their employees.**

   A. place
   B. its
   C. employees
   D. No change is necessary.

13. **For example, whereas such jobs as accounting and bookkeeping require mathematical ability; graphic design requires creative/artistic ability.**

   A. For example
   B. whereas,
   C. ability,
   D. No change is necessary.

14. **Doing good at one job does not usually guarantee success at another.**

   A. well
   B. usually
   C. succeeding
   D. No change is necessary.

15. **However,** one of the elements crucial to all jobs **are** especially **notable:** the accomplishment of a goal.

A. However
B. is
C. notable;
D. No change is necessary.

16. The **accomplishment** of the **employees varies** according to the job.

A. accomplishment,
B. employee's
C. vary
D. No change is necessary.

17. In many jobs, the employees **become accustom** to the accomplishment **provided** by the work they do every day.

A. became
B. accustomed
C. provides
D. No change is necessary.

18. In medicine, for example, every doctor **tests** **him self** by treating badly-injured and critically-ill people.

A. test
B. himself
C. critical
D. No change is necessary.

19. In the **operating room,** a team of **Surgeons, is** responsible for operating on many of **these** patients.

A. operating room:
B. surgeons is
C. those
D. No change is necessary.

20. In addition to the feeling of accomplishment that the workers **achieve,** some jobs also **give** a sense of self-identity to the **employees'.**

A. achieve
B. gave
C. employees
D. No change is necessary.

21. **Profesions** like law, **education,** and sales **offer** huge financial and emotional rewards.

A. Professions
B. education;
C. offered
D. No change is necessary.

22. Politicians **are** public **servants: who work** for the federal and state governments.

A. were
B. servants who
C. worked
D. No change is necessary.

23. President bush is basically employed <u>by</u> the American people to <u>make</u> laws and run the country.

   A. Bush
   B. to
   C. made
   D.No change is necessary.

24. <u>Finally;</u> the contributions that employees make to <u>their</u> companies and to the world cannot be <u>taken</u> for granted.

   A. Finally,
   B. their
   C. took
   D. No change is necessary.

DIRECTIONS: *For the underlined sentence(s), choose the option that expresses the meaning with the most fluency and the clearest logic within the context. If the underlined sentence should not be changed, choose Option A, which shows no change.*

25. Selecting members of a President's cabinet can often be an aggravating process. <u>Either there are too many or too few qualified candidates for a certain position, and then they have to be confirmed by the Senate, where there is the possibility of rejection.</u>

   A. Either there are too many or too few qualified candidates for a certain position, and then they have to be confirmed by the Senate, where there is the possibility of rejection.

   B. Qualified candidates for certain positions face the possibility of rejection, when they have to be confirmed by the Senate.

   C. The Senate has to confirm qualified candidates, who face the possibility of rejection.

   D. Because the Senate has to confirm qualified candidates; they face the possibility of rejection.

26. **Treating patients for drug and/or alcohol abuse is a sometimes difficult process. <u>Even though there are a number of different methods for helping the patient overcome a dependency, there is no way of knowing which is best in the long-run</u>.**

   A. Even though there are a number of different methods for helping the patient overcome a dependency, there is no way of knowing which is best in the long-run.

   B. Even though different methods can help a patient overcome a dependency, there is no way to know which is best in the long-run.

   C. Even though there is no way to know which way is best in the long run, patients can overcome their dependencies when they are helped.

   D. There is no way to know which method will help the patient overcome a dependency in the long-run, even though there are many different ones.

27. **Many factors account for the decline in the quality of public education. <u>Overcrowding, budget cutbacks, and societal deterioration which have greatly affected student learning</u>.**

   A. Overcrowding, budget cutbacks, and societal deterioration which have greatly affected student learning.

   B. Student learning has been greatly affected by overcrowding, budget cutbacks, and societal deterioration.

   C. Due to overcrowding, budget cutbacks, and societal deterioration, student learning has been greatly affected.

   D. Overcrowding, budget cutbacks, and societal deterioration have affected students learning greatly.

28. **Which of the following sentences logically and correctly expresses the comparison?**

    A. The Empire State Building in New York is taller than buildings in the city.

    B. The Empire State Building in New York is taller than any other building in the city.

    C. The Empire State Building in New York is tallest than other buildings in the city.

DIRECTIONS: *Choose the most effective word within the context of the sentence.*

29. **Many of the clubs in Boca Raton are noted for their _____ elegance.**

    A. vulgar
    B. tasteful
    C. ordinary

30. **When a student is expelled from school, the parents are usually _____ in advance.**

    A. rewarded
    B. congratulated
    C. notified

31. **Before appearing in court, the witness was _____ the papers requiring her to show up.**

    A. condemned
    B. served
    C. criticized

DIRECTIONS: *Choose the underlined word or phrase that is unnecessary within the context of the passage.*

32. **Considered by many to be one of the worst terrorist incidents on American soil was the bombing of the Oklahoma City Federal Building, which will be remembered for years to come.**

   A. considered by many to be
   B. terrorist
   C. on American soil
   D. for years to come

33. **The flu epidemic struck most of the respected faculty and students of The Woolbright School, forcing the Boynton Beach School Superintendent to close it down for two weeks.**

   A. flu
   B. most of
   C. respected
   D. for two weeks

34. **The expanding number of television channels has prompted cable operators to raise their prices, even though many consumers do not want to pay a higher increased amount for their service.**

   A. expanding
   B. prompted
   C. even though
   D. increased

DIRECTIONS: *The passage below contains several errors. Read the passage. Then, answer each test item by choosing the option that corrects an error in the underlined portion(s). No more than one underlined error will appear in each item. If no error exists, choose "No change is necessary."*

The discovery of a body at Paris Point marina in Boca Raton shocked the residents of Palmetto Pines, a luxury condominium complex located next door to the marina.

The victim is a thirty-five year old woman who had been apparently bludgeoned to death and dumped in the ocean late last night. Many neighbors reported terrible screams, gunshots: as well as the sound of a car backfiring loudly to Boca Raton Police shortly after midnight. The woman had been spotted in the lobby of Palmetto Pines around ten thirty, along with an older man, estimated to be in his fifties, and a younger man, in his late twenties.

"Apparently, the victim had been driven to the complex by the older man and was seen arguing with him when the younger man intervened," said Sheriff Fred Adams, "all three of them left the building together and walked to the marina, where gunshots rang out an hour later." Deputies found five bullets on the sidewalk and some blood, along with a steel pipe that is assumed to be the murder weapon. Two men were seen fleeing the scene in a red Mercedes shortly after, rushing toward the Interstate.

The Palm Beach County Coroner, Melvin Watts, said he concluded the victim's skull had been crushed by a blunt tool, which resulted in a brain hemorrhage. As of now, there is no clear motive for the murder.

35. **The discovery of a body at Paris Point marina in Boca Raton shocked the residents of Palmetto Pines, a luxury condominium complex located next door to the marina.**

    A. Marina
    B. residence
    C. condominium
    D. No change is necessary.

36. **The victim is a thirty-five-year-old who had been apparently bludgeoned to death and dumped in the ocean late last night.**

    A. was
    B. bludgoned
    C. ocean: late
    D. No change is necessary .

37. **Many neighbors reported terrible screams, gunshots: as well as the sound of a car backfiring loudly to Boca Raton Police shortly after midnight.**

    A. nieghbors
    B. gunshots, as
    C. loud
    D. No change is necessary.

38. **The woman had been spotted in the lobby of Palmetto Pines around ten thirty, along with an older man, estimated to be in his fifties, and a younger man in his late twenties.**

    A. has
    B. thirty;
    C. man estimated
    D. No change is necessary.

39. **"Apparently, the victim had been driven to the complex by the older man and was seen arguing with him when the younger man intervened," said Sheriff Fred Adams, "all three of them left the building together and walked to the marina, where gunshots rang out an hour later."**

    A. sheriff Fred Adams, "all
    B. sheriff Fred Adams, "All
    C. Sheriff Fred Adams." All
    D. No change is necessary.

40. **Deputies found five bullets on the sidewalk and some blood, along with a steel pipe that is assumed to be the murder weapon.**

    A. blood;
    B. assuming
    C. to have been
    D. No change is necessary.

Answer Key: Communication Skills

1.	A		21.	A
2.	B		22.	B
3.	A		23.	A
4.	D		24.	A
5.	D		25.	C
6.	D		26.	B
7.	C		27.	B
8.	B		28.	B
9.	C		29.	B
10.	A		30.	C
11.	A		31.	B
12.	B		32.	A
13.	C		33.	C
14.	A		34.	D
15.	B		35.	A
16.	C		36.	A
17.	B		37.	B
18.	B		38.	C
19.	B		39.	C
20.	C		40.	C

Answers with Rationale: Communication Skills

1. **A**   A comma is needed between *adventure* and *one* to avoid creating a fragment of the second part. In Option B, a comma after *everyone* would not be appropriate when the dash is used on the other side of *not*. In Option C, the singular verb *seems* is needed to agree with the singular subject *everyone*.

2. **B**   A semicolon, not a comma, is needed to separate the first independent clause from the second independent clause. Option A is incorrect because the plural subject *trails* needs the singular verb *stretch*. Option C is incorrect because the adverb form *usually* is needed to modify the adjective *frigid*.

3. **A**   The word *several* is misspelled in the text. Option B is incorrect because a comma, not a colon, is needed to set off the modifying phrase. Option C is incorrect because no apostrophe is needed after *hikers* since possession is not involved.

4. **D**   The present tense must be used consistently throughout; therefore, Option C is incorrect. Option A is incorrect because the singular pronoun *his* does not agree with the plural antecedent *climbers*. Option B is incorrect because a comma, not a semicolon, is needed to separate the dependent clause from the main clause.

5. **D**   No change is needed. Option A is incorrect because a comma would make the phrase *who take precautions* seem less restrictive or less essential to the sentence. Option B is incorrect because *less* is appropriate when two items--the prepared and the unprepared--are compared. Option C is incorrect because the comparative adverb *than*, not *then*, is needed.

6. **D**   No change is necessary.

7. **C**   The word *necessities* is misspelled in the text. Option A is incorrect because the singular verb *is* must agree with the singular noun *pair* (a collective singular). Option B is incorrect because *if also* is set off with commas (potential correction); it should be set off on both sides.

8. **B**   The plural verb *are* must be used with the plural subject *beverages*. Option A is incorrect because *becoming* has only one *m*. Option C is incorrect because the plural pronoun *them* is needed to agree with the referent *climbers*.

9. **C** The adverb form *comfortably* is needed to modify the verb phrase *can enjoy*. Option A is incorrect because the possessive plural pronoun is spelled *their*. Option B is incorrect because a semi-colon would make the first half of the item seem like an independent clause when the subordinating conjunction *once* makes that clause dependent.

10. **A** An apostrophe is needed to show the plural possessive form *observers' eyes*. Option B is incorrect because the semicolon would make the second half of the item seem like an independent clause when the subordinating conjunction *while* makes that clause dependent. Option C is incorrect because *formed* is in the wrong tense.

11. **A** The singular verb *is* agrees with the singular subject *each.* Option B is incorrect because *magnificence* is misspelled. Option C is incorrect because an apostrophe is needed to show possession.

12. **B** The singular possessive pronoun *its* must agree with its antecedent *job*, which is singular also. Option A is incorrect because *place* is a plural form, and the subject, *job*, is singular. Option C is incorrect because the correct spelling of employees is given in the sentence.

13. **C** An introductory dependent clause is set off with a comma, not a semicolon. Option A is incorrect because the transitional phrase *for example* should be set off with a comma. Option B is incorrect because the adverb *whereas* functions like *while* and does not take a comma after it.

14. **A** The adverb *well* modifies the word *doing*. Option B is incorrect because *usually* is spelled correctly in the sentence. Option C is incorrect because *succeeding* is in the wrong tense.

15. **B** The singular verb *is* is needed to agree with the singular subject *one.* Option A is incorrect because a comma is needed to set off the transitional word *however.* Option C is incorrect because a colon, not a semicolon, is needed to set off an item.

16. **C** The singular verb *vary* is needed to agree with the singular subject *accomplishment.* Option A is incorrect because a comma after *accomplishment* would suggest that the modifying phrase *of the employees* is additional instead of essential. Option B is incorrect because *employees* is not possessive.

17. **B** The past participle *accustomed* is needed with the verb *become.* Option A is incorrect because the verb tense does not need to change to the past *became.* Option C is incorrect because *provides* is the wrong tense.

18. **B** The reflexive pronoun *himself* is needed. (Him self is nonstandard and never correct.) Option A is incorrect because the singular verb *test* is needed to agree with the singular subject *doctor*. Option C is incorrect because the adverb *critically* is needed to modify the verb *ill*.

19. **B** *Surgeons* is not a proper name, so it does not need to be capitalized. A comma is not needed to break up *a team of surgeons* from the rest of the sentence. Option A is incorrect because a comma ,not a colon, is needed to set off an item. Option C is incorrect because *those* is an incorrect pronoun.

20. **C** Option C is correct because *employees* is not possessive. Option A is incorrect because *achieve* is spelled correctly in the sentence. Option B is incorrect because *gave* is the wrong tense.

21. **A** Option A is correct because *professions* is misspelled in the sentence. Option B is incorrect because a comma, not a semi-colon, is needed after *education*. In Option C, *offered*, is in the wrong tense.

22. **B** A colon is not needed to set off the introduction of the sentence. In Option A, *were*, is the incorrect tense of the verb. In Option C, *worked*, is in the wrong tense.

23. **A** *Bush* is a proper name and should be capitalized. In Option B, *to* does not fit with the verb *employed*. Option C uses the wrong form of the verb *make*.

24. **A** A comma is needed to separate *Finally* from the rest of the sentence. *Finally* is a preposition which usually heads a dependent sentence, hence a comma is needed. Option B is incorrect because *their* is misspelled. Option C is incorrect because *took* is the wrong form of the verb.

25. **C** Option C is the most straightforward and concise sentence. Option A is too unwieldy with the wordy *Either...or* phrase at the beginning. Option B doesn't make clear the fact that candidates face rejection by the Senate. Option D illogically implies that candidates face rejection because they have to be confirmed by the Senate.

26. **B** Option B is concise and logical. Option A tends to ramble with the use of *there are* and the verbs *helping* and *knowing*. Option C is awkwardly worded and repetitive in the first part of the sentence, and vague in the second because it never indicates how the patients can be helped. Option D contains the unnecessary phrase *even though there are many different ones*.

27. **B** Option B is concise and best explains the causes of the decline in student education. The unnecessary use of *which* in Option A makes the sentence feel incomplete. Option C has weak coordination between the reasons for the decline in public education and the fact that student learning has been affected. Option D incorrectly places the adverb *greatly* after learning, instead of before *affected.*

28. **B** Because the Empire State Building is a building in New York City, the phrase *any other* must be included. Option A is incorrect because the Empire State Building is implicitly compared to itself since it is one of the buildings. Option C is incorrect because *tallest* is the incorrect form of the adjective.

29. **B** *Tasteful* means beautiful or charming, which would correspond to an elegant club. The words *vulgar* and *ordinary* have negative connotations.

30. **C** *Notified* means informed or told, which fits into the logic of the sentence. The words *rewarded* and *congratulated* are positive actions, which don't make sense regarding someone being expelled from school.

31. **B** *Served* means given, which makes sense in the context of the sentence. *Condemned* and *criticized* do not make sense within the context of the sentence.

32. **A** *Considered by many to be* is a wordy phrase and unnecessary in the context of the sentence. All other words are necessary within the context of the sentence.

33. **C** The fact that the faculty might have been *respected* is not really necessary to mention in the sentence. The other words and phrases are all necessary to complete the meaning of the sentence.

34. **D** The word *increased* is redundant with *higher* and should be removed. All the other words are necessary within the context of the sentence.

35. **A** *Marina* is a name that needs to be capitalized. Options B and C create misspellings.

36. **A** The past tense *was* is needed to maintain consistency. Option B creates a misspelling. Option C incorrectly uses a colon when none is needed.

37. **B** Option B correctly uses a comma, not a colon to separate the items. Option A creates a misspelling. Option C incorrectly changes the adverb into an adjective.

38. **C**   A comma is not needed to separate the item because *an older man estimated to be in his fifties* is one complete fragment. Option A incorrectly uses the present tense *has* instead of the past tense *had.* Option B incorrectly uses a colon when a comma is needed.

39. **C**   The quote's source comes in the middle of two independent clauses, so a period should follow *Adams.* Option A is incorrect because titles, when they come before a name, must be capitalized. Punctuation is also faulty. Option B is incorrect because the word *Adams* ends a sentence; a comma is not strong enough to support two sentences.

40. **C**   The past tense *to have been* is needed to maintain consistency. Option A incorrectly uses a colon, instead of a comma. Option B uses the wrong form of the verb *assumed.*

SUBAREA III.   **MATHEMATICS**

**COMPETENCY 9.0   SOLVE PROBLEMS INVOLVING DATA
                              INTERPRETATION AND ANALYSIS**

**Skill 9.1   Interpret information from line graphs, bar graphs, histograms,
              pictographs, pie charts and tables.**

To make a **bar graph** or a **pictograph**, determine the scale to be used for the
graph. Then determine the length of each bar on the graph or determine the
number of pictures needed to represent each item of information. Be sure to
include an explanation of the scale in the legend.

Example: A class had the following grades:
            4 A's, 9 B's, 8 C's, 1 D, 3 F's.
            Graph these on a bar graph and a pictograph.

Pictograph

Grade	Number of Students
A	☺☺☺☺
B	☺☺☺☺☺☺☺☺☺
C	☺☺☺☺☺☺☺☺
D	☺
F	☺☺☺

Bar graph

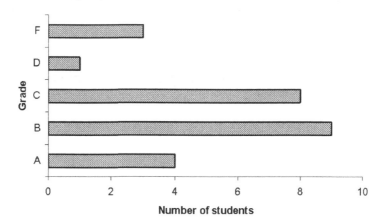

To make a **line graph**, determine appropriate scales for both the vertical and horizontal axes (based on the information to be graphed). Describe what each axis represents and mark the scale periodically on each axis. Graph the individual points of the graph and connect the points on the graph from left to right.

Example: Graph the following information using a line graph.

The number of National Merit finalists/school year

	90-91	91-92	92-93	93-94	94-95	95-96
Central	3	5	1	4	6	8
Wilson	4	2	3	2	3	2

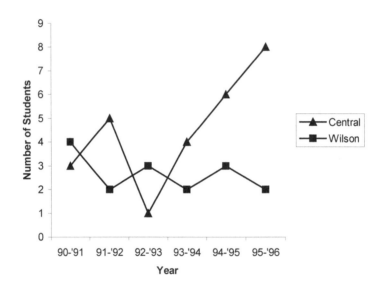

To make a **circle graph**, total all the information that is to be included on the graph. Determine the central angle to be used for each sector of the graph using the following formula:

$$\frac{\text{information}}{\text{total information}} \times 360^\circ = \text{degrees in central} \sphericalangle$$

Lay out the central angles to these sizes, label each section and include its percent.

Example: Graph this information on a circle graph:

Monthly expenses:

Rent, $400
Food, $150
Utilities, $75
Clothes, $75
Church, $100
Misc., $200

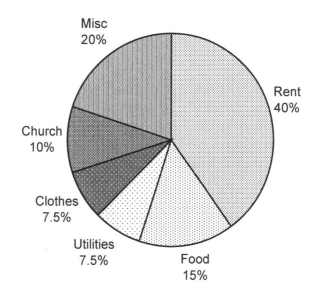

Scatter plots compare two characteristics of the same group of things or people and usually consist of a large body of data. They show how much one variable is affected by another. The relationship between the two variables is their **correlation**. The closer the data points come to making a straight line when plotted, the closer the correlation.

Stem and leaf plots are visually similar to line plots. The **stems** are the digits in the greatest place value of the data values, and the **leaves** are the digits in the next greatest place values. Stem and leaf plots are best suited for small sets of data and are especially useful for comparing two sets of data. The following is an example using test scores:

4	9
5	4 9
6	1 2 3 4 6 7 8 8
7	0 3 4 6 6 6 7 7 7 8 8 8 8
8	3 5 5 7 8
9	0 0 3 4 5
10	0 0

Histograms are used to summarize information from large sets of data that can be naturally grouped into intervals. The vertical axis indicates **frequency** (the number of times any particular data value occurs), and the horizontal axis indicates data values or ranges of data values. The number of data values in any interval is the **frequency of the interval**.

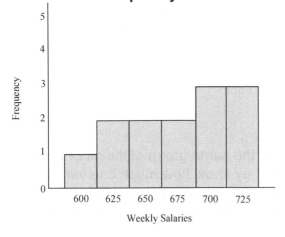

Skill 9.2   Recognize appropriate representations of various data in graphic form

A **trend** line on a line graph shows the correlation between two sets of data. A trend may show positive correlation (both sets of data get bigger together) negative correlation (one set of data gets bigger while the other gets smaller), or no correlation.

An **inference** is a statement which is derived from reasoning. When reading a graph, inferences help with interpretation of the data that is being presented. From this information, a **conclusion** and even **predictions** about what the data actually means is possible.

Example: Katherine and Tom were both doing poorly in math class. Their teacher had a conference with each of them in November. The following graph shows their math test scores during the school year.

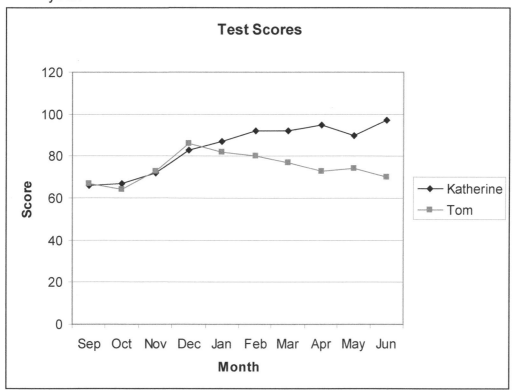

What kind of trend does this graph show?

This graph shows that there is a positive trend in Katherine's test scores and a negative trend in Tom's test scores.

What inferences can you make from this graph?

We can infer that Katherine's test scores rose steadily after November. Tom's test scores spiked in December but then began to fall again and became negatively trended.

What conclusion can you draw based upon this graph?

We can conclude that Katherine took her teacher's meeting seriously and began to study in order to do better on the exams. It seems as though Tom tried harder for a bit, but his test scores eventually slipped back down to the level where he began.

COMPETENCY 10.0 APPLY MATHEMATICAL REASONING SKILLS TO ANALYZE PATTERNS AND SOLVE PROBLEMS

Skill 10.1 Draw conclusions using inductive reasoning.

A simple statement represents a simple idea, that can be described as either "true" or "false", but not both. A simple statement is represented by a small letter of the alphabet.

Example: "Today is Monday." This is a simple statement since it can be determine that this statement is either true or false. We can write p = "Today is Monday".

Example: "John, please be quite". This is not considered a simple statement in our study of logic, since we cannot assign a truth value to it.

Simple statements joined together by **connectives** ("and", "or", "not", "if then", and "if and only if") result in compound statements. Note that compound statements can also be formed using "but", "however", or "never the less". A compound statement can be assigned a truth value.

Conditional statements are frequently written in "if-then" form. The "if" clause of the conditional is known as the **hypothesis**, and the "then" clause is called the **conclusion**. In a proof, the hypothesis is the information that is assumed to be true, while the conclusion is what is to be proven true. A conditional is considered to be of the form: **If p, then q** where p is the hypothesis and q is the conclusion.

$p \rightarrow q$ is read "if p then q".
~ (statement) is read "it is not true that (statement)".

Quantifiers are words describing a quantity under discussion. These include words like "all", "none" (or "no"), and "some".

Negation of a Statement- If a statement is true, then its negation must be false (and vice versa).

A Summary of Negation Rules:

statement	negation
(1) q	(1) <u>not</u> q
(2) <u>not</u> q	(2) q
(3) π <u>and</u> s	(3) (not π) <u>or</u> (not s)
(4) π <u>or</u> s	(4) (not π) <u>and</u> (not s)
(5) if p, then q	(5) (p) <u>and</u> (not q)

Example: Select the statement that is the negation of "some winter nights are not cold".

        A. All winter nights are not cold.
        B. Some winter nights are cold.
        C. All winter nights are cold.
        D. None of the winter nights are cold.

        Negation of "some are" is "none are". So the negation statement is "none of the winter night is cold". So the answer is D.

Example: Select the statement that is the negation of "if it rains, then the beach party will not be held".

        A. If it does not rain, then the beach party will be held.
        B. If the beach party is held, then it will not rain.
        C. It does not rain and the beach party will be held.
        D. It rains and the beach party will be held.

        Negation of "if p, then q" is "p and (not q)". So the negation of the given statement is "it rains and the beach party will be held". So select D.

Example: Select the negation of the statement "If they get elected, then all politicians go back on election promises".

        A. If they get elected, then many politicians go back on election promises.
        B. They get elected and some politicians go back on election promises.
        C. If they do not get elected, some politicians do not go back on election promises.
        D. None of the above statements is the negation of the given statement.

        Identify the key words of "if...then" and "all...go back". The negation of the given statement is "they get elected and none of the politicians go back on election promises". So select response D, since A, B, and C, statements are not the negations.

Example: Select the statement that is the negation of "the sun is shining bright and I feel great".

A. If the sun is not shining bright. I do not feel great.
B. The sun is not shining bright and I do not feel great.
C. The sun is not shining bring or I do not feel great.
D. the sun is shining bright and I do not feel great.

The negation of "r and s" is "(not r) or (not s)". So the negation of the given statement is "the sun is <u>not</u> shining bright <u>or</u> I do not feel great". We select response C.

Conditional statements can be diagrammed using a **Venn diagram**. A diagram can be drawn with one circle inside another circle. The inner circle represents the hypothesis. The outer circle represents the conclusion. If the hypothesis is taken to be true, then you are located inside the inner circle. If you are located in the inner circle then you are also inside the outer circle, so that proves the conclusion is true.

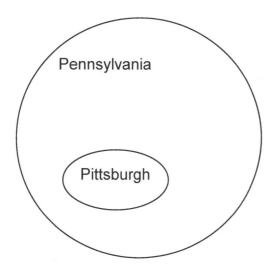

Example: If an angle has a measure of 90 degrees, then it is a right angle.

In this statement "an angle has a measure of 90 degrees" is the hypothesis. In this statement "it is a right angle" is the conclusion.

Example: If you are in Pittsburgh, then you are in Pennsylvania.

In this statement "you are in Pittsburgh" is the hypothesis.
In this statement "you are in Pennsylvania" is the conclusion.

Skill 10.2 Draw conclusions using deductive reasoning.

Deductive reasoning is the process of arriving at a conclusion based on other statements that are all known to be true.

A symbolic argument consists of a set of premises and a conclusion in the format of of if [Premise 1 and premise 2] then [conclusion].

An argument is **valid** when the conclusion follows necessarily from the premises. An argument is **invalid** or a fallacy when the conclusion does not follow from the premises.

There are 4 standard forms of valid arguments which must be remembered.

1. Law of Detachment	If p, then q p, Therefore, q	(premise 1) (premise 2)
2. Law of Contraposition	If p, then q not q, Therefore not p	
3. Law of Syllogism	If p, then q If q, then r Therefore if p, then r	
4. Disjunctive Syllogism	p or q not p Therefore, q	

Example: Can a conclusion be reached from these two statements?

   A.   All swimmers are athletes.
          All athletes are scholars.

In "if-then" form, these would be:
    If you are a swimmer, then you are an athlete.
    If you are an athlete, then you are a scholar.

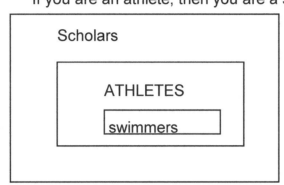

Clearly, if you are a swimmer, then you are also an athlete. This includes you in the group of scholars.

   B.   All swimmers are athletes.
          All wrestlers are athletes.

In "if-then" form, these would be:
    If you are a swimmer, then you are an athlete.
    If you are a wrestler, then you are an athlete.

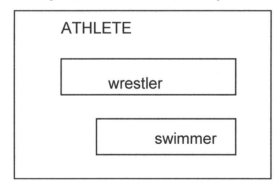

Clearly, if you are a swimmer or a wrestler, then you are also an athlete. This does NOT allow you to come to any other conclusions.

A swimmer may or may NOT also be a wrestler. Therefore, NO CONCLUSION IS POSSIBLE.

Suppose that these statements were given to you, and you are asked to try to reach a conclusion. The statements are:

Example: Determine whether statement A, B, C, or D can be deduced from the following:

(i)If John drives the big truck, then the shipment will be delivered.

(ii)The shipment will not be delivered.

a.John does not drive the big truck.
b.John drives the big truck.
c.The shipment will not be delivered.
d.None of the above conclusion is true. .

Let   p: John drives the big truck.
        q: The shipment is delivered.

statement (i) gives $p \rightarrow q$, statement (ii) gives $\sim q$. This is the Law of Contraposition.

Therefore, the logical conclusion is $\sim p$ or "John does not drive the big truck". So the answer is response A.

Example: Given that:
(i)Peter is a Jet Pilot or Peter is a Navigator.
(ii)Peter is not a Jet Pilot

Determine which conclusion can be logically deduced.

a.Peter is not a Navigator.
b.Peter is a Navigator.
c.Peter is neither a Jet Pilot nor a Navigator.
d.None of the above is true.

Let   p: Peter is a Jet Pilot
        q: Peter is a Navigator.

So we have $p \lor q$ from statement (i)
        $\sim p$ from statement (ii)

So choose response B.

COMPETENCY 11.0   SOLVE APPLIED PROBLEMS USING A COMBINATION OF MATHEMATICAL SKILLS

Skill 11.1   Apply combinations of algebraic skills to solve problems.

See COMPETENCY 12.0

Skill 11.2   Apply combinations of mathematical skills to solve a series of related problems.

Properties are rules that apply for addition, subtraction, multiplication, or division of real numbers. These properties are:

Commutative: You can change the order of the terms or factors as follows.

For addition: $a + b = b + a$
For multiplication: $ab = ba$

Since addition is the inverse operation of subtraction and multiplication is the inverse operation of division, no separate laws are needed for subtraction and division.

Example: $5 + ^-8 = ^-8 + 5 = ^-3$

Example: $^-2 \times 6 = 6 \times ^-2 = ^-12$

Associative: You can regroup the terms as you like.

For addition: $a + (b + c) = (a + b) + c$
For multiplication: $a(bc) = (ab)c$

This rule does not apply for division and subtraction.

Example: $(^-2 + 7) + 5 = ^-2 + (7 + 5)$
$5 + 5 = ^-2 + 12 = 10$

Example: $(3 \times ^-7) \times 5 = 3 \times (^-7 \times 5)$
$^-21 \times 5 = 3 \times ^-35 = ^-105$

Identity: Finding a number so that when added to a term results in that number (additive identity); finding a number such that when multiplied by a term results in that number (multiplicative identity).

For addition: $a + 0 = a$ (zero is additive identity)
For multiplication: $a \cdot 1 = a$ (one is multiplicative)

Example: $17 + 0 = 17$

Example: $^-34 \times 1 = {^-}34$
The product of any number and one is that number.

Inverse: Finding a number such that when added to the number it results in zero; or when multiplied by the number results in 1.

For addition: $a + (-a) = 0$
For multiplication: $a \cdot (1/a) = 1$

$(-a)$ is the additive inverse of a; $(1/a)$, also called the reciprocal, is the multiplicative inverse of a.

Example: $25 + {^-}25 = 0$

Example: $5 \times \frac{1}{5} = 1$ The product of any number and its reciprocal is one.

Distributive: This technique allows us to operate on terms within a parenthesis without first performing operations within the parentheses. This is especially helpful when terms within the parentheses cannot be combined.

$a (b + c) = ab + ac$

Example: $6 \times ({^-}4 + 9) = (6 \times {^-}4) + (6 \times 9)$
           $6 \times 5 = {^-}24 + 54 = 30$

To multiply a sum by a number, multiply each addend by the number, then add the products.

Addition of whole numbers

Example: At the end of a day of shopping, a shopper had $24 remaining in his wallet. He spent $45 on various goods. How much money did the shopper have at the beginning of the day?

The total amount of money the shopper started with is the sum of the amount spent and the amount remaining at the end of the day.

$$
\begin{array}{r}
24 \\
+\ 45 \\
\hline
69
\end{array}
$$
→ The original total was $69.

Example: A race took the winner 1 hr. 58 min. 12 sec. on the first half of the race and 2 hr. 9 min. 57 sec. on the second half of the race. How much time did the entire race take?

1 hr. 58 min. 12 sec.
+ 2 hr. 9 min. 57 sec.   Add these numbers
　　3 hr. 67 min. 69 sec.
+ 1 min -60 sec.   Change 60 seconds to 1 min.

3 hr. 68 min. 9 sec.
+ 1 hr.-60 min.   .   Change 60 minutes to 1 hr.
　4 hr. 8 min. 9 sec. ←final answer

Subtraction of Whole Numbers

Example: At the end of his shift, a cashier has $96 in the cash register. At the beginning of his shift, he had $15. How much money did the cashier collect during his shift?

The total collected is the difference of the ending amount and the starting amount.

$$
\begin{array}{r}
96 \\
-\ 15 \\
\hline
81
\end{array}
$$
→ The total collected was $81.

Multiplication of whole numbers

Multiplication is one of the four basic number operations. In simple terms, multiplication is the addition of a number to itself a certain number of times. For example, 4 multiplied by 3 is the equal to 4 + 4 + 4 or 3 + 3 + 3 +3. Another way of conceptualizing multiplication is to think in terms of groups. For example, if we have 4 groups of 3 students, the total number of students is 4 multiplied by 3. We call the solution to a multiplication problem the product.

The basic algorithm for whole number multiplication begins with aligning the numbers by place value with the number containing more places on top.

172
x 43 ⟶   Note that we placed 122 on top because it has more
places than 43 does.

Next, we multiply the ones' place of the second number by each place value of the top number sequentially.

(2)
172   {3 x 2 = 6, 3 x 7 = 21, 3 x 1 = 3}
x 43 ⟶   Note that we had to carry a 2 to the hundreds' column
516   because 3 x 7 = 21. Note also that we add, not
multiply, carried numbers to the product.

Next, we multiply the number in the tens' place of the second number by each place value of the top number sequentially. Because we are multiplying by a number in the tens' place, we place a zero at the end of this product.

(2)
172
x 43 ⟶   {4 x 2 = 8, 4 x 7 = 28, 4 x 1 = 4}
516
6880

Finally, to determine the final product we add the two partial products.

172
x 43
516
+ 6880
7396 ⟶   The product of 172 and 43 is 7396.

Example: A student buys 4 boxes of crayons. Each box contains 16 crayons. How many total crayons does the student have?

The total number of crayons is 16 x 4.

$$\begin{array}{r} 16 \\ \times\ 4 \\ \hline 64 \end{array}$$ → Total number of crayons equals 64.

Division of whole numbers

Division, the inverse of multiplication, is another of the four basic number operations. When we divide one number by another, we determine how many times we can multiply the divisor (number divided by) before we exceed the number we are dividing (dividend). For example, 8 divided by 2 equals 4 because we can multiply 2 four times to reach 8 (2 x 4 = 8 or 2 + 2 + 2 + 2 = 8). Using the grouping conceptualization we used with multiplication, we can divide 8 into 4 groups of 2 or 2 groups of 4. We call the answer to a division problem the quotient.

If the divisor does not divide evenly into the dividend, we express the leftover amount either as a remainder or as a fraction with the divisor as the denominator. For example, 9 divided by 2 equals 4 with a remainder of 1 or 4 ½.

The basic algorithm for division is long division. We start by representing the quotient as follows.

$14\overline{)293}$ → 14 is the divisor and 293 is the dividend.

This represents 293 ÷ 14.

Next, we divide the divisor into the dividend starting from the left.

$14\overline{)293}^{\ \ 2}$ → 14 divides into 29 two times with a remainder.

Next, we multiply the partial quotient by the divisor, subtract this value from the first digits of the dividend, and bring down the remaining dividend digits to complete the number.

$$\begin{array}{r} 2 \\ 14\overline{)293} \\ -28 \\ \hline 13 \end{array}$$ → 2 x 14 = 28, 29 – 28 = 1, and bringing down the 3 yields 13.

Finally, we divide again (the divisor into the remaining value) and repeat the preceding process. The number left after the subtraction represents the remainder.

$$
\begin{array}{r}
20 \\
14\overline{)293} \\
-28 \\
\hline
13 \\
-0 \\
\hline
13
\end{array}
$$

⟶ The final quotient is 20 with a remainder of 13. We can also represent this quotient as 20 13/14.

Example: Each box of apples contains 24 apples. How many boxes must a grocer purchase to supply a group of 252 people with one apple each?

The grocer needs 252 apples. Because he must buy apples in groups of 24, we divide 252 by 24 to determine how many boxes he needs to buy.

$$
\begin{array}{r}
10 \\
24\overline{)252} \\
-24 \\
\hline
12 \\
-0 \\
\hline
12
\end{array}
$$

⟶ The quotient is 10 with a remainder of 12.

Thus, the grocer needs 10 boxes plus 12 more apples. Therefore, the minimum number of boxes the grocer can purchase is 11.

Example: At his job, John gets paid $20 for every hour he works. If John made $940 in a week, how many hours did he work?

This is a division problem. To determine the number of hours John worked, we divide the total amount made ($940) by the hourly rate of pay ($20). Thus, the number of hours worked equals 940 divided by 20.

$$
\begin{array}{r}
47 \\
20\overline{)940} \\
-80 \\
\hline
140 \\
-140 \\
\hline
0
\end{array}
$$

⟶ 20 divides into 940, 47 times with no remainder.

John worked 47 hours.

Addition and Subtraction of Decimals

When adding and subtracting decimals, we align the numbers by place value as we do with whole numbers. After adding or subtracting each column, we bring the decimal down, placing it in the same location as in the numbers added or subtracted.

Example: Find the sum of 152.3 and 36.342.

$$
\begin{array}{r}
152.300 \\
+36.342 \\
\hline
188.642
\end{array}
$$

Note that we placed two zeroes after the final place value in 152.3 to clarify the column addition.

Example: Find the difference of 152.3 and 36.342.

$$
\begin{array}{cc}
\begin{array}{r}
2\;9\;10 \\
152.\cancel{300} \\
-36.342 \\
\hline
58
\end{array}
&
\begin{array}{r}
(4)11(12) \\
15\cancel{2}.\cancel{300} \\
-36.342 \\
\hline
115.958
\end{array}
\end{array}
$$

Note how we borrowed to subtract from the zeroes in the hundredths' and thousandths' place of 152.300.

Multiplication of Decimals

When multiplying decimal numbers, we multiply exactly as with whole numbers and place the decimal moving in from the left the total number of decimal places contained in the two numbers multiplied. For example, when multiplying 1.5 and 2.35, we place the decimal in the product 3 places in from the left (3.525).

Example: Find the product of 3.52 and 4.1.

$$
\begin{array}{r}
3.52 \\
\times4.1 \\
\hline
352 \\
+\;14080 \\
\hline
14432
\end{array}
$$

Note that there are 3 total decimal places in the two numbers.

We place the decimal 3 places in from the left.

Thus, the final product is 14.432.

Example: A shopper has 5 one-dollar bills, 6 quarters, 3 nickels, and 4 pennies in his pocket. How much money does he have?

$$
\begin{array}{cccc}
 & 3 & & \\
5 \times \$1.00 = \$5.00 \quad & \$0.25 & \$0.05 & \$0.01 \\
 & \underline{\times \quad 6} & \underline{\times \quad 3} & \underline{\times \quad 4} \\
 & \$1.50 & \$0.15 & \$0.04 \\
\end{array}
$$

Note the placement of the decimals in the multiplication products. Thus, the total amount of money in the shopper's pocket is:

$$
\begin{array}{r}
\$5.00 \\
1.50 \\
0.15 \\
\underline{+\ 0.04} \\
\$6.69 \\
\end{array}
$$

Division of Decimals

When dividing decimal numbers, we first remove the decimal in the divisor by moving the decimal in the dividend the same number of spaces to the right. For example, when dividing 1.45 into 5.3 we convert the numbers to 145 and 530 and perform normal whole number division.

Example: Find the quotient of 5.3 divided by 1.45.
Convert to 145 and 530.

Divide.

$$
\begin{array}{r}
3 \\
145\overline{)530} \\
\underline{-435} \\
95 \\
\end{array}
\longrightarrow
\begin{array}{r}
3.65 \\
145\overline{)530.00} \\
\underline{-435} \\
950 \\
\underline{-870} \\
800 \\
\end{array}
\longrightarrow
$$

Note that we insert the decimal to continue division.

Because one of the numbers divided contained one decimal place, we round the quotient to one decimal place. Thus, the final quotient is 3.7.

Operating with Percents

Example: 5 is what percent of 20?

This is the same as converting $\dfrac{5}{20}$ to % form.

$$\frac{5}{20} \times \frac{100}{1} = \frac{5}{1} \times \frac{5}{1} = 25\%$$

Example: There are 64 dogs in the kennel. 48 are collies. What percent are collies?

Restate the problem.	48 is what percent of 64?
Write an equation.	$48 = n \times 64$
Solve.	$\dfrac{48}{64} = n$

$n = \dfrac{3}{4} = 75\%$

75% of the dogs are collies.

Example: The auditorium was filled to 90% capacity. There were 558 seats occupied. What is the capacity of the auditorium?

Restate the problem.	90% of what number is 558?
Write an equation.	$0.9n = 558$
Solve.	$n = \dfrac{558}{.9}$
	$n = 620$

The capacity of the auditorium is 620 people.

Example: A pair of shoes costs $42.00. Sales tax is 6%. What is the total cost of the shoes?

Restate the problem.	What is 6% of 42?
Write an equation.	$n = 0.06 \times 42$
Solve.	$n = 2.52$

Add the sales tax to the cost. $42.00 + $2.52 = $44.52

The total cost of the shoes, including sales tax, is $44.52.

Skill 11.3 **Identify the algebraic equivalent of a stated relationship.**

Procedure for solving algebraic equations.

Example: $3(x+3) = {}^-2x+4$ Solve for x.

1) Expand to eliminate all parentheses.

$3x+9 = {}^-2x+4$

2) Multiply each term by the LCD to eliminate all denominators.

3) Combine like terms on each side when possible.

4) Use the properties to put all variables on one side and all constants on the other side.

$\rightarrow 3x+9-9 = {}^-2x+4-9$ (subtract nine from both sides)

$\rightarrow 3x = {}^-2x-5$

$\rightarrow 3x+2x = {}^-2x+2x-5$ (add $2x$ to both sides)

$\rightarrow 5x = {}^-5$

$\rightarrow \dfrac{5x}{5} = \dfrac{{}^-5}{5}$ (divide both sides by 5)

$\rightarrow x = {}^-1$

Example: Solve: $3(2x+5)-4x = 5(x+9)$

$6x+15-4x = 5x+45$

$2x+15 = 5x+45$

${}^-3x+15 = 45$

${}^-3x = 30$

$x = {}^-10$

The solution **set of linear equations** is all the ordered pairs of real numbers that satisfy both equations, thus the intersection of the lines There are two methods for solving linear equations: **linear combinations** and **substitution**.

In the **substitution** method, an equation is solved for either variable. Then, that solution is substituted in the other equation to find the remaining variable.

Example: (1) $2x + 8y = 4$
            (2) $x - 3y = 5$

            (2a) $x = 3y + 5$ Solve equation (2) for x

            (1a) $2(3y + 5) + 8y = 4$ Substitute x in equation (1)
                   $6y + 10 + 8y = 4$ Solve.
                   $14y = -6$
                   $y = \frac{-3}{7}$ Solution

            (2) $x - 3y = 5$
                   $x - 3(\frac{-3}{7}) = 5$ Substitute the value of y.

                   $x = \frac{26}{7} = 3\frac{5}{7}$ Solution

Thus the solution set of the system of equations is $(3\frac{5}{7}, \frac{-3}{7})$.

In the **linear combinations** method, one or both of the equations are replaced with an equivalent equation in order that the two equations can be combined (added or subtracted) to eliminate one variable.

Example: (1) $4x + 3y = -2$
            (2) $5x - y = 7$

            (1) $4x + 3y = -2$
            (2a) $15x - 3y = 21$ Multiply equation (2) by 3

            $19x = 19$ Combining (1) and (2a)
            $x = 1$ Solve.
            To find y, substitute the value of x in equation 1 (or 2).
            (1) $4x + 3y = -2$
                   $4(1) + 3y = -2$
                   $4 + 3y = -2$
                   $3y = -2$
                   $y = -2$

Thus the solution is $x = 1$ and $y = -2$ or the order pair $(1, -2)$.

Example: Solve for x and y.

$$4x + 6y = 340$$
$$3x + 8y = 360$$

To solve by addition-subtraction:

Multiply the first equation by 4: $4(4x + 6y = 340)$

Multiply the other equation by $^-3$: $^-3(3x + 8y = 360)$

By doing this, the equations can be added to each other to eliminate one variable and solve for the other variable.

$$16x + 24y = 1360$$
$$\underline{-9x - 24y = {}^-1080}$$
$$7x = 280$$
$$x = 40$$

solving for y, $y = 30$

Skill 11.4   Identify the proper equation or expression to solve word problems involving one and two variables.

Example: Mark and Mike are twins. Three times Mark's age plus four equals four times Mike's age minus 14. How old are the boys?

Since the boys are twins, their ages are the same. "Translate" the English into Algebra. Let x = their age.

$3x + 4 = 4x - 14$

$18 = x$

The boys are each 18 years old.

Example: The YMCA wants to sell raffle tickets to raise $32,000. If they must pay $7,250 in expenses and prizes out of the money collected from the tickets, how many tickets worth $25 each must they sell?

Let x = number of tickets sold
Then $25x$ = total money collected for x tickets

Total money minus expenses is greater than $32,000.

$25x - 7250 = 32,000$
$25x = 39350$
$x = 1570$

If they sell 1,570 tickets, they will raise $32,000.

Example: The Simpsons went out for dinner. All 4 of them ordered the aardvark steak dinner. Bert paid for the 4 meals and included a tip of $12 for a total of $84.60. How much was an aardvark steak dinner?

Let x = the price of one aardvark dinner.
So $4x$ = the price of 4 aardvark dinners.

$$4x + 12 = 84.60$$

$$4x = 72.60$$

$$x = \$18.50 \text{ for each dinner.}$$

Some word problems can be solved using a system (group) of equations or inequalities. Watch for words like greater than, less than, at least, or no more than which indicate the need for inequalities.

Example: Farmer Greenjeans bought 4 cows and 6 sheep for $1700. Mr. Ziffel bought 3 cows and 12 sheep for $2400. If all the cows were the same price and all the sheep were another price, find the price charged for a cow or for a sheep.

Let x = price of a cow
Let y = price of a sheep

Then Farmer Greenjeans' equation would be: $4x + 6y = 1700$
Mr. Ziffel's equation would be: $3x + 12y = 2400$

To solve by **addition-subtraction**:

Multiply the first equation by $^-2$: $^-2(4x + 6y = 1700)$
Keep the other equation the same : $(3x + 12y = 2400)$
By doing this, the equations can be added to each other to eliminate one variable and solve for the other variable.

$$
\begin{aligned}
^-8x - 12y &= {}^-3400 \\
3x + 12y &= 2400 \qquad \text{Add these equations.} \\
\hline
^-5x &= {}^-1000
\end{aligned}
$$

$x = 200 \leftarrow$ the price of a cow was \$200.
Solving for y, $y = 150 \leftarrow$ the price of a sheep, \$150.

To solve by **substitution**:

Solve one of the equations for a variable. (Try to make an equation without fractions if possible.) Substitute this expression into the equation that you have not yet used. Solve the resulting equation for the value of the remaining variable.

$4x + 6y = 1700$
$3x + 12y = 2400 \leftarrow$ Solve this equation for x.

It becomes $x = 800 - 4y$. Now substitute $800 - 4y$ in place of x in the OTHER equation. $4x + 6y = 1700$ now becomes:

$$
\begin{aligned}
4(800 - 4y) + 6y &= 1700 \\
3200 - 16y + 6y &= 1700 \\
3200 - 10y &= 1700 \\
^-10y &= {}^-1500
\end{aligned}
$$

$y = 150$, or \$150 for a sheep.

Substituting 150 back into an equation for y, find x.
$4x + 6(150) = 1700$
$4x + 900 = 1700$
$4x = 800$ so $x = 200$ for a cow.

Example: Sharon's Bike Shoppe can assemble a 3 speed bike in 30 minutes or a 10 speed bike in 60 minutes. The profit on each bike sold is $60 for a 3 speed or $75 for a 10 speed bike. How many of each type of bike should they assemble during an 8 hour day (480 minutes) to make the maximum profit? Total daily profit must be at least $300.

Let x = number of 3 speed bikes.
y = number of 10 speed bikes.

Since there are only 480 minutes to use each day,

$30x + 60y \leq 480$ is the first inequality.

Since the total daily profit must be at least $300,

$60x + 75y \geq 300$ is the second inequality.

$30x + 60y \leq 480$ solves to $y \leq 8 - 1/2\,x$
$60y \leq -30x + 480$

$$y \leq -\frac{1}{2}x + 8$$

$60x + 75y \geq 300$ solves to $y \geq 4 - 4/5\,x$
$75y + 60x \geq 300$

$75y \geq -60x + 300$

$$y \geq -\frac{4}{5}x + 4$$

This problem can be solved by graphing these two inequalities.

Graph these 2 inequalities:

$$y \leq 8 - 1/2\,x$$
$$y \geq 4 - 4/5\,x$$

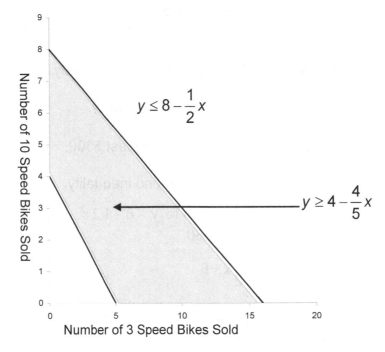

Realize that $x \geq 0$ and $y \geq 0$, since the number of bikes assembled can not be a negative number. Graph these as additional constraints on the problem. The number of bikes assembled must always be an integer value, so points within the shaded area of the graph must have integer values. The maximum profit will occur at or near a corner of the shaded portion of this graph. Those points occur at (0,4), (0,8), (16,0), or (5,0).

Since profits are $60/3$-speed or $75/10$-speed, the profit would be :

$$
\begin{aligned}
(0,4) \quad & 60(0) + 75(4) = 300 \\
(0,8) \quad & 60(0) + 75(8) = 600 \\
(16,0) \quad & 60(16) + 75(0) = 960 \leftarrow \text{Maximum profit} \\
(5,0) \quad & 60(5) + 75(0) = 300
\end{aligned}
$$

The maximum profit would occur if 16 3-speed bikes are made daily.

COMPETENCY 12.0   SOLVE WORD PROBLEMS INVOLVING INTEGERS, FRACTIONS, DECIMALS, AND UNITS OF MEASUREMENT.

Skill 12.1   Solve word problems involving integers, fractions, and decimals

Rational numbers can be expressed as the ratio of two integers, $\frac{a}{b}$ where b ≠ 0, for example $\frac{2}{3}$, $-\frac{4}{5}$, 5 = $\frac{5}{1}$.

The rational numbers include integers, fractions and mixed numbers, terminating and repeating decimals. Every rational number can be expressed as a repeating or terminating decimal and can be shown on a number line.

Integers are positive and negative whole numbers and zero.
    ...-6, -5, -4, -3, -2, -1, 0, 1, 2, 3, 4, 5, 6, ...

Whole numbers are natural numbers and zero.
    0, 1, 2, 3, ,4 ,5 ,6 ...

Natural numbers are the counting numbers.
    1, 2, 3, 4, 5, 6, ...

Irrational numbers are real numbers that cannot be written as the ratio of two integers. These are infinite non-repeating decimals.
    <u>Examples</u>: $\sqrt{5}$ = 2.2360..,   pi =∏ = 3.1415927...

A **fraction** is an expression of numbers in the form of x/y , where **x** is the numerator and **y** is the denominator, which cannot be zero.

Example: $\dfrac{3}{7}$ 3 is the numerator; 7 is the denominator

If the fraction has common factors for the numerator and denominator, divide both by the common factor to reduce the fraction to its lowest form.

Example:

$$\frac{13}{39} = \frac{1 \times 13}{3 \times 13} = \frac{1}{3}$$ Divide by the common factor 13

A **mixed** number has an integer part and a fractional part.

Example: $2\frac{1}{4}, \ ^-5\frac{1}{6}, \ 7\frac{1}{3}$

Percent = per 100 (written with the symbol %). Thus $10\% = \frac{10}{100} = \frac{1}{10}$.

Decimals = deci = part of ten. To find the decimal equivalent of a fraction, use the denominator to divide the numerator as shown in the following example.

Example: Find the decimal equivalent of $\frac{7}{10}$.

Since 10 cannot divide into 7 evenly

$$\frac{7}{10} = 0.7$$

Addition and subtraction of fractions

Key Points

1.   You need a common denominator in order to add and subtract reduced and improper fractions.

Example: $\dfrac{1}{3} + \dfrac{7}{3} = \dfrac{1+7}{3} = \dfrac{8}{3} = 2\dfrac{2}{3}$

Example: $\dfrac{4}{12} + \dfrac{6}{12} - \dfrac{3}{12} = \dfrac{4+6-3}{12} = \dfrac{7}{12}$

2.   Adding an integer and a fraction of the <u>same</u> sign results directly in a mixed fraction.

Example: $2 + \dfrac{2}{3} = 2\dfrac{2}{3}$

Example: $^-2 - \dfrac{3}{4} = \ ^-2\dfrac{3}{4}$

3.   Adding an integer and a fraction with different signs involves the following steps.

-get a common denominator
-add or subtract as needed
-change to a mixed fraction if possible

Example: $$2 - \frac{1}{3} = \frac{2 \times 3 - 1}{3} = \frac{6 - 1}{3} = \frac{5}{3} = 1\frac{2}{3}$$

Example: Add $7\frac{3}{8} + 5\frac{2}{7}$

Add the whole numbers; add the fractions and combine the two results:

$$7\frac{3}{8} + 5\frac{2}{7} = (7 + 5) + (\frac{3}{8} + \frac{2}{7})$$

$$= 12 + \frac{(7 \times 3) + (8 \times 2)}{56} \quad \text{(LCM of 8 and 7)}$$

$$= 12 + \frac{21 + 16}{56} = 12 + \frac{37}{56} = 12\frac{37}{56}$$

Example: Perform the operation.

$$\frac{2}{3} - \frac{5}{6}$$

We first find the LCM of 3 and 6 which is 6.

$$\frac{2 \times 2}{3 \times 2} - \frac{5}{6} \rightarrow \frac{4 - 5}{6} = \frac{^-1}{6} \quad \text{(Using method A)}$$

Example: $-7\frac{1}{4}+2\frac{7}{8}$

$$-7\frac{1}{4}+2\frac{7}{8}=(-7+2)+(\frac{-1}{4}+\frac{7}{8})$$

$$=(-5)+\frac{(-2+7)}{8}=(-5)+(\frac{5}{8})$$

$$=(-5)+\frac{5}{8}=\frac{-5\times8}{1\times8}+\frac{5}{8}=\frac{-40+5}{8}$$

$$=\frac{-35}{8}=-4\frac{3}{8}$$

Divide 35 by 8 to get 4, remainder 3.

Caution: Common error would be

$$-7\frac{1}{4}+2\frac{7}{8}=-7\frac{2}{8}+2\frac{7}{8}=-5\frac{9}{8}$$ Wrong.

It is correct to add -7 and 2 to get -5, but adding $\frac{2}{8}+\frac{7}{8}=\frac{9}{8}$

is wrong. It should have been $\frac{-2}{8}+\frac{7}{8}=\frac{5}{8}$. Then,

$$-5+\frac{5}{8}=-4\frac{3}{8}$$ as before.

Skill 12.2   Solve word problems involving ratio and proportions.

A **ratio** is a comparison of 2 numbers. If a class had 11 boys and 14 girls, we can write the ratio of boys to girls in 3 ways:

11:14   or   11 to 14   or $\frac{11}{14}$

The ratio of girls to boys is:

14:11, 14 to 11 or $\frac{14}{11}$

We should reduce ratios when possible. A ratio of 12 cats to 18 dogs reduces to 2:3, 2 to 3, or 2/3.

Note: Read ratio questions carefully. Given a group of 6 adults and 5 children, the ratio of children to the entire group would be 5:11.

A **proportion** is an equation in which one fraction is set equal to another. To solve the proportion, multiply each numerator by the other fraction's denominator. Set these two products equal to each other and solve the resulting equation. This is called **cross-multiplying** the proportion.

Example: $\dfrac{4}{15} = \dfrac{x}{60}$ is a proportion.

To solve, cross multiply.

$(4)(60) = (15)(x)$

$240 = 15x$

$16 = x$

Example: $\dfrac{x+3}{3x+4} = \dfrac{2}{5}$ is a proportion.

To solve, cross multiply.

$5(x + 3) = 2(3x + 4)$

$5x + 15 = 6x + 8$

$7 = x$

Example: $\dfrac{x+2}{8} = \dfrac{2}{x-4}$ is another proportion.

To solve, cross multiply.

$(x + 2)(x - 4) = 8(2)$

$x^2 - 2x - 8 = 16$

$x^2 - 2x - 24 = 0$

$(x - 6)(x + 4) = 0$

$x = 6$ or $x = {}^-4$

We can use **proportions** to solve word problems that involve comparisons of relationships. Some situations include scale drawings and maps, similar polygons, speed, time and distance, cost, and comparison shopping.

Example: Which is the better buy, 6 items for $1.29 or 8 items for $1.69?

Find the unit price.

$$\frac{6}{1.29} = \frac{1}{x}$$
$$6x = 1.29$$
$$x = 0.215$$

$$\frac{8}{1.69} = \frac{1}{x}$$
$$8x = 1.69$$
$$x = 0.21125$$

Thus, 8 items for $1.69 is the better buy (lower unit price).

Example: A car travels 125 miles in 2.5 hours. How far will it go in 6 hours?

Write a proportion comparing the distance and time.

$$\frac{miles}{hours} \qquad \frac{125}{2.5} = \frac{x}{6}$$

$$2.5x = 750$$
$$x = 300$$

Thus, the car can travel 300 miles in 6 hours.

Example: The scale on a map is ¾ inch = 6 miles. What is the actual distance between two cities if they are 1 ½ inches apart on the map?

Write a proportion comparing the scale to the actual distance.

scale   actual

$$\frac{\frac{3}{4}}{1\frac{1}{2}} = \frac{6}{x}$$

$$\frac{3}{4}x = 1\frac{1}{2} \times 6$$

$$\frac{3}{4}x = 9$$

$$x = 12$$

Thus, the actual distance between the cities is 12 miles.

Skill 12.3   Solve word problems involving units of measurement and conversions

Measurements of length (English system)

12 inches (in)	=	1 foot (ft)
3 feet (ft)	=	1 yard (yd)
1760 yards (yd)	=	1 mile (mi)

Measurements of length (Metric system)

1 kilometer (km)	=	1000 meters (m)
1 hectometer (hm)	=	100 meters (m)
1 decameter (dam)	=	10 meters (m)
1 meter (m)	=	1 meter (m)
1 decimeter (dm)	=	1/10 meter (m)
1 centimeter (cm)	=	1/100 meter (m)
1 millimeter (mm)	=	1/1000 meter (m)

Conversion of length from English to Metric

1 inch	=	2.54 centimeters
1 foot	≈	30 centimeters
1 yard	≈	0.9 meters
1 mile	≈	1.6 kilometers

Measurements of weight (English system)

28 grams (g)	=	1 ounce (oz)
16 ounces (oz)	=	1 pound (lb)
2000 pounds (lb)	=	1 ton (t)

Measurements of weight (Metric system)

1 kilogram (kg)	=	1000 grams (g)
1 gram (g)	=	1 gram (g)
1 milligram (mg)	=	1/1000 gram (g)

Conversion of weight from English to Metric

1 ounce	≈	28 grams
1 pound	≈	0.45 kilograms
	≈	454 grams

Measurement of volume (English system)

8 fluid ounces (oz)	=	1 cup (c)
2 cups (c)	=	1 pint (pt)
2 pints (pt)	=	1 quart (qt)
4 quarts (qt)	=	1 gallon (gal)

Measurement of volume (Metric system)

1 kiloliter (kl)	=	1000 liters (l)
1 liter (l)	=	1 liter (l)
1 milliliter (ml)	=	1/1000 liters (ml)

Conversion of volume from English to Metric

1 teaspoon (tsp)	≈	5 milliliters
1 fluid ounce	≈	15 milliliters
1 cup	≈	0.24 liters
1 pint	≈	0.47 liters
1 quart	≈	0.95 liters
1 gallon	≈	3.8 liters

Measurement of time

1 minute	=	60 seconds
1 hour	=	60 minutes
1 day	=	24 hours
1 week	=	7 days
1 year	=	365 days
1 century	=	100 years

Note: (') represents feet and (") represents inches.

COMPETENCY 13.0 GRAPH AND SOLVE ALGEBRAIC EQUATIONS WITH ONE AND TWO VARIABLES.

Skill 13.1 Graph numbers or number relationships.

A relationship between two quantities can be shown using a table, graph or rule. In this example, the rule y= 9x describes the relationship between the total amount earned, y, and the total amount of $9 sunglasses sold, x.

A table using this data would appear as:

number of sunglasses sold	1	5	10	15
total dollars earned	9	45	90	135

Each *(x,y)* relationship between a pair of values is called the coordinate pair and can be plotted on a graph. The coordinate pairs *(1,9)*, *(5,45)*, *(10,90)*, and *(15,135)*, are plotted on the graph below.

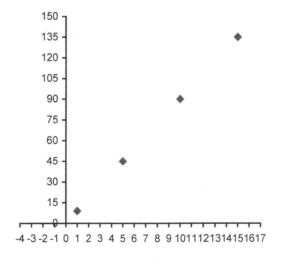

The graph above shows a linear relationship. A linear relationship is one in which two quantities are proportional to each other. Doubling *x* also doubles *y*. On a graph, a straight line depicts a linear relationship.

Coordinate plane - A plane with a point selected as an origin, some length selected as a unit of distance, and two perpendicular lines that intersect at the origin, with positive and negative direction selected on each line. Traditionally, the lines are called x (drawn from left to right, with positive direction to the right of the origin) and y (drawn from bottom to top, with positive direction upward of the origin). Coordinates of a point are determined by the distance of this point from the lines, and the signs of the coordinates are determined by whether the point is in the positive or in the negative direction from the origin. The standard coordinate plane consists of a plane divided into 4 quadrants by the intersection of two axis, the x-axis (horizontal axis), and the y-axis (vertical axis).

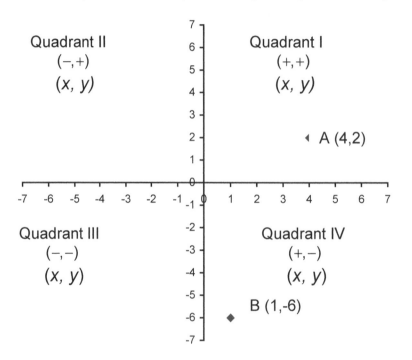

Coordinates - A unique **ordered pair** of numbers that identifies a point on the coordinate plane. The first number in the ordered pair identifies the position with regard to the x-axis while the second number identifies the position on the y-axis (x ,y)

In the coordinate plane shown above, point A has the ordered pair (4,2); point B has the ordered pair (1,-6).

Slope – The slope of a line is the "slant" of a line. A downward left to right slant means a negative slope. An upward slant is a positive slope.
The formula for calculating the slope of a line with coordinates $(x_1, y_1) and (x_2, y_2)$ is:

$$\text{slope} = \frac{y_2 - y_1}{x_2 - x_1}$$

The top of the fraction represents the change in the y coordinates; it is called the **rise**.
The bottom of the fraction represents the change in the x coordinates, it is called the **run.**

Example: Find the slope of a line with points at (2,2) and (7,8).

$\dfrac{(8)-(2)}{(7)-(2)}$ plug the values into the formula

$\dfrac{6}{5}$ solve the rise over run

= 1.2   solve for the slope

The length of a line segment is the **distance** between two different points, A and B. The formula for the length of a line is:

$$\text{length} = \sqrt{(x_1 - x_2)^2 + (y_1 - y_2)^2}$$

Example: Find the length between the points (2,2) and (7,8)

$= \sqrt{(2-7)^2 + (2-8)^2}$ plug the values into the formula

$= \sqrt{(-5)^2 + (-6)^2}$ calculate the x and y differences

$= \sqrt{25 + 36}$ square the values

$= \sqrt{61}$ add the two values

$= 7.81$ calculate the square root

A first degree equation has an equation of the form $ax + by = c$. To find the slope of a line, solve the equation for y. This gets the equation into **slope intercept form**, $y = mx + b$. **m is the line's slope.**

The y-intercept is the coordinate of the point where a line crosses the y axis. To find the y intercept, substitute 0 for x and solve for y. This is the y-intercept. In slope intercept form, $y = mx + b$, b is the y-intercept.
To find the x intercept, substitute 0 for y and solve for x. This is the x-intercept.

If the equation solves to x = **any number**, then the graph is a **vertical line**. It only has an x-intercept. Its slope is **undefined**.

If the equation solves to y = **any number**, then the graph is a **horizontal line**. It only has a y-intercept. Its slope is 0 (zero).

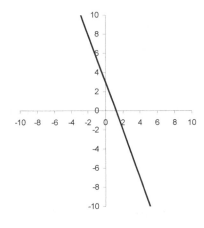

$$5x + 2y = 6$$
$$y = {}^-5/2\,x + 3$$

We can find the equation of a line from its graph by finding its slope (see Skill 3.2 for the slope formula) and its y-intercept.

$$Y - y_a = m(X - x_a)$$

(x_a, y_a) can be (x_1, y_1) or (x_2, y_2). If we distribute **m**, the value of the slope, through the parentheses, we can rewrite the equation into other forms.

Example: Find the equation of a line through $(9, {}^-6)$ and $({}^-1, 2)$.

$$\text{slope} = \frac{y_2 - y_1}{x_2 - x_1} = \frac{2 - {}^-6}{{}^-1 - 9} = \frac{8}{{}^-10} = -\frac{4}{5}$$

$Y - y_a = m(X - x_a) \rightarrow Y - 2 = {}^-4/5 (X - {}^-1) \rightarrow$

$Y - 2 = {}^-4/5 (X + 1) \rightarrow Y - 2 = {}^-4/5 X - 4/5 \rightarrow$

$Y = {}^-4/5 \ X + 6/5$ This is the slope-intercept form.

Multiplying by 5 to eliminate fractions, it is:

$5Y = {}^-4X + 6 \rightarrow 4X + 5Y = 6$ Standard form.

Example: Find the slope and intercepts of $3x + 2y = 14$.

$3x + 2y = 14$

$2y = {}^-3x + 14$

$y = {}^-3/2 \ x + 7$

The slope of the line is ${}^-3/2$. The y-intercept of the line is 7.

We can also find the intercepts by substituting 0 in place of the other variable in the equation.

To find the y intercept:	To find the x intercept:
let $x = 0$; $3(0) + 2y = 14$	let $y = 0$; $3x + 2(0) = 14$
$0 + 2y = 14$	$3x + 0 = 14$
$2y = 14$	$3x = 14$
$y = 7$	$x = 14/3$
$(0,7)$ is the y-intercept.	$(14/3, 0)$ is the x-intercept.

Example: Sketch the graph of the line represented by $2x + 3y = 6$.

Let $x = 0 \rightarrow 2(0) + 3y = 6$
$\rightarrow 3y = 6$
$\rightarrow y = 2$
$\rightarrow (0,2)$ is the y-intercept.

Let $y = 0 \rightarrow 2x + 3(0) = 6$
$\rightarrow 2x = 6$
$\rightarrow x = 3$
$\rightarrow (3,0)$ is the x-intercept.

Let $x = 1 \rightarrow 2(1) + 3y = 6$
$\rightarrow 2 + 3y = 6$
$\rightarrow 3y = 4$
$\rightarrow y = \dfrac{4}{3}$
$\rightarrow \left(1, \dfrac{4}{3}\right)$ is the third point.

Plotting the three points on the coordinate system, we get the following:

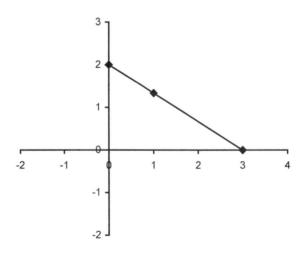

Skill 13.2   Find the value of the unknown in a given one-variable equation.

See Skills 11.2 and 11.3.

Skill 13.3   Express one variable in terms of a second variable in two-variable equations.

See Skills 11.2 and 11.3.

COMPETENCY 14.0   SOLVE PROBLEMS INVOLVING GEOMETRIC FIGURES.

Skill 14.1   Solve problems involving two-dimensional geometric figures

Polygons are simple closed **two-dimensional figures** composed of line segments. Their names correlate to the number of sides they have.

A **quadrilateral** is a polygon with four sides.
The sum of the measures of the angles of a quadrilateral is 360°.

A **trapezoid** is a quadrilateral with exactly <u>one</u> pair of parallel sides.

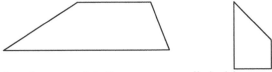

In an **isosceles trapezoid**, the non-parallel sides are congruent.

A **parallelogram** is a quadrilateral with <u>two</u> pairs of parallel sides.

In a parallelogram:
The diagonals bisect each other.
Each diagonal divides the parallelogram into two congruent triangles.
Both pairs of opposite sides are congruent.
Both pairs of opposite angles are congruent.
Two adjacent angles are supplementary.

A **rectangle** is a parallelogram with a right angle.

A **rhombus** is a parallelogram with all sides of equal length.

A **square** is a rectangle with all sides of equal length.

Example: True or false?

All squares are rhombuses.	True
All parallelograms are rectangles.	False - <u>some</u> parallelograms are rectangles
All rectangles are parallelograms.	True
Some rhombuses are squares.	True
Some rectangles are trapezoids.	False - only <u>one</u> pair of parallel sides
All quadrilaterals are parallelograms.	False -some quadrilaterals are parallelograms
Some squares are rectangles.	False - all squares are rectangles
Some parallelograms are rhombuses.	True

A **triangle** is a polygon with three sides.

We can classify triangles by the types of angles or the lengths of their sides.

An **acute** triangle has exactly three *acute* angles.
A **right** triangle has one *right* angle.
An **obtuse** triangle has one *obtuse* angle.

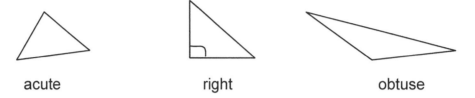

acute   right   obtuse

All *three* sides of an **equilateral** triangle are the same length.
Two sides of an **isosceles** triangle are the same length.
None of the sides of a **scalene** triangle are the same length.

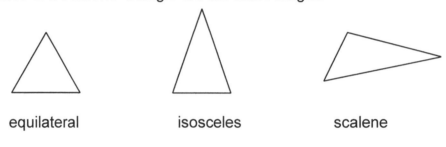

equilateral   isosceles   scalene

Example: Can a triangle have two right angles?
No. A right angle measures 90°, therefore the sum of two right angles would be 180° and there could not be third angle.

Example: Can a triangle have two obtuse angles?
No. Since an obtuse angle measures more than 90° the sum of two obtuse angles would be greater than 180°.

The **perimeter** of any polygon is the sum of the lengths of the sides.

The **area** of a polygon is the number of square units covered by the figure.

FIGURE	AREA FORMULA	PERIMETER FORMULA
Rectangle	Length x Width	2(Length + Width)
Triangle	$\frac{1}{2}bh$ (b = base, h = height)	$a+b+c$ (where a, b, and c are legs of the triangle)
Parallelogram	bh	sum of the lengths of the sides
Trapezoid	$\frac{1}{2}h(a+b)$ (where a and b are the bases)	sum of the lengths of the sides

Perimeter of a Polygon

Example: A farmer has a piece of land shaped as shown below. He wishes to fence this land. The estimated cost is $25 per linear foot. What is the total cost of fencing this property to the nearest foot.

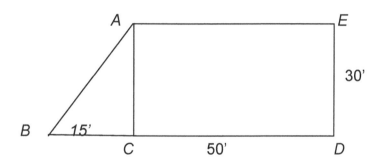

From the right triangle ABC, AC = 30 and BC = 15.

Since $(AB)^2 = (AC)^2 + (BC)^2$
$(AB)^2 = (30)^2 + (15)^2$

So, $\sqrt{(AB)^2} = AB = \sqrt{30^2 + 15^2} = \sqrt{1125} = 33.5410$ feet

To the nearest foot AB = 34 feet.

Perimeter of the piece of land is $= AB + BC + CD + DE + EA$

$= 34 + 15 + 50 + 30 + 50 = 179$ feet

cost of fencing = $25 x 179 = $4, 475.00

Area of a Polygon

Example: What is the cost of carpeting a rectangular office that measures 12 feet by 15 feet if the carpet costs $12.50 per square yard?

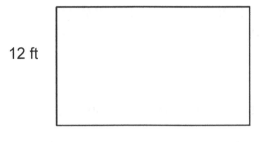

12 ft

15 ft

This is a basic area problem. To solve this problem you must first determine the area of the office. The area of a rectangle is the *length* times the *width*.

Substitute the given values in the equation $A = lw$

$$A = (12 \text{ ft})(15 \text{ ft})$$

$$A = 180 \text{ ft}^2$$

The problem asked you to determine the cost of carpet at $12.50 per square yard.

First, you need to convert 180 ft.^{2} into yards^2.

1 yd. = 3 ft.

(1 yard)(1 yard) = (3 feet)(3 feet)

$1 \text{ yd}^2 = 9 \text{ ft}^2$

Hence, $180 \text{ ft}^2 = 20 \text{ yd}^2$ $(180 \div 9)$

The carpet cost $12.50 per square yard; thus, the cost of carpeting the office is $12.50 x 20 yd^2 = $250.00.

Example: Find the area of a parallelogram with bases 6.5 cm long and altitude 3.7 cm long. (note: the altitude is the line perpendicular to the bases)

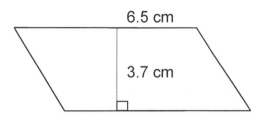

6.5 cm

3.7 cm

$$A_{parallelogram} = bh$$
$$= (3.7)(6.5)$$
$$= 24.05 \text{ cm}^2$$

Example: Find the area of this triangle.

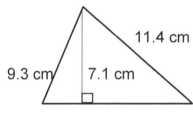

11.4 cm

9.3 cm   7.1 cm

16.8 cm

$$A_{triangle} = \frac{1}{2}bh$$
$$= 0.5 (16.8)(7.1)$$
$$= 59.64 \text{ cm}^2$$

Example: Find the area of this trapezoid.

17.5 cm

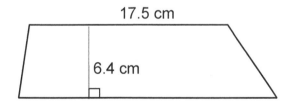

6.4 cm

23.7 cm

The area of a trapezoid equals one-half the sum of the bases times the altitude.

$$A_{trapezoid} = \frac{1}{2}h(b_1 + b_2)$$
$$= 0.5 (6.4)(17.5 + 23.7)$$
$$= 131.84 \text{ cm}^2$$

Circles

The distance around a circle is the **circumference**. The ratio of the circumference to the diameter is represented by the Greek letter pi (π).

$$\pi \approx 3.14 \approx \frac{22}{7}$$

The formula used to find the circumference of a circle is $C = 2\pi r$ or $C = \pi d$ where r is the radius of the circle and d is the diameter.

The formula used to find the **area** of a circle is $A = \pi r^2$.

Example: Find the circumference and area of a circle whose radius is 7 meters.

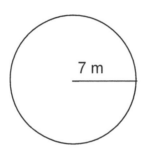

7 m

$C = 2\pi r$	$A = \pi r^2$
$= 2(3.14)(7)$	$= 3.14(7)(7)$
$= 43.96$ m	$= 153.86$ m^2

Skill 14.2   Solve problems involving three-dimensional geometric figures

A **cylinder** has two congruent circular bases that are parallel.

A **sphere** is a three-dimensional figure having all its points the same distance from the center.

A **cone** is a three-dimensional figure having a circular base and a single vertex.

A **pyramid** is a three-dimensional figure with a square base and 4 triangle-shaped sides.

A **tetrahedron** is a 4-sided three-dimensional triangle. Each face is a triangle.

A **prism** is a three-dimensional figure with two congruent, parallel bases that are polygons.

The following are formulas used to compute **Volume** and **Surface area**:

FIGURE	VOLUME	TOTAL SURFACE AREA
Right Cylinder	$\pi r^2 h$	$2\pi rh + 2\pi r^2$
Right Cone	$\dfrac{\pi r^2 h}{3}$	$\pi r\sqrt{r^2 + h^2} + \pi r^2$
Sphere	$\dfrac{4}{3}\pi r^3$	$4\pi r^2$
Rectangular Solid	LWH	$2LW + 2WH + 2LH$

FIGURE	LATERAL AREA	TOTAL AREA	VOLUME
Regular Pyramid	1/2Pl	1/2Pl+B	1/3Bh

P = Perimeter
h = height
B = Area of Base
l = slant height

Example: What is the volume of a shoe box with a length of 35 cm, a width of 20 cm and a height of 15 cm?

Volume of a rectangular solid
= Length x Width x Height
= 35 x 20 x 15
= 10500 cm^3

Example: A water company is trying to decide whether to use traditional cylindrical paper cups or to offer conical paper cups since both cost the same amount. The traditional cups are 8 cm wide and 14 cm high. The conical cups are 12 cm wide and 19 cm high. The company will use the cup that holds the most water.

Draw and label a sketch of each.

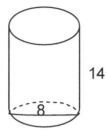 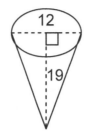

$V = \pi r^2 h$ $\qquad$ $V = \dfrac{\pi r^2 h}{3}$ $\qquad$ 1. write formula

$V = \pi(4)^2(14)$ $\qquad$ $V = \dfrac{1}{3}\pi(6)^2(19)$ $\qquad$ 2. substitute

$V = 703.717 \text{ cm}^3$ $\qquad$ $V = 716.283 \text{ cm}^3$ $\qquad$ 3. solve

The choice should be the conical cup, because it has a greater volume and can hold more water.

Example: How much material is needed to make a basketball that has a diameter of 15 inches? How much air is needed to fill the basketball?

Draw and label a sketch.

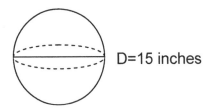 D=15 inches

The amount of material needed is equal to the surface area and the amount of air needed is equal to the volume.

Total surface area   Volume

$\text{TSA} = 4\pi r^2$ $V = \dfrac{4}{3}\pi r^3$ 1. write formula

$\quad = 4\pi(7.5)^2$ $\quad = \dfrac{4}{3}\pi(7.5)^3$ 2. substitute

$\quad = 706.8 \text{ in}^2$ $\quad = 1767.1 \text{ in}^3$ 3. solve

Sample Test: Mathematics and Computation Skills

1. $\left(\dfrac{^-4}{9}\right) + \left(\dfrac{^-7}{10}\right) =$

    A. $\dfrac{23}{90}$

    B. $\dfrac{^-23}{90}$

    C. $\dfrac{103}{90}$

    D. $\dfrac{^-103}{90}$

2. $0.74 =$

    A. $\dfrac{74}{100}$

    B. 7.4%

    C. $\dfrac{33}{50}$

    D. $\dfrac{74}{10}$

3. $^-9\dfrac{1}{4}$ ☐ $^-8\dfrac{2}{3}$

    A. $=$

    B. $<$

    C. $>$

    D. $\leq$

4. **303 is what percent of 600?**

    A. 0.505%

    B. 5.05%

    C. 505%

    D. 50.5%

5. **An item that sells for $375 is put on sale at $120. What is the percent of decrease?**

    A. 25%

    B. 28%

    C. 68%

    D. 34%

6. **Two mathematics classes have a total of 410 students. The 8:00 am class has 40 more than the 10:00 am class. How many students are in the 10:00 am class?**

    A. 123.3

    B. 370

    C. 185

    D. 330

7. A restaurant employs 465 people. There are 280 waiters and 185 cooks. If 168 waiters and 85 cooks receive pay raises, what percent of the waiters will receive a pay raise?

    A.   36.13%

    B.   60%

    C.   60.22%

    D.   40%

8. A car gets 25.36 miles per gallon. The car has been driven 83,310 miles. What is a reasonable estimate for the number of gallons of gas used?

    A.   2,087 gallons

    B.   3,000 gallons

    C.   1,800 gallons

    D.   164 gallons

9. Round $1\frac{13}{16}$ of an inch to the nearest quarter of an inch.

    A. $1\frac{1}{4}$ inch

    B. $1\frac{5}{8}$ inch

    C. $1\frac{3}{4}$ inch

    D.   2 inches

10. The owner of a rectangular piece of land 40 yards in length and 30 yards in width wants to divide it into two parts. She plans to join two opposite corners with a fence as shown in the diagram below. The cost of the fence will be approximately $25 per linear foot. What is the estimated cost for the fence needed by the owner?

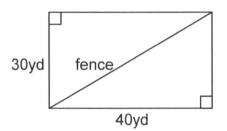

    A. $1,250

    B. $62,500

    C. $5,250

    D. $3,750

11. **What unit of measurement could we use to report the distance traveled walking around a track?**

   A. degrees

   B. square meters

   C. kilometers

   D. cubic feet

12. **What is the area of a square whose side is 13 feet?**

   A. 169 feet

   B. 169 square feet

   C. 52 feet

   D. 52 square feet

13. **The trunk of a tree has a 2.1 meter radius. What is its circumference?**

   A. 2.1π square meters

   B. 4.2π meters

   C. $2.1\ \pi$ meters

   D. 4.2π square meters

14. **The figure below shows a running track and the shape of an inscribed rectangle with semicircles at each end.**

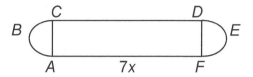

   Calculate the distance around the track.

   A. $6\pi y + 14x$

   B. $3\pi y + 7x$

   C. $6\pi y + 7x$

   D. $3\pi y + 14x$

15. **What type of triangle is $\triangle ABC$?**

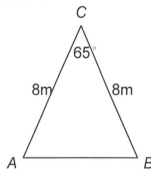

   A. right

   B. equilateral

   C. scalene

   D. isosceles

16. Choose the expression that is not equivalent to 5x + 3y + 15z:

   A. 5(x + 3z) + 3y

   B. 3(x + y + 5z)

   C. 3y + 5(x + 3z)

   D. 5x + 3(y + 5z)

17. $\dfrac{7}{9} + \dfrac{1}{3} \div \dfrac{2}{3} =$

   A. $\dfrac{5}{3}$

   B. $\dfrac{3}{2}$

   C. 2

   D. $\dfrac{23}{18}$

18. Choose the statement that is true for all real numbers.

   A. $a = 0, b \neq 0$, then $\dfrac{b}{a}$ = undefined.

   B. $^-(a + (^-a)) = 2a$

   C. $2(ab) = ^-(2a)b$

   D. $^-a(b + 1) = ab - a$

19. Choose the equation that is equivalent to the following:

   $$\dfrac{3x}{5} - 5 = 5x$$

   A. $3x - 25 = 25x$

   B. $x - \dfrac{25}{3} = 25x$

   C. $6x - 50 = 75x$

   D. $x + 25 = 25x$

20. If $4x - (3 - x) = 7(x - 3) + 10$, then

   A. $x = 8$

   B. $x = -8$

   C. $x = 4$

   D. $x = -4$

21. Given the formula *d =rt*, (where *d* = distance, *r* =rate, and *t* =time), calculate the time required for a vehicle to travel 585 miles at a rate of 65 miles per hour.

   A. 8.5 hours

   B. 6.5 hours

   C. 9.5 hours

   D. 9 hours

22. The price of gas was $3.27 per gallon. Your tank holds 15 gallons of fuel. You are using two tanks a week. How much will you save weekly if the price of gas goes down to $2.30 per gallon.

A. $26.00

B. $29.00

C. $15.00

D. $17.00

23. What is the area of this triangle?

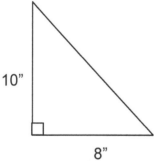

10"

8"

A. 80 square inches

B. 20 square inches

C. 40 square inches

D. 30 square inches

24. What unit of measurement would describe the spread of a forest fire in a unit time?

A. 10 square yards per second

B. 10 yards per minute

C. 10 feet per hour

D. 10 cubit feet per hour

25. In a sample of 40 full-time employees at a particular company, 35 were also holding down a part-time job requiring at least 10 hours/week. If this proportion holds for the entire company of 25000 employees, how many full-time employees at this company are actually holding down a part-time job of at least 10 hours per week.

A. 714

B. 625

C. 21,875

D. 28,571

26. A student organization is interested in determining how strong the support is among registered voters in the United States for the president's education plan. Which of the following procedures would be most appropriate for selecting a statistically unbiased sample?

   A. Having viewers call in to a nationally broad-cast talk show and give their opinions.

   B. Survey registered voters selected by blind drawing in the three largest states.

   C. Select regions of the country by blind drawing and then select people from the voters registration list by blind drawing.

   D. Pass out survey forms at the front entrance of schools selected by blind drawing and ask people entering and exiting to fill them in.

27. The following chart shows the yearly average number of international tourists visiting Palm Beach for 1990-1994. How many more international tourists visited Palm Beach in 1994 than in 1991?

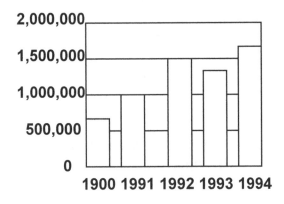

   A. 100,000

   B. 600,000

   C. 1,600,000

   D. 8,000,000

28. Consider the graph of the distribution of the length of time it took individuals to complete an employment form.

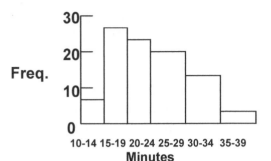

Approximately how many individuals took less than 15 minutes to complete the employment form?

A. 35
B. 28
C. 7
D. 4

29. Solve for x.

$$3x - \frac{2}{3} = \frac{5x}{2} + 2$$

A. $5\frac{1}{3}$

B. $\frac{17}{3}$

C. 2

D. $\frac{16}{2}$

30. For the following statements

I. All parallelograms are rectangles
II. Some rhombi are squares

A. Both statements are correct

B. Both statements are incorrect

C. Only II is correct

D. Only I is correct

31. What is the equation that expresses the relationship between x and y in the table below?

x	y
-2	4
-1	1
0	-2
1	-5
2	-8

A. $y = -x - 2$

B. $y = -3x - 2$

C. $y = 3x - 2$

D. $y = \frac{1}{3}x - 1$

32. Set A, B, C, and U are related as shown in the diagram.

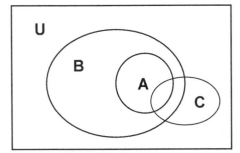

Which of the following is true, assuming not one of the six regions is empty?

A. Any element that is a member of set B is also a member of set A.

B. No element is a member of all three sets A, B, and C.

C. Any element that is a member of set U is also a member of set B.

D. None of the above statements is true.

33. Select the statement that is the negation of the statement, "If the weather is cold, then the soccer game will be played."

A. If the weather is not cold, then the soccer game will be played.

B. The weather is cold and the soccer game was not played.

C. If the soccer game is played, then the weather is not cold.

D. The weather is cold and the soccer game will be played.

34. Select the statement below that is NOT logically equivalent to "If Mary works late, then Bill will prepare lunch."

A. Bill prepares lunch or Mary does not work late.

B. If Bill does not prepare lunch, then Mary did not work late.

C. If Bill prepares lunch, then Mary works late.

D. Mary does not work late or Bill prepares lunch.

35. **Select the rule of logical equivalence that directly (in one step) transforms the statement (i) into statement (ii),**

   i. Not all the students have books.
   ii. Some students do not have books.

   A.   "If p, then q" is equivalent to "if not q, then b."

   B.   "Not all are p" is equivalent to "some are not p."

   C.   "Not q" is equivalent to "p."

   D.   "All are not p" is equivalent to "none are p ."

36. **Given that:**
   i. No athletes are weak.
   ii. All football players are athletes.

   Determine which conclusion can be logically deduced.

   A.   Some football players are weak.

   B.   All football players are weak.

   C.   No football player is weak.

   D.   None of the above is true.

37. **Study the information given below. If a logical conclusion is given, select that conclusion.**

   Bob eats donuts or he eats yogurt. If Bob eats yogurt, then he is healthy. If Bob is healthy, then he can run the marathon. Bob does not eat yogurt.

   A.   Bob does not eat donuts.

   B.   Bob is healthy.

   C.   If Bob runs the marathon then he eats yogurt.

   D.   None of the above is warranted.

38. **A sofa sells for $520. If the retailer makes a 30% profit, what was the wholesale price?**

   A. $400

   B. $676

   C. $490

   D. $364

39. **Corporate salaries are listed for several employees. Which is the best measure of central tendency?**

   $24,000 $24,000 $26,000

   $28,000 $30,000 $120,000

   A. Mean

   B. median

   C. mode

   D. no difference

40. **Which statement is true about George's budget?**

   A. George spends the greatest portion of his income on food.
   B. George spends twice as much on utilities as he does on his mortgage.
   C. George spends twice as much on utilities as he does on food.
   D. George spends the same amount on food and utilities as he does on mortgage.

Answer Key: Mathematics and Computation Skills

1.   D
2.   A
3.   B
4.   D
5.   C
6.   C
7.   B
8.   B
9.   C
10. D
11. C
12. B
13. B
14. D
15. D
16. B
17. D
18. A
19. A
20. C
21. D
22. B
23. C
24. A
25. C
26. C
27. B
28. C
29. A
30. C
31. B
32. D
33. B
34. B
35. B
36. C
37. D
38. A
39. B
40. C

Answers with Rationale: Mathematics and Computation Skills

1. Find the LCD of $\dfrac{-4}{9}$ and $\dfrac{-7}{10}$. The LCD is 90, so you get

   $\dfrac{-40}{90} + \dfrac{-63}{90} = \dfrac{-103}{90}$, which is answer **D**.

2. 0.74⑧ the 4 is in the hundredths place, so the answer is $\dfrac{74}{100}$, which is **A**.

3. The larger the absolute value of a negative number, the smaller the negative number is. The absolute value of $-9\dfrac{1}{4}$ is $9\dfrac{1}{4}$ which is larger than the absolute value of $-8\dfrac{2}{3}$, which is $8\dfrac{2}{3}$. Therefore, the relationship should be $-9\dfrac{1}{4} < -8\dfrac{2}{3}$, which is answer **B**.

4. Use x for the percent. $600x = 303$. $\dfrac{600x}{600} = \dfrac{303}{600} \rightarrow x = 0.505 = 50.5\%$, which is answer **D**.

5. Use $(1 - x)$ as the discount. $375x = 120$.
   $375(1 - x) = 120 \rightarrow 375 - 375x = 120 \rightarrow 375x = 255 \rightarrow x = 0.68 = 68\%$
   which is answer **C**.

6. Let x = # of students in the 8 am class and $x - 40$ = # of students in the 10 am class. $x + (x - 40) = 410 \rightarrow 2x - 40 = 410 \rightarrow 2x = 450 \rightarrow x = 225$. So there are 225 students in the 8 am class, and 225 − 40 = 185 in the 10 am class, which is answer **C**.

7. The total number of waiters is 280 and only 168 of them get a pay raise. Divide the number getting a raise by the total number of waiters to get the percent. $\dfrac{168}{280} = 0.6 = 60\%$, which is answer **B**.

8. Divide the number of miles by the miles per gallon to determine the approximate number of gallons of gas used.
   $\dfrac{83310 \text{ miles}}{25.36 \text{ miles per gallon}} = 3285$ gallons. This is approximately 3000 gallons, which is answer **B**.

9. $1\dfrac{13}{16}$ inches is approximately $1\dfrac{12}{16}$, which is also $1\dfrac{3}{4}$, which is the nearest $\dfrac{1}{4}$ of an inch, so the answer is **C**.

10. Find the length of the diagonal by using the Pythagorean theorem. Let x be the length of the diagonal.

$$30^2 + 40^2 = x^2 \rightarrow 900 + 1600 = x^2$$
$$2500 = x^2 \rightarrow \sqrt{2500} = \sqrt{x^2}$$
$$x = 50 \text{ yards}$$

Convert to feet. $\dfrac{50 \text{ yards}}{x \text{ feet}} = \dfrac{1 \text{ yard}}{3 \text{ feet}} \rightarrow 1500 \text{ feet}$

It cost \$25.00 per linear foot, so the cost is (1500 ft)(\$25) = \$3750, which is answer **D.**

11. Degrees measures angles, square meters measures area, cubic feet measure volume, and kilometers measures length. Kilometers is the only reasonable answer, which is **C.**

12. Area = length times width (*lw*).
Length = 13 feet
Width = 13 feet (square, so length and width are the same).
Area = $13 \times 13 = 169$ square feet.
Area is measured in square feet. So the answer is **B.**

13. Circumference is $2\pi r$, where r is the radius. The circumference is $2\pi 2.1 = 4.2\pi$ meters (not square meters because we are not measuring area), which is answer **B.**

14. The two semicircles of the track create one circle with a diameter 3y. The circumference of a circle is $C = \pi d$ so $C = 3\pi y$. The length of both sides of the track is 7x each side, so the total circumference around the track is $3\pi y + 7x + 7x = 3\pi y + 14x$, which is answer **D.**

15. Two of the sides are the same length, so we know the triangle is either equilateral or isosceles. $\angle CAB$ and $\angle CBA$ are equal, because their sides are. Therefore, $180° = 65° - 2x = \dfrac{115°}{2} = 57.5°$. Because all three angles are not equal, the triangle is isosceles, so the answer is **D.**

16. 5x + 3y + 15z = (5x + 15z) + 3y = 5(x + 3z) + 3y   A. is true
            = 5x + (3y + 15z) = 5x + 3(y + 5z)   D. is true
            = 37 + (5x + 15z) = 37 + 5(x + 3z)   C is true
We can solve all of these using the associative property and then factoring. However, in B 3(x + y + 5z) by distributive property = 3x + 3y + 15z, which does not equal 5x + 37 + 15z. The answer is **B.**

17. First, do the division.
$$\frac{1}{3} \div \frac{2}{3} = \frac{1}{3} \times \frac{3}{2} = \frac{1}{2}$$
Add.
$$\frac{7}{9} + \frac{1}{2} = \frac{14}{18} + \frac{9}{18} = \frac{23}{18}, \text{ which is answer } \mathbf{D.}$$

18. **A** is the correct answer because any number divided by 0 is undefined.

19. **A** is the correct answer because it is the original equation multiplied by 5. The other choices alter the answer to the original equation.

20. Solve for x.

$$4x - (3 - x) = 7(x - 3) + 10$$
$$4x - 3 + x = 7x - 21 + 10$$
$$5x - 3 = 7x - 11$$
$$5x = 7x - 11 + 3 \qquad \text{The answer is } \mathbf{C.}$$
$$5x - 7x = {}^-8$$
$$^-2x = {}^-8$$
$$x = 4$$

21. We are given d = 585 miles and r = 65 miles per hour and $d = rt$. Solve for t. $585 = 65t \rightarrow t = 9$ hours, which is answer **D.**

22. 15 gallons x 2 tanks = 30 gallons a week
= 30 gallons x \$3.27 = \$98.10
30 gallons x \$2.30 = \$69.00
\$98.10 - \$69.00 = \$29.10 is approximately \$29.00. The answer is **B.**

23. The area of a triangle is $\frac{1}{2}bh$.

$\frac{1}{2} x 8 x 10 = 40$ square inches. The answer is **C.**

24. The only appropriate answer is one that describes "an area" of forest consumed per unit time. All answers are not units of area measurement except answer **A.**

25. $\frac{35}{40}$ full time employees have a part time job also. Out of 25,000 full time employees, the number that also have a part time job is

$\frac{35}{40} = \frac{x}{25000} \rightarrow 40x = 875000 \rightarrow x = 21875$, so 21875 full time employees also have a part time job. The answer is **C.**

26. **C** is the best answer because it is random and it surveys a larger population.

27. The number of tourists in 1991 was 1,000,000 and the number in 1994 was 1,600,000. Subtract to get a difference of 600,000, which is answer **B.**

28. According to the chart, the number of people who took under 15 minutes is 7, which is answer **C.**

29. $3x(6) - \dfrac{2}{3}(6) = \dfrac{5x}{2}(6) + 2(6)$ 6 is the LCD of 2 and 3

$18x - 4 = 15x + 12$

$18x = 15x + 16$

$3x = 16$

$x = \dfrac{16}{3} = 5\dfrac{1}{3}$ which is answer **A.**

30. I is false because only some parallelograms are rectangles. II is true. So only II is correct, which is answer **C**.

31. Solve by plugging the values of x and y into the equations to see if they work. The answer is **B** because it is the only equation for which the values of x and y are correct.

32. Answer A is incorrect because not all members of set B are also in set A. Answer B is incorrect because there are elements that are members of all three sets A, B, and C. Answer C is incorrect because not all members of set U are members of set B. This leaves answer **D**, which states that none of the above choices are true.

33. **B**

34. **B**

35. **B**

36. **C**

37. **D**

38. $400; Let x be the wholesale price, then x + .30x = 520, 1.30x = 520. divide both sides by 1.30. **A**

39. The median provides the best measure of central tendency in this case where the mode is the lowest number and the mean is disproportionately skewed by the outlier $120,000. **B**

40. George spends twice as much on utilities as he does on food. **C**

SUBAREA V.   **LIBERAL STUDIES: SCIENCE, ART AND LITERATURE, SOCIAL SCIENCES**

COMPETENCY 15.0   UNDERSTAND AND ANALYZE MAJOR SCIENTIFIC PRINCIPLES, CONCEPTS, AND THEORIES, AND APPLY SKILLS, PRINCIPLES, AND PROCEDURES ASSOCIATED WITH SCIENTIFIC INQUIRY.

Skill 15.1   Analyze the nature of scientific thought and inquiry.

Investigation is an essential component of science. Science investigation consists of a number of steps designed to solve a problem. This is important because it helps in solving scientific problems and in gathering new information. Scientists start with a problem and solve it in an orderly fashion called the scientific method. This is made up of a series of steps, which, when applied properly, solve scientific problems. The key to the success of this method lies in minimizing human prejudice. As human beings, we tend to have biases. The steps consist of identifying the problem, gathering information, formulating a hypothesis, designing an experiment, interpreting data, and drawing conclusions.

The first step in a science investigation is identifying the problem. As we observe, we notice interesting things that arouse our curiosity. We ask ourselves the basic questions of enquiry – how, why, what, when, which, and where. The two most important questions are how and why. We can classify observations into two types. The first is qualitative, which we describe in words. No mention of numbers or quantities is made – the water is very hot, the solution is sour, etc. The second type is quantitative, where numbers and quantities are used. This is more precise – mass: format is 125 kg., distance: 500 km, etc.

The second step is gathering information. As much information as possible is collected from various sources, such as the internet, books, journals, knowledgeable people, newspapers, etc. This lays a solid foundation for formulating a hypothesis.

The third step is hypothesizing. This is making a statement about the problem with the knowledge acquired and using the two important words *if* and *when*.

The next step is designing an experiment. Before this is done, one needs to identify the control, the constants, the independent variables, and the dependent variables.

For beginners, the simplest investigation would be to manipulate only one variable at a time. In this way, the experiment doesn't get too complicated and is easier to handle. The control has to be identified and then the variable that can affect the outcome of the results. For an experiment to be authentic and reliable, constants have to be identified and kept constant throughout the experiment. Finally, the dependent variable, which is dependent on the independent variable, has to be identified. The dependent variable is the factor that is being measured in an experiment – e.g., height of plant, number of leaves, etc. For an experiment to be successful, it should be completed in 10-12 days. The results are noted carefully. At the end of the experiment, the data has to be analyzed and searched for patterns. Any science investigation has to be repeated at least twice to get reproducible results. After the analysis, conclusions must be drawn based on the data.

In order to draw conclusions, we need to study the data on hand. The data tell us whether or not the hypothesis is correct. If the hypothesis is not correct, another hypothesis has to be formulated, and an experiment has to be done.
If the hypothesis is tested, and the results are repeated in further experimentation, a theory could be formulated. A theory is a hypothesis that is tested repeatedly by different scientists and has yielded the same results. A theory has more validity because it could be used to predict future events.

Scientific inquiries should end in formulating an explanation or model. Models should be physical, conceptual, and mathematical. While drawing conclusions, a lot of discussion and arguments are generated. There may be several possible explanations for any given sets of results: not all of them are reasonable. Carefully evaluating and analyzing the data creates a reasonable conclusion. The conclusion needs to be backed up by scientific criteria.

After the conclusion is drawn, the final step is communication. In this age, much emphasis is put on the method of communication. The conclusions must be communicated by clearly describing the information using accurate data and visual representations, such as graphs (bar/line/pie), tables/charts, diagrams, artwork, and other appropriate media, including PowerPoint presentations. Modern technology must be used whenever it is necessary. The method of communication must be suitable to the audience.

Written communication is as important as oral communication. This is essential for submitting research papers to scientific journals, newspapers, other magazines, etc.

Characteristics and uses of various types of scientific investigations

Scientific investigations come in all sizes and forms. One can conduct a simple survey over the course of a large population with the hopes of gaining an understanding of the entire population. This method is often used by medical and pharmaceutical companies and may include a questionnaire that asks about health and lifestyle. Ecologists use field observations. Like the medical questionnaire, they study small sample sizes to gain a better understanding of a larger group. For example, they may track one animal to follow its migratory patterns, or they may place cameras in one area in the hopes of capturing footage of a roaming animal or pack. Ecologists are studying an area and all of the organisms within it, but this is too broad to study, so they often limit sampling size and use a representative of the population. Whenever possible, a scientist would prefer to use controlled experiments. This can happen most readily in a laboratory and is near impossible to achieve in nature. In a controlled experiment, only one variable is manipulated at once, and a control, or normal variable under normal conditions, is always present. This control group gives the scientist something to compare the variable against. It tells him what would normally have happened under the experimental conditions, had he not altered/introduced the variable.

An experiment is proposed and performed with the sole objective of testing a hypothesis. When evaluating an experiment, it is important to first look at the question it was supposed to answer. How logically did the experiment flow from there? How many variables existed? (It is best to only test one variable at a time.)

You discover a scientist conducting an experiment with the following characteristics. He has two rows each set up with four stations. The first row has a piece of tile as the base at each station. The second row has a piece of linoleum as the base at each station. The scientist has eight eggs and is prepared to drop one over each station. What is he testing? He is trying to answer whether or not the egg is more likely to break when dropped over one material as opposed to the other. His hypothesis might have been: The egg will be less likely to break when dropped on linoleum. This is a simple experiment. If the experiment was more complicated, or for example, conducted on a microscopic level, one might want to examine the appropriateness of the instruments utilized and their calibration.

Properly collecting data yields information that appropriately answers the original question. For example, one wouldn't try to use a graduated cylinder to measure mass, nor would one use a ruler to measure a microscopic item. Utilizing appropriate measuring devices, using proper units, and careful mathematics will provide strong results. Carefully evaluating and analyzing the data creates a reasonable conclusion. The conclusion needs to be backed up by scientific criteria and then finally communicated to the audience.

Sources of error or uncertainty in an investigation

Unavoidable experimental error is the random error inherent in scientific experiments regardless of the methods used. One source of unavoidable error is measurement and the use of measurement devices. Using measurement devices is an imprecise process because it is often impossible to accurately read measurements. For example, when using a ruler to measure the length of an object, if the length falls between markings on the ruler, we must estimate the true value. Another source of unavoidable error is the randomness of population sampling and the behavior of any random variable. For example, when sampling a population, we cannot guarantee that our sample is completely representative of the larger population. In addition, because we cannot constantly monitor the behavior of a random variable, any observations necessarily contain some level of unavoidable error.

Statistical variability is the deviation of an individual in a population from the mean of the population. Variability is inherent in biology because living things are innately unique. For example, the individual weights of humans vary greatly from the mean weight of the population. Thus, when conducting experiments involving the study of living things, we must control for innate variability. Control groups are identical to the experimental group in every way, with the exception of the variable being studied. Comparing the experimental group to the control group allows us to determine the effects of the manipulated variable in relation to statistical variability.

The procedure used to obtain data is important to the outcome. Experiments consist of **controls** and **variables**. A control is the experiment run under normal conditions. The variable includes a factor that is changed. In biology, the variable may be light, temperature, pH, time, etc. The differences in tested variables may be used to make a prediction or form a hypothesis. Only one variable should be tested at a time. One would not alter both the temperature and pH of the experimental subject.

An **independent variable** is one that is changed or manipulated by the researcher. This could be the amount of light given to a plant or the temperature at which bacteria is grown. The **dependent variable** is that which is influenced by the independent variable.

Measurements may be taken in different ways. There is an appropriate measuring device for each aspect of biology. A graduated cylinder is used to measure volume. A balance is used to measure mass. A microscope is used to view microscopic objects. A centrifuge is used to separate two or more parts in a liquid sample. The list goes on, but you get the point. For each variable, there is an appropriate way to measure it. The internet and teaching guides are virtually unlimited resources for laboratory ideas. You should be imparting on the students the importance of the method with which they conduct the study, the resources they use to do so, the concept of double checking their work, and the use of appropriate units.

Biologists use a variety of tools and technologies to perform tests, collect and display data, and analyze relationships. Examples of commonly used tools include computer-linked probes, spreadsheets, and graphing calculators.

Biologists use computer-linked probes to measure various environmental factors, including temperature, dissolved oxygen, pH, ionic concentration, and pressure. The advantage of computer-linked probes, as compared to more traditional observational tools, is that the probes automatically gather data and present it in an accessible format. This property of computer-linked probes eliminates the need for constant human observation and manipulation.

Biologists use spreadsheets to organize, analyze, and display data. For example, conservation ecologists use spreadsheets to model population growth and development, apply sampling techniques, and create statistical distributions to analyze relationships. Spreadsheet use simplifies data collection and manipulation and allows the presentation of data in a logical and understandable format.

Graphing calculators are another technology with many applications to biology. For example, biologists use algebraic functions to analyze growth, development, and other natural processes. Graphing calculators can manipulate algebraic data and create graphs for analysis and observation. In addition, biologists use the matrix function of graphing calculators to model problems in genetics. The use of graphing calculators simplifies the creation of graphical displays, including histograms, scatter plots, and line graphs. Biologists can also transfer data and displays to computers for further analysis. Finally, biologists connect computer-linked probes, used to collect data, to graphing calculators to ease the collection, transmission, and analysis of data.

Appropriate methods and criteria for organizing and displaying data

The type of graphic representation used to display observations depends on the data that is collected. **Line graphs** are used to compare different sets of related data or to predict data that has not yet been measured. An example of a line graph would be comparing the rate of activity of different enzymes at varying temperatures. A **bar graph** or **histogram** is used to compare different items and make comparisons based on this data. An example of a bar graph would be comparing the ages of children in a classroom. A **pie chart** is useful when organizing data as part of a whole. A good use for a pie chart would be displaying the percent of time students spend on various after school activities.

As noted before, the independent variable is controlled by the experimenter. This variable is placed on the x-axis (horizontal axis). The dependent variable is influenced by the independent variable and is placed on the y-axis (vertical axis). It is important to choose the appropriate units for labeling the axes. It is best to take the largest value to be plotted and divide it by the number of blocks and then round to the nearest whole number.

Precision, accuracy, and error

Accuracy is the degree of conformity of a measured, calculated quantity to its actual (true) value. Precision, also called reproducibility or repeatability, is the degree to which further measurements or calculations will show the same or similar results.

Accuracy is the degree of veracity, while precision is the degree of reproducibility.

The best analogy to explain accuracy and precision is the target comparison.

Repeated measurements are compared to arrows that are fired at a target. Accuracy describes the closeness of arrows to the bull's eye at the target center. Arrows that strike closer to the bull's eye are considered more accurate.

All experimental uncertainty is due to either random errors or systematic errors.

Random errors are statistical fluctuations in the measured data due to the precision limitations of the measurement device. Random errors usually result from the experimenter's inability to take the same measurement in exactly the same way to get exactly the same number.

Systematic errors, by contrast, are reproducible inaccuracies that are consistently in the same direction. Systematic errors are often due to a problem that persists throughout the entire experiment.

Systematic and random errors refer to problems associated with making measurements. Mistakes made in the calculations or in reading the instrument are not considered in error analysis.

Skill 15.2   Use an appropriate illustration or physical model to represent a scientific theory or concept.

The tools of modeling and mathematics can be used to help us understand and predict behavior of natural systems. Let's look at an example: the movement of carbon through the biological and geological world.

The first step in preparing our model is to draw a diagram representing the various components and the relationships between them. Below, carbon reserves are shown as squares and converting processes as circles. This is a simplified diagram, with only a few of the important components of the carbon cycle:

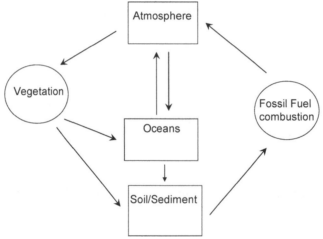

Next, we would like to attach mathematical quantities and equations to describe these relationships. In this and many other situations in the natural world, not all these quantities and exact relationships will be known. Thus, the equations and their coefficients must be approximated and estimated. In the carbon cycle, we can write chemical equations for the various exchanges of carbon, such as that for aerobic respiration: $C_6H_{12}O_6 + 6O_2 \rightarrow 6CO_2 + 6H_2O$. Additionally, we can make yearly estimates for how much carbon is stored in the various reservoirs and how much is transformed by the processes.

To make visualization simple, we can add these numbers to our diagram. (All quantities are in GigaTons or GigaTons/yr.):

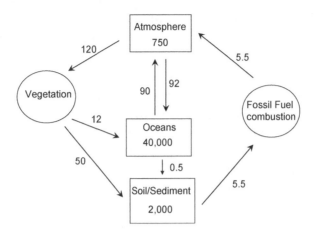

Finally, with all the relationships elucidated, we can use our model to make predictions. In the carbon cycle example, we can predict what might happen if fossil fuel combustion rates were increased or vegetation was killed. The ability to make predictions about the results of changes in a system, without actually performing an experiment, is one of the most useful aspects of modeling. Computer simulations are often employed for highly complex natural systems, in which the number of relationships is high, and the equations are complicated.

Skill 15.3 Relate major scientific principles, concepts, or theories to everyday phenomena.

See Skill 15.4.

Skill 15.4 Apply scientific methods and principles to assess real-world questions or problems.

Humans have a tremendous impact on the world's natural resources. The world's natural water supplies are affected by human use. Waterways are major sources for recreation and freight transportation. Oil and wastes from boats and cargo ships pollute the aquatic environment. The aquatic plant and animal life is affected by this contamination. To obtain drinking water, contaminants such as parasites, pollutants, and bacteria are removed from raw water through a purification process involving various screening, conditioning, and chlorination steps. Most uses of water resources, such as drinking and crop irrigation, require fresh water. Only 2.5% of water on Earth is fresh water, and more than two thirds of this fresh water is frozen in glaciers and polar ice caps. Consequently, in many parts of the world, water use greatly exceeds supply. This problem is expected to increase in the future.

Plant resources also make up a large part of the world's natural resources. Plant resources are renewable and can be re-grown and restocked. Plant resources can be used by humans to make clothing, buildings, and medicines and can also be directly consumed. Forestry is the study and management of growing forests. This industry provides the wood that is essential for use as construction timber or paper. Cotton is a common plant found on farms of the Southern United States. Cotton is used to produce fabric for clothing, sheets, furniture, etc. Another example of a plant resource that is not directly consumed is straw, which is harvested for use in plant growth and farm animal care. The list of plants grown to provide food for the people of the world is extensive. Major crops include corn, potatoes, wheat, sugar, barley, peas, beans, beets, flax, lentils, sunflowers, soybeans, canola, and rice. These crops may have alternate uses as well. For example, corn is used to manufacture cornstarch, ethanol fuel, high fructose corn syrup, ink, biodegradable plastics, chemicals used in cosmetics and pharmaceuticals, adhesives, and paper products.

Other resources used by humans are known as "non-renewable" resources. Such resources, including fossil fuels, cannot be re-made and do not naturally reform at a rate that could sustain human use. Non-renewable resources are therefore depleted and not restored. Presently, non-renewable resources provide the main source of energy for humans. Common fossil fuels used by humans are coal, petroleum, and natural gas, which all form from the remains of dead plants and animals through natural processes after millions of years. Because of their high carbon content, when burnt, these substances generate high amounts of energy as well as carbon dioxide, which is released back into the atmosphere, increasing global warming. To create electricity, energy from the burning of fossil fuels is harnessed to power a rotary engine called a turbine. Implementation of the use of fossil fuels as an energy source provided for large-scale industrial development.

Mineral resources are concentrations of naturally occurring inorganic elements and compounds located in the Earth's crust that are extracted through mining for human use. Minerals have a definite chemical composition and are stable over a range of temperatures and pressures. Construction and manufacturing rely heavily on metals and industrial mineral resources. These metals may include iron, bronze, lead, zinc, nickel, copper, tin, etc. Other industrial minerals are divided into two categories: bulk rocks and ore minerals. Bulk rocks, including limestone, clay, shale, and sandstone, are used as aggregate in construction, in ceramics, or in concrete. Common ore minerals include calcite, barite, and gypsum. Energy from some minerals can be utilized to produce electricity fuel and industrial materials. Mineral resources are also used as fertilizers and pesticides in the industrial context.

Deforestation for urban development has resulted in the extinction or relocation of several species of plants and animals. Animals are forced to leave their forest homes or perish amongst the destruction. The number of plant and animal species that have become extinct due to deforestation is unknown. Scientists have only identified a fraction of the species on Earth. It is known that if the destruction of natural resources continues, there may be no plants or animals successfully reproducing in the wild.

The current energy crisis is largely centered on the uncertain future of fossil fuels. The supplies of fossil fuels are limited and are quickly declining. Additionally, most oil is now derived from a politically volatile area of the world. Finally, continuing to produce energy from fossils fuels is unwise given the damage done by both the disruption to the environment necessary to harvest them and by the byproducts of their combustion, which cause pollution. The various detrimental effects of fossil fuels are listed later in this section.

It is important to recognize that a real energy crisis has vast economic implications. Oil, currently the most important fossil fuel, is needed for heating, electricity, and as a raw material for the manufacture of many items, particularly plastics. Additionally, the gasoline made from oil is important in transporting people and goods, including food and other items necessary for life. A disruption in the oil supply often causes rising prices in all sectors and may eventually trigger recession.

Alternative, sustainable energy sources must be found for both economic and ecological reasons.

COMPETENCY 16.0   UNDERSTAND AND ANALYZE THE HISTORICAL DEVELOPMENT AND CULTURAL CONTEXTS OF SCIENCE AND TECHNOLOGY AND THE IMPACT OF SCIENCE ON SOCIETY.

Skill 16.1   Analyze the historical development and impact of key scientific ideas and discoveries.

Interrelationships among science and other disciplines

Math, science, and technology have common themes in how they are applied and understood. All three use models, diagrams, and graphs to simplify a concept for analysis and interpretation. Patterns observed in these systems lead to predictions based on these observations. Another common theme among these three systems is equilibrium. **Equilibrium** is a state in which forces are balanced, resulting in stability. Static equilibrium is stability due to a lack of changes, and dynamic equilibrium is stability due to a balance between opposite forces.

The fundamental relationship between the natural and social sciences is the use of the scientific method and the rigorous standards of proof that both disciplines require. This emphasis on organization and evidence separates the sciences from the arts and humanities. Natural science, particularly biology, is closely related to social science, the study of human behavior. Biological and environmental factors often dictate human behavior, and accurate assessment of behavior requires a sound understanding of biological factors.

Concepts and methods that are common to science and technology

Biological science is closely connected to technology and the other sciences and greatly impacts society and everyday life. Scientific discoveries often lead to technological advances and, conversely, technology is often necessary for scientific investigation, as advances in technology often expand the reach of scientific discoveries. In addition, biology and the other scientific disciplines share several concepts and processes that help unify the study of science. Finally, because biology is the science of living systems, biology directly impacts society and everyday life.

Science and technology, while distinct concepts, are closely related. Science attempts to investigate and explain the natural world, while technology attempts to solve human adaptation problems. Technology often results from the application of scientific discoveries, and advances in technology can increase the impact of scientific discoveries. For example, Watson and Crick used science to discover the structure of DNA, and their discovery led to many biotechnological advances in the manipulation of DNA. These technological advances greatly influenced the medical and pharmaceutical fields. The success of Watson and Crick's experiments, however, was dependent on the technology available. Without the necessary technology, the experiments would have failed.

The combination of biology and technology has improved the human standard of living in many ways. However, the negative impact of increasing human life expectancy and population on the environment is problematic. In addition, advances in biotechnology (e.g., genetic engineering, cloning) produce ethical dilemmas that society must consider.

(See Skill 15.1 for more information on how biology and technology are linked.)

Key events in the history of science and the science contributions of people from a variety of social and ethnic backgrounds

The history of biology follows man's understanding of the living world from the earliest recorded history to modern times. Though the concept of biology as a field of science arose only in the 19th century, its origins could be traced back to the ancient Greeks (Galen and Aristotle).

During the Renaissance and Age of Discovery, renewed interest in the rapidly increasing number of known organisms generated a great deal of interest in biology.

Andreas Vesalius (1514-1564) was a Belgian anatomist and physician whose dissections of the human body and the descriptions of his findings helped correct the misconceptions of science. The books Vesalius wrote on anatomy were the most accurate and comprehensive anatomical texts of the time.

Anton van Leeuwenhoek is known as the father of microscopy. In the 1650s, Leeuwenhoek began making tiny lenses that gave magnifications up to 300x. He was the first to see and describe bacteria, yeast plants, and the microscopic life found in water. Over the years, light microscopes have advanced to produce greater clarity and magnification. The scanning electron microscope (SEM) was developed in the 1950s. Instead of light, a beam of electrons passes through the specimen. Scanning electron microscopes have a resolution about one thousand times greater than light microscopes. The disadvantage of the SEM is that the chemical and physical methods used to prepare the sample result in the death of the specimen.

Carl Von Linnaeus (1707-1778), a Swedish botanist, physician, and zoologist, is well known for his contributions in ecology and taxonomy. Linnaeus is famous for his binomial system of nomenclature, in which each living organism has two names, a genus and a species name. He is considered the father of modern ecology and taxonomy.

In the late 1800s, Pasteur discovered the role of microorganisms in the cause of disease, pasteurization, and the rabies vaccine. Koch took his observations one step further by postulating that specific diseases were caused by specific pathogens. **Koch's postulates** are still used as guidelines in the field of microbiology. They state that the same pathogen must be found in every diseased person, the pathogen must be isolated and grown in culture, the disease must be induced in experimental animals from the culture, and the same pathogen must be isolated from the experimental animal.

In the 18th century, many fields of science, such as botany, zoology, and geology, began to evolve as scientific disciplines in the modern sense.

In the 20th century, the rediscovery of Mendel's work led to the rapid development of genetics by Thomas Hunt Morgan and his students.

DNA structure was another key event in biological study. In the 1950s, James Watson and Francis Crick discovered the structure of a DNA molecule as that of a double helix. This structure made it possible to explain DNA's ability to replicate and to control the synthesis of proteins.

Following the cracking of the genetic code, biology has largely split between organismal biology—consisting of ecology, ethology, systematics, paleontology, evolutionary biology, developmental biology, and other disciplines that deal with whole organisms or group of organisms—and the disciplines related to molecular biology, which include cell biology, biophysics, biochemistry, neuroscience, and immunology.

The use of animals in biological research has expedited many scientific discoveries. Animal research has allowed scientists to learn more animal biological systems, including the circulatory and reproductive systems. One significant use of animals is for the testing of drugs, vaccines, and other products (such as perfumes and shampoos) before use or consumption by humans. There are both significant pros and cons of animal research. The debate about the ethical treatment of animals has been ongoing since the introduction of animals to research. Many people believe the use of animals in research is cruel and unnecessary. Animal use is federally and locally regulated. The purpose of the Institutional Animal Care and Use Committee (IACUC) is to oversee and evaluate all aspects of an institution's animal care and use program.

Skill 16.2   Evaluate factors that have promoted or hindered developments in science and technology.

The influence of social and cultural factors on science and technology

Curiosity is the heart of science. Maybe this is why so many diverse people are drawn to it. In the area of zoology, one of the most recognized scientists is Jane Goodall. Miss Goodall is known for her research with chimpanzees in Africa. Jane has spent many years abroad conducting long-term studies of chimp interactions and returns from Africa to lecture and provide information about Africa, the chimpanzees, and her institute, which is located in Tanzania.

In the area of chemistry, we recognize Dorothy Crowfoot Hodgkin. She studied at Oxford and won the Nobel Prize of Chemistry in 1964 for recognizing the shape of the vitamin B 12.

Have you ever heard of Florence Nightingale? She was a true person living in the 1800's, and she shaped the nursing profession. Florence was born into wealth and shocked her family by choosing to study health reforms for the poor in lieu of attending the expected social events. Florence studied nursing in Paris and became involved in the Crimean war. The British lacked supplies, and the secretary of war asked for Florence's assistance. She earned her nickname walking the floors at night, checking on patients, and writing letters to British officials demanding supplies.

In 1903, the Nobel Prize in Physics was jointly awarded to three individuals: Marie Curie, Pierre Curie, and Becquerel. Marie was the first woman ever to receive this prestigious award. In addition, she received the Nobel Prize in chemistry in 1911, making her the only person to receive two Nobel awards in science. Ironically, her cause of death in 1934 was of overexposure to radioactivity, the research for which she was so respected.

Neil Armstrong is an American icon. He will always be symbolically linked to our aeronautics program. This astronaut and naval aviator is known for being the first human to set foot on the Moon.

Sir Alexander Fleming was a pharmacologist from Scotland who isolated the antibiotic penicillin from a fungus in 1928. Fleming also noted that bacteria developed resistance whenever too little penicillin was used or when it was used for too short a period, a key problem we still face today.

It is important to realize that many of the most complex scientific questions have been answered in a collaborative form. The human genome project is a great example of research conducted and shared by multiple countries world wide.

It is also interesting to note that because of differing cultural beliefs, some cultures may be more likely to allow areas of research that other cultures may be unlikely to examine.

Society and culture are very closely related. They are in fact closely intertwined. Together they have influenced every aspect of the human life. Science and technology are no exception to this.

Let us examine **the influence of social and cultural factors on science** first, and then we will see their effect on technology.

The influence of social and cultural factors on science is profound. In a way, we can say that society has changed the face of science by absorbing scientific innovations. Science has always been a big part of society. The difference is that in ancient societies, people did not realize that it was science, but took it as a part of their lives. In the modern society, everything has a label and a name, so that people are aware of science and other disciplines.

Societies have had trouble accepting science, especially where the science exposed some cultural aspects as myths. There was a big dilemma of whether to accept the proven facts provided by scientific investigations or to cling to cultural norms. This went on for centuries. It took a long time for societies to accept these facts and to leave some of the cultural practices behind or to modify them. At the same time, we must give full credit to cultural practices, which are scientifically correct, but which are sometimes connected to religion and taken very seriously by believers. We can conclude that there are two factors - one is cultural practices by societies which are scientifically correct, and the second one is cultural practices which have no scientific foundation (myths and superstitions). A society's progress depends on distinguishing between these two. Some indigenous societies suffered when they were not quick to adjust since their cultures are very ancient, and the people found it difficult to accept new challenges and adapt to new changes. At the same time, ancient cultures, like the Chinese, Egyptian, Greek, Asian, and Indian had well-developed science that was recorded in their ancient writings.

Let's take a look at **the effect of society and culture on technology.** If we compare science to a volcano, technology is like lava spewing out of the volcano. This was the scenario in the last few centuries in terms of rapid strides in the development of technology. Technology greatly influenced society and culture, and at the same time, science and culture exercised their influence on technology. It is like a two-way street.

It became extremely difficult for some societies to come to terms with technological advances. Even today, some cultures are not using modern technology, but at the same time, they are using technology in principle - using simple machines for farming rather than using complex machines like tractors, etc. Other cultures have so readily adapted to technology that lives are intertwined with it. Intertwined so much that we utilize the computer, television, microwave, dishwasher, washing machine, cell phone, etc. on a daily basis. It is surprising to realize that we began with no technology and now are enslaved to it. Cultures that are not in tune with modern technology are falling behind. It is often argued that to live without technology yields peace of mind, serenity, and happiness, but such cultures are also losing valuable opportunities in this age of communication.

Positive contributions of technology are that it revolutionized education, medicine, communication, travel, etc. The world has seemed to shrink in that we don't seem as far apart, and we have means to stay connected. As a result of this technology, man is exploring space to find out what it is like and to learn and gain knowledge, which used to be elusive and as distant as the planets themselves.

When we take a critical look at these facts, we have to commend societies for trying to keep their own culture, as culture is a very important aspect of humanity. We also need to appreciate cultures that accepted or incorporated science and technology.

Differences between ethical and unethical uses of science

To understand scientific ethics, we need to have a clear understanding of ethics. Ethics is defined as a system of public, general rules for guiding human conduct (Gert, 1988). The rules are general because they are supposed to apply to all people at all times, and they are public because they are not secret codes or practices.

Philosophers have given a number of moral theories to justify moral rules, which range from utilitarianism (a theory of ethics that prescribes the quantitative maximization of good consequences for a population. It is a form of consequentialism. This theory was proposed by Mozi, a Chinese philosopher who lived during BC 471-381.) to Kantianism (a theory proposed by Immanuel Kant, a German philosopher who lived during 1724-1804, which ascribes intrinsic value to rational beings and is the philosophical foundation of contemporary human rights) to social contract theory (a view of the ancient Greeks which states that the person's moral and/or political obligations are dependent upon a contract or agreement between them to form society).

The following are some of the guiding principles of scientific ethics:

1. Scientific Honesty: not to fraud, fabricate, or misinterpret data for personal gain
2. Caution: to avoid errors and sloppiness in all scientific experimentation
3. Credit: to give credit where credit is due and not to copy
4. Responsibility: to only report reliable information to the public and not to mislead in the name of science
5. Freedom: freedom to criticize old ideas, question new research, and conduct research

Many more principles could be added to this list. Though these principles seem straightforward and clear, it is very difficult to put them into practice since they could be interpreted in more ways than one. Nevertheless, it is not an excuse for scientists to overlook these guiding principles of scientific ethics.

Scientists are expected to show good conduct in their scientific pursuits. Conduct here refers to all aspects of scientific activity, including experimentation, testing, education, data evaluation, data analysis, data storing, peer review, government funding, the staff, etc.

The common ethical code described above could be applied to many areas, including science. When the general code is applied to a particular area of human life, it then becomes an institutional code. Hence, scientific ethics is an institutional code of conduct that reflects the chief concerns and goals of science.

To discuss scientific ethics, we can look at natural phenomena like rain. Rain, in the normal sense, is extremely useful to us, and it is absolutely vital that there is a water cycle. When rain gets polluted with acid, it becomes acid rain. Here lies the ethical issue of releasing all these pollutants into the atmosphere. Should the scientists communicate the whole truth about acid rain or withhold some information because it may alarm the public? There are many issues like this. Whatever may be the case, scientists are expected to be honest and forthright with the public.

Skill 16.3   Assess the implications of recent developments in science and technology.

The effects of scientific and technological developments on the environment, human biology, society, and culture

In the last century, the advances in the fields of science and technology were amazing and have changed the lives of human beings forever. Lifestyles were greatly affected, and the society experienced dramatic changes.   People started to take science technology very seriously. The advances in these two interrelated fields are no longer the domain of the elite few. The average person started to use the advances in the field of technology in their daily lives. Because of this, the societal structure is changing rapidly to the extent that even young children are using technology.

With any rapid change, there are always positive and negative aspects associated with it. Caution and care are the two words we need to associate with these giant strides in technology. At the same time, we need high technology in our lives, and we can't afford not to make use of these developments and not to reap the benefits for the good of humanity.

The environment in which we live, human biology, society at large, and our culture are being affected. Let us take each point and examine very carefully the effects of science and technology on the above.

Environment

The environment we live in is constantly and rapidly undergoing tremendous changes.

The positive effects include the ability to predict hurricanes; measure the changes in terms of radioactivity present in our environment; the remedial measures for that problem; predicting the levels of gases, like carbon monoxide, carbon dioxide, and other harmful gases; various estimates, like the green house effect, ozone layer, and UV radiation, to name a few. With the help of modern technology, it is possible to know their quantities and to monitor and plan and implement measures to deal with them. Even with the most advanced technology available to us, it is impossible to go back to the clean, green Earth, since man has made a mark on it in a negative way. It is possible, to a limited extent, to alleviate the problem, but it is impossible to eradicate it.

The negative aspects of the effects of technology on our environment are numerous. The first and foremost is pollution of various kinds - water, air, noise etc.--including the greenhouse effect, the indiscriminate use of fertilizers, the spraying of pesticides, the use of various additives to our food, deforestation, unprecedented exploitation of non-renewable energy resources, to name a few.

As we discussed earlier, it is not possible to solve these problems with money, human resources, etc., but educating the society and making them aware of these negative aspects will go a long way. For example, as teachers, we need to educate students about using natural resources cautiously, trying to save those resources, and we also need to teach that little steps in the right direction will go a long way, e.g., car pooling, not wasting paper, walking whenever possible (if it is safe). It is important to teach the students to have trees if they have space or at least to have house plants, as they change the quality of the air we breath.

Human biology

The strides science and technology made have lasting effects on human biology. A few examples are organ transplants, in vitro fertilization, cloning, new drugs, a new understanding of various diseases using scientific knowledge, cosmetic surgery, reconstructive surgery, use of computers in operations, lasers in medicine, forensic science, etc. These changes have made a lasting difference to humanity.

As always, there are pros and cons to these changes.

One positive aspects is that people with organ transplants have renewed hope. Their life spans are increased, and their quality of life has changed with the use of technology, including pace makers. Another pro is that couples who experienced infertility are having babies now. Corrective and cosmetic surgery are giving new confidence to patients. Glasses to correct vision problems are being replaced slowly by laser surgery.

The negative aspects are paternity issues arising out of in vitro fertilization, some medical blunders, which are expensive and heart wrenching (when a wrong egg is implanted), the indiscriminate use of corrective and cosmetic surgery, older mothers and young orphans, etc.

Society

Society is not the same as it used to be even 25 years ago. The use of technology has changed our patterns of lifestyle, our behavior, our ethical and moral thinking, our economy and career opportunities, to name a few.

The positive effects are the economy booming due to the high tech industry, more career opportunities for people to select, raising of standard of living, prolonged life with quality, closeness even though we are separated by thousands of kilometers/miles, quicker and faster communication, etc. The computer has contributed a great deal to these changes. Normal household chores are being done by machines, giving relief and a cost-effective and time-saving means for upkeep of the kitchen and the home.

The negative aspects are far reaching. The breakdown in family structure could be attributed partly to high tech. Family meals and family togetherness are being replace with gadgets. Some would argue that as a result of this, our young people are becoming insecure, indirectly affecting their problem solving skills. Young people are becoming increasingly vulnerable due to internet programs, including chat rooms and online pornography, etc. There must be stringent measures to protect our younger generation from these internet predators. The effects of various high tech gadgets like the microwave are not entirely positive.

Constant game playing utilizing new technology (Gameboy, Xbox, etc.) encourage a sedentary lifestyle and childhood obesity.

Culture

This is a very sensitive yet very important issue. The above listed factors are affecting the cultures of people.

The positive aspects are that technology is uniting us to a certain extent - e.g., it is possible to communicate with a person of any culture even when we are not seeing them face to face. It makes business and personal communication much easier over long distances. Some people were not comfortable with communicating with other cultures since they were closed societies, but email has changed that. When we all use the same pieces of technology, we understand better and a common ground is established. Internet can definitely boast of some successful cross-cultural marriages. Sharing opinions and information has also been enhanced.

With modern technology, travel is changing the way we think, as well as career opportunities. It is helping us to know other cultures, different ways of doing the same things, and to learn the positive values of other cultures.

The negative aspects include moral and ethical values, as increased awareness is allowing for a new wave of thinking. Care must be exercised in how much of our past culture we are willing to trade for the modern. Positive aspects of any culture must be guarded carefully and passed on to generations to come.

On the whole, we can safely conclude that science and technology are part of our lives, and we must always exercise caution and be careful when we are adapting to new ideas and new thinking. It is possible that awareness and incorporation of other cultural practices will make us a better nation, which our founding fathers envisioned and dreamed of.

The relationships between personal choices and health

While genetics plays an important role in health, human behaviors can greatly affect short- and long-term health both positively and negatively. Behaviors that negatively affect health include smoking, excessive alcohol consumption, substance abuse, and poor eating habits. Behaviors that positively affect health include good nutrition and regular exercise.

Smoking negatively affects health in many ways. First, smoking decreases lung capacity, causes persistent coughing, and limits the ability to engage in strenuous physical activity. In addition, the long-term effects are even more damaging. Long-term smoking can cause lung cancer, heart disease, and emphysema (a lung disease).

Alcohol is the most abused legal drug. Excessive alcohol consumption has both short- and long-term negative effects. Drunkenness can lead to reckless behavior and distorted judgment that can cause injury or death. In addition, extreme alcohol abuse can cause alcohol poisoning that can result in immediate death. Long-term alcohol abuse is also extremely hazardous. The potential effects of long-term alcohol abuse include liver cirrhosis, heart problems, high blood pressure, stomach ulcers, and cancer.

The abuse of illegal substances can also negatively affect health. Commonly abused drugs include cocaine, heroin, opiates, methamphetamines, and marijuana. Drug abuse can cause immediate death or injury and, if used for a long time, can cause many physical and psychological health problems.

A healthy diet and regular exercise are the cornerstones of a healthy lifestyle. A diet rich in whole grains, fruits, vegetables, polyunsaturated fats, and lean protein and low in saturated fat and sugar, can positively affect overall health. Such diets can reduce cholesterol levels, lower blood pressure, and help manage body weight. Conversely, diets high in saturated fat and sugar can contribute to weight gain, heart disease, strokes, and cancer.

Finally, regular exercise has both short- and long-term health benefits. Exercise increases physical fitness, improving energy levels, overall body function, and mental well-being. Long-term, exercise helps protect against chronic diseases, maintains healthy bones and muscles, helps maintain a healthy body weight, and strengthens the body's immune system.

COMPETENCY 17.0   UNDERSTAND, INTERPRET, AND COMPARE REPRESENTATIONS FROM THE VISUAL AND PERFORMING ARTS FROM DIFFERENT PERIODS AND CULTURES, AND UNDERSTAND THE RELATIONSHIP OF WORKS OF ART TO THEIR SOCIAL AND HISTORICAL CONTEXTS.

Skill 17.1   Identify and evaluate major historical and contemporary developments and movements in the arts.

The various *styles* of **dance** can be explained as follows:

- ☐ Creative dance
- ☐ Modern dance
- ☐ Social dance
- ☐ Dance of other cultures
- ☐ Structured dance
- ☐ Ritual Dance
- ☐ Ballet

Creative dance is the one that is most natural to a young child. Creative dance depicts feelings through movement. It is the initial reaction to sound and movement. The older elementary student will incorporate mood and expressiveness. Stories can be told to release the dancer into imagination.

Isadora Duncan is credited with being the mother of modern dance. **Modern dance** today refers to a concept of dance where the expressions of opposites are developed, such as fast-slow, contract-release, vary height and level to fall and recover. Modern dance is based on four principles, which are substance, dynamism, metakinesis, and form.

Social dance requires a steadier capability than the previous levels. The social aspect of dance, rather than romantic aspect, represents customs and pastimes. Adults laugh when they hear little ones go "eweeee". Changing partners frequently within the dance is something that is subtly important to maintain. Social dance refers to a cooperative form of dance with respect to one sharing the dance floor with others and to have respect for one's partner. Social dance may be in the form of marches, the waltz, and the two-step.

The upper level elementary student can learn dance in connection with historical **cultures**, such as the minuet. The minuet was introduced to the court in Paris in 1650, and it dominated the ballroom until the end of the eighteenth century. The waltz was introduced around 1775 and was an occasion of fashion and courtship. The pomp and ceremony of it all makes for fun classroom experiences.

Dance traditionally is central to many cultures, and the interrelatedness of teaching history, such as the Native American Indians' dance, the Mexican hat dance, or Japanese theater, which incorporates both theater of masks and dance, are all important exposures to dance and culture.

Structured dances are recognized by particular patterns, such as the Tango or waltz, and were made popular in dance studios and gym classes alike. Arthur Murray promoted dance lessons for adults.

Ritual dances are often of a religious nature that celebrate a significant life event, such as a harvest season, the rainy season, glorifying the gods, asking for favors in hunting, and birth and death dances. Many of these themes are carried out in movies and theaters today, but they have their roots in Africa, where circle dances and chants summoned the gods and sometimes produced trance-like states, where periods of divine contact convey the spiritual cleansing of the experience.

Dancing at weddings today is a prime example of ritual dance. The father dances with the bride. Then, the husband dances with the bride. And finally, the two families dance with each other.

Ballet uses a barre to hold to practice the five basic positions used in ballet. Alignment is the way in which various parts of the dancer's body are in line with one another while the dancer is moving. It is very precise and executed with grace and form. The mood and expressions of the music are very important to ballet and form the canvas upon which the dance is performed.

Theatre

Greek History

The history of theatre can be dated back to early sixth century B.C. in Greece. The Greek theatre was the earliest known theater experience. Drama was expressed in many Greek spiritual ceremonies. There are two main dramatic forms that have both evolved in their own time.

Tragedy is typically conflict between characters. **Comedy** is typically paradoxical relationships between humans and the unknown gods, such as Sophocles and Euripides.

Comedies and Tragedies were seldom mixed by playwrights. Plays such as these were designed to entertain and contained little violence and were based on the knowledge and teachings of Aristotle.

Roman History

The history of theatre in Roman times was discovered in the third century. These theatre shows were also based on religious aspects of the lives of Roman gods and goddesses. Drama wasn't able to withstand the fall of the Roman Empire in 476 A.D. By the end of the sixth century, drama was nearly dead in Rome.

Medieval Drama

Medieval theatre was a new revelation of drama that appeared around the tenth century. New phases of religion were introduced in many holiday services, such as Christmas and Easter. In the church itself, drama was noticed in many troupes that toured churches presenting religious narratives and life stories of moral deeds. Over time, the once small traveling groups grew into full-sized plays, presentations, and elaborate passions. Performances became spectacles at outdoor theaters, marketplaces, and any place large audiences could gather. The main focus of these presentations of drama was to glorify God and humanity and to celebrate local artisan trades.

Puritan Commonwealth

The Puritan Commonwealth was ruled by Oliver Cromwell, who outlawed dramatic performances, and that ban lasted for nearly twenty years. Following the Puritan era was the restoration of the English monarchy, and new, more well-rounded plays became the focus of art. For the first time in history, women were allowed to participate.

Melodrama

Melodrama eventually took over the stage of acting, in which the good always triumphed over the evil. This form of acting was usually pleasing to the audience yet sometimes unrealistic.

Serious Drama

Serious Drama emerged late in the nineteenth and twentieth centuries. It came following the movement of realism. Realism attempted to combine the dealings of nature with realistic and ordinary situations on stage.

Realism

Today, realism is the most common form of stage presence. The techniques used today to stage drama combine many of the past histories and cultures of drama.

The greatest works in art, literature, music, theater, and dance all mirror universal themes. Universal themes are themes that reflect the human experience, regardless of time period, location, or socio-economic standing. Universal themes tend to fall into broad categories, such as Man vs. Society, Man vs. Himself, Man vs. God, Man vs. Nature, and Good vs. Evil, to name the most obvious. The general themes listed below all fall into one of these broad categories.

Prehistoric Arts, (circa 1,000,000-circa 8,000 B.C)
Major themes of this vast period appear to center around religious fertility rites and sympathetic magic, consisting of imagery of pregnant animals and faceless, pregnant women.

Mesopotamian Arts, (circa 8,000-400 B.C.)
The prayer statues and cult deities of the period point to the theme of polytheism in religious worship.

Egyptian Arts, (circa 3,000-100 B.C.)
The predominance of funerary art from ancient Egypt illustrates the theme of preparation for the afterlife and polytheistic worship. Another dominant theme, reflected by artistic convention, is the divinity of the pharaohs. In architecture, the themes were monumentality and adherence to ritual.

Greek Arts, (800-100 B.C.)
The sculpture of ancient Greece is replete with human figures, most nude and some draped. Most of these sculptures represent athletes and various gods and goddesses. The predominant theme is that of the ideal human, in both mind and body. In architecture, the theme was scale, based on the ideal human proportions.

Roman Arts, (circa 480 B.C.- 476 A.D.)
Judging from Roman arts, the predominant themes of the period deal with the realistic depiction of human beings and how they relate to Greek classical ideals. The emphasis is on practical realism. Another major theme is the glory in serving the Roman state. In architecture, the theme was rugged practicality mixed with Greek proportions and elements.

Middle Ages Arts, (300-1400 A.D.)

Although the time span is expansive, the major themes remain relatively constant. Since the Roman Catholic Church was the primary patron of the arts, most work was religious in nature. The purpose of much of the art was to educate. Specific themes varied from the illustration of Bible stories to interpretations of theological allegory, to lives of the saints, to consequences of good and evil. Depictions of the Holy Family were popular. Themes found in secular art and literature centered on chivalric love and warfare. In architecture, the theme was glorification of God and education of congregation to religious principles.

Renaissance Arts, (circa 1400-1630 A.D.)

Renaissance themes include Christian religious depiction (see Middle Ages), but tend to reflect a renewed interest in all things classical. Specific themes include Greek and Roman mythological and philosophic figures, ancient battles, and legends. Dominant themes mirror the philosophic beliefs of Humanism, emphasizing individuality and human reason, such as those of the High Renaissance, which center around the psychological attributes of individuals. In architecture, the theme was scale, based on human proportions.

Baroque Arts, (1630-1700 A.D.)

The predominant themes found in the arts of the Baroque period include the dramatic climaxes of well-known stories, legends, and battles and the grand spectacle of mythology. Religious themes are found frequently, but it is drama and insight that are emphasized and not the medieval "salvation factor." Baroque artists and authors incorporated various types of characters into their works, careful to include minute details. Portraiture focused on the psychology of the sitters. In architecture, the theme was large scale grandeur and splendor.

Eighteenth Century Arts, (1700-1800 A.D.)

Rococo themes of this century focused on religion, light mythology, portraiture of aristocrats, pleasure and escapism, and occasionally, satire. In architecture, the theme was artifice and gaiety, combined with an organic quality of form. Neo-classic themes centered on examples of virtue and heroism, usually in classical settings, and historical stories. In architecture, classical simplicity and utility of design were regained.

Nineteenth Century Arts, (1800-1900 A.D.)

Romantic themes included human freedom, equality, and civil rights, a love for nature, and a tendency toward the melancholic and mystic. The underlying theme is that the most important discoveries are made within the self, and not in the exterior world. In architecture, the theme was fantasy and whimsy, known as "picturesque." Realistic themes included social awareness and a focus on society victimizing individuals. The themes behind Impressionism were the constant flux of the universe and the immediacy of the moment. In architecture, the themes were strength, simplicity, and upward thrust, as skyscrapers entered the scene.

Twentieth Century Arts, (1900-2000 A.D.)

Diverse artistic themes of the century reflect a parting with traditional religious values and a painful awareness of man's inhumanity to man. Themes also illustrate a growing reliance on science, while simultaneously expressing disillusionment with man's failure to adequately control science. A constant theme is the quest for originality and self-expression, while seeking to express the universal in human experience. In architecture, "form follows function."

Genres By Historical Periods

Ancient Greek Art, (circa 800-323 B.C.)

Dominant genres from this period were vase paintings, both black-figure and red-figure, and classical sculpture.

Roman Art, (circa 480 B.C.-476 A.D.)

Major genres from the Romans include frescoes (murals done in fresh plaster to affix the paint), classical sculpture, funerary art, state propaganda art, and relief work on cameos.

Middle Ages Art, (circa 300-1400 A.D.)

Significant genres during the Middle Ages include Byzantine mosaics, illuminated manuscripts, ivory relief, altarpieces, cathedral sculpture, and fresco paintings in various styles.

Renaissance Art, (1400-1630 A.D.)

Important genres from the Renaissance included Florentine fresco painting (mostly religious), High Renaissance painting and sculpture, Northern oil painting, Flemish miniature painting, and Northern printmaking.

Baroque Art, (1630-1700 A.D.)

Pivotal genres during the Baroque era include Mannerism, Italian Baroque painting and sculpture, Spanish Baroque, Flemish Baroque, and Dutch portraiture. Genre paintings in still-life and landscape appear prominently in this period.

Eighteenth Century Art, (1700-1800 A.D.)

Predominant genres of the century include Rococo painting, portraiture, social satire, Romantic painting, and Neoclassic painting and sculpture.

Nineteenth Century Art, (1800-1900 A.D.)

Important genres include Romantic painting, academic painting and sculpture, landscape painting of many varieties, realistic painting of many varieties, impressionism, and many varieties of post-impressionism.

Twentieth Century Art, (1900-2000 A.D.)

Major genres of the twentieth century include symbolism, art nouveau, fauvism, expressionism, cubism (both analytical and synthetic), futurism, non-objective art, abstract art, surrealism, social realism, constructivism in sculpture, Pop and Op art, and conceptual art.

Paleolithic/Neolithic Arts, (circa 1,000,000 B.C.- 8,000 B.C.)

Although the span of years that separate us from the earliest artists is formidable, those men and women still speak to us eloquently from the far-reaches of prehistory. Paleolithic and Neolithic cave artists were probably community shamans who utilized their paintings and sculptures for religious rituals, specifically sympathetic magic. Their images are predominated by animals and faceless pregnant women, probably rendered for use in fertility rites. The fact that most paintings are located in inaccessible parts of caves leads historians to speculate that the paintings were sacred in some way. Natural materials, such as charcoal, stone, and bone are the mediums that have survived to present day. Early artists utilized outcroppings of stone to simulate a three-dimensional quality. Since some of the images appear to be renderings of dancing people, historians conclude that dance was also a Paleolithic activity, perhaps used in religious activities.

Remnants of musical instruments, also made from natural materials, indicate that music was also a part of Paleolithic life.

Arts of Mesopotamia and Egypt, (circa 8,000 B.C.-800 B.C.)

Of the two ancient civilizations to span thousands of years along the banks of the Tigris-Euphrates Rivers (Mesopotamia) and the Nile River (Egypt), the older was Mesopotamia.

Due to geographic factors, Mesopotamia was inhabited by a series of cultures, from the Sumerians to the Persians. Cylinder seals and vases were decorated with processions of animals and human figures. Sumerians created stylized votive statues with hands clasped in prayer and staring eyes. Temple-like ziggurats served both as shrines to cult statues and as grain warehouses. Inlaid harps and goat figures were decorated with gold and lapis lazuli.

During the Babylonian era, The Epic of Gilgamesh, originally an oral narrative replete with repetition, was written.

The Assyrian era was marked by imposing, war-like sculpture and relief work that reflected the chief quality of the society. Lyres, harps, flutes and dulcimers were depicted in the visual arts of the period. Dance appears to have been included in religious ceremonies, most notably in the Fire Festival, a fertility rite.

In Egypt, geographic factors induced a more stable culture whose cultural continuity spanned thousands of years. Egyptian architecture was most notable for the monumental building scale of tombs, temples, and pyramids in stone, many decorated inside and out with paintings and reliefs.

Tomb murals, although depicting the realistic life of the deceased, utilized artistic conventions in the portrayal of the human body. Pharaohs were always depicted with divine attributes, with the exception of Pharaoh Amenhotep IV and Tutankhamun, who apparently insisted on a more realistic rendering. Sarcophagi of painted wood and works in gold and alabaster typify the royal funerary equipment of the period.

The visual arts illustrate the existence of stringed, wind, and percussion musical instruments, as well as "stride" dances used for both funerary and fertility rites. Literature of the period is collectively called the *Book of the Dead* because it consists mainly of prayers, chants, and magical information needed by the Ka to traverse to the afterlife.

Arts of Ancient Greece, (800 B.C.- 323 B.C).
The earliest artists known to us as specific individuals herald from the days of the ancient Greeks. Following a long sculptural tradition, Myron and Polyclitus produced bronze sculpture in the classical style, which stressed simplicity, dignity, proportion, and appeal to the intellect. Later, Praxiteles utilized his famous S-curve (contrapposto) in the marble torsos he produced. The sculptures, many of nude athletes, were idealized, a reflection of the philosophy of the period. From approximately 340 B.C. on, Hellenistic sculpture possessed a more dramatic, narrative quality. Two-dimensional work appears on vases of various styles.

The most notable architecture was created from stone, using post and lintel technique (horizontal blocks laid across vertical supports) to form temples, treasuries, and monuments, also in the classical style. The Classical Orders of Doric, Ionic, and Corinthian were developed. The Doric column was thick, topped with a plain capital, the Ionic column was slender, topped with a volute-carved capital, while the Corinthian column, also slender, terminated in an elaborately carved capital, encrusted with plants and leaves.

Theater, originally associated with the religious festivals of Dionysus, consisted of both tragic and comic plays, also reflecting classical ideals. These heroic tales were performed, with a chorus to provide background and mood, in auditoriums cut into the hillsides.

Arts of Ancient Rome, (480 B.C.- 476 A.D.)

Due to the Roman penchant for all things Greek, most early Roman sculpture was copied from Greek originals. When the Romans did develop their unique style, it was, like its creators, solidly grounded in realism. Portraiture was an Etruscan tradition that found its way into Roman sculpture and cameos, also with a naturalistic basis. Most two-dimensional work is found on domestic murals. Roman architecture was practical, utilizing the arch to build structures that could bear more weight, such as aqueducts and coliseums. The classical orders in architecture were also borrowed from the Greeks.

Music was regarded as entertainment and used extensively in society.

Early literature again relied on Greek structure, but writers, such as Cicero and Virgil, adapted the epic to Roman use.

Byzantine Arts, (610-1453 A.D.)

Much two-dimensional work of the Byzantine era appeared in mosaic form, which tended to produce work of a stylized, impersonal nature. Increasingly, religious subjects were emphasized, leading to the hieratic style, which was an elongated representation of humans in an effort to portray spirituality.

In architecture, the domed church with pendentives (spherical triangles of masonry which couple the square corners of the church with the circular dome) and a cross-in-square floor plan were predominant.

In literature, three genres appear: historiography (written in Greek, following Greek models), hagiography (anecdotes and life accounts of monks and saints), and vernacular poems of fifteen-syllable verse.

Theater seems to have disappeared from the scene.

Early Middle Ages Arts, (300-1300 A.D.)

The early Middle Ages corresponded with the rise of Christianity across Europe. Because the Roman Catholic Church was increasing in wealth and influence, many of the arts found patronage in its expansionism. Two-dimensional art followed local (usually Roman) traditions across Europe, but was generally decorative, narrative, and religious in nature. The hieratic elongation found in Byzantine works also made its way to European painting and sculpture. Illuminated manuscripts, crucifixes, cathedral doors, and tympanums were all sites for the interpretation of Biblical scenes.

The massive-feeling, dark Romanesque style churches (basilica), with their Roman arches and small clerestory windows, were springing up across Europe. New musical forms included the hymns, with poetic lyrics set to popular songs, and the Gregorian chant, also called "plainsong," which is marked by a single line of melody, sung in unison, with a single syllable often sung across several notes.

In the field of literature, Christian writers, such as St. Augustine, St. Jerome, and St. Benedict were predominant. Secular sources for stories were the wandering troubadours, with their fantastic heroic stories, such as the *Song of Roland*. Folk stories, such as *Nibelungenlied*, were also popular.

Late Middle Ages Arts, (1100-1453 A.D.)
The visual arts began to illustrate a better awareness of space, although the laws of perspective were still to be mastered. Late medieval artists incorporated more movement in their works and a greater sense of naturalism.
In architecture, the trend was away from Romanesque toward the new building style of Gothic. Gothic cathedrals were noted for the heavenward sweep of the building itself, the height of the roof and spires, the lightness of the interior (due mainly to the increased use of stained glass), and the efficiency of the flying buttresses, which made thin walls possible.

Theater of the day included "mystery" plays, which were essentially Bible stories, "miracle" plays, which were plays about the lives of the saints, and "morality" plays, featuring various sins as characters.

In literature, the influence of the church was still felt, as in Dante's *Divine Comedy*, based on the various levels of heaven, hell, and purgatory. Simultaneously, as more people learned to read and write, authors attempted to accommodate them by writing in the vernacular. Petrarch, innovator of the sonnet form, wrote in both Latin and Tuscan Italian. The medieval chronicle, a somewhat fictional account of various people and places, was also a secular genre.

Musical notation was developed, and along with it, polyphony, or music with many harmonious voices. Musical structure became more formalized, and conventions of key, harmony, and rhythm became more consistent. Motets and madrigals were the predominant musical forms.

Early Renaissance Arts, (1300-1495 A.D.)
The Renaissance in Italy produced a myriad of artists who not only rediscovered the classical Greco-Roman arts, but, in an effort to surpass the classical masters, also refined various artistic techniques.

Early Renaissance two-dimensional art was characterized by shallow depth, usually depicted by overlapping of objects, symmetrical balance, other-worldly figures, and over-all diffused lighting. Subject matter began to reflect a new intellectual direction, as evidenced by Botticelli's inclusion of mythological characters in his paintings. Masaccio used light (chiaroscuro), perspective, and mathematics in new ways to illuminate human forms and to create an illusion of new depth, foreshadowing the High Renaissance.

In the field of architecture, Brunelleschi developed the laws of linear perspective that artists have continued to use. Both he and Alberti reinstated classical proportions in the buildings they designed.

The sculptor Donatello used the classical contrapposto stance in his sculptures but also endowed them with a new sense of humanity and self-awareness.

Writers, such as Petrarch and Boccaccio, also looked to literary classics for form and ethics and then emphasized the vernacular in their own works.

In the field of music, the contrapuntal style was developed for sacred motets, while the mass was given a polyphonic approach.

High Renaissance Arts, (1495-1527 A.D.)
By the sixteenth century, the pervasive theme in the arts was Humanism. The giants of the age, including da Vinci, Michelangelo, and Raphael, made significant strides in achieving psychological awareness through their art. The works of da Vinci achieve this, in part, through his subtle use of "sfumato," while Michelangelo's figures in both paint and marble reflect the humanistic ideals glorifying the individual.

Architecture also reflected the ideals of humanism as architects, such as Bramante, sought to define the perfect proportions of buildings in relation to the human body.

Music in the high Renaissance continued to develop with the genius of Palestrina, who composed elaborate polyphonic choral pieces for the Catholic Church.

Literary figures, such as Machiavelli and Castiglione, wrote about political theory and personal conduct, again reflections of humanistic thought.

The Renaissance was not confined to Italy, but spread throughout Europe. In Flanders, van der Weyden, Durer, and van Eyck were producing works that incorporated new technologies in engraving and oil painting. The intellectuals Erasmus and More wrote in the Christian humanist vein, believing that mankind had lost sight of the teachings of Jesus, and encouraging a return to more Christian philosophy.

The late Renaissance art in Italy (1515-1630) was characterized by the work of Bronzino and El Greco, in a style known as Mannerism. Emotional turmoil, spirituality, and an altered, affected reality were hallmarks of these artists.

Baroque Arts, (1630-1750 A.D.)
Baroque painters across Europe shared similar traits in their works. Italy's Caravaggio, Flander's Rubens, and Rembrandt van Rijn used dramatic chiaroscuro (strong lighting) and strong diagonals to illustrate the climax of well-known myths and stories, while their portraiture often gave insight into the minds of their sitters.

Baroque architecture was often ornamental, with emphasis on light and dark, movement, emotion, and affluence. The large scale of Baroque building lent a feeling of drama to the architecture, as evidenced by Louis XIV's Palace of Versailles.

Some of the most spectacular Baroque achievements were in the field of music. Opera incorporated the Baroque characteristics of dramatic storytelling and sensational shifts from soft to loud, joy to suffering. Bach's cantatas powerfully express the profound religious faith of the Reformation, usually in a contrapuntal mode for four voices. His music for keyboard, in the form of fugues, also reflects the Baroque penchant for ornamentation, dramatic shifts, and large-scale performance. Oratorios and sonatas also tended toward the dramatic, with an emphasis on contrasting passages and tempos and instrumental experimentation.

The reign of Elizabeth I ushered in an era of splendor for English literature. Shakespeare's plays focused on the drama of human psychology, dealing with the turbulent and often contradictory emotions experienced in life. In the process, he vastly enriched the English language with original vocabulary and eloquent phrasing. Elsewhere in Europe, lyric poetry and sonnets took on new, more dramatic characteristics, while the novel developed into a more popular, easy-to-read format, as exemplified by Cervantes' *Don Quixote*.

Eighteenth Century, (1700-1800 A.D.)
The eighteenth century spawned several artistic styles, the first of which was an offshoot of Baroque, known as Rococo (rocks and shells), which utilized decorative motifs.

In architecture, it referred generally to a style of interior design, featuring a light, delicate feeling, enhanced with curvilinear furniture and gilt tracery, often based on a shell motif. In exterior design, it featured undulating walls, reliance on light and shadow for dramatic effect, and caryatid ornamentation.

In painting, Rococo exuded sentimentality, love of pleasure, and delight in love. Rococo musicians improvised pretty "ornaments" or additions to the musical scores, and composers included delicate and artificial passages in their works.

Simultaneously with rococo, in music, a style known as Expressive developed. This style was original and uncomplicated, yet well-proportioned and logical, as evidenced in many works by C.P.E. Bach. Also in music rose the classical style, which was based on classical ideals, not classical models. A highly-defined structure, a predominant melody, and an increase in contrasts of rhythm marked the classical style, as evidenced by many of the works by Mozart. Many musical forms, such as opera and sonata, changed to accommodate these classical requirements. Haydn, Mozart, and Beethoven all composed in their own manner within the classical constraints.

Other painting styles of the eighteenth century included Humanitarianism, the chief characteristic of which was social commentary, and Neo-classicism, the works of which not only detail historical subject matter, but also strive to embrace the classical ideals of proportion, harmony, and rationalism. Neo-classicism in architecture reflected the idea that while ancient architectural styles enhance present building, architects are free to mix elements from various periods with their own creative expressions to produce unique architecture, thus producing a kind of eclecticism.

Nineteenth Century, (1800-1900 A.D.)
The Industrial Age brought with it a myriad of changes, as Europe dealt with the ever-quickening pace of modern life. This was mirrored by the multiplicity of styles that surfaced during the century.

Romanticism in the visual arts implied a variety of sub-styles, most of which were characterized by a sense of melancholy, love of nature, emotionalism, and a sense of the exotic. Romanticism was often regarded as a reaction against the cool restraint of neo-classicism.

In music, however, this "rebellion" was not as clear. Romantic music was an extension of classical music, with the emphasis on spontaneous, poignant, and lyrical melodies. Emotion was suggested by rhythmic patterns, key changes, chromatics, and dissonance.

Romantic authors also emphasized love of nature, emotionalism, and the exotic and bizarre in their works, as evidenced by Wordsworth, Byron, and Shelley.

Realism in the visual arts, emerging during the second half of the century, referred to both a realistic depiction technically and subject matter derived from a genuine source. As the century progressed, however, the line between realism and romanticism blurred, as romantic artists used realism-style techniques to portray their romantic subject matter more accurately. Realistic authors, such as Dickens and Balzac, wrote novels that depict human beings caught in an uncompromising society.

The painting style known as Impressionism was inspired by scientific studies of light and the philosophy that the universe is constantly changing. Artists attempted to capture the transitory aspect of the world by recording a particular moment or "impression," usually working out-of-doors and fairly quickly. Increasingly aware of the plurality of colors in nature, they developed color theories as they sought to record light and atmosphere. Many of the impressionist paintings have a candid quality to them, probably a direct influence of the new medium of photography. Strong diagonals in the composition reflect the influence of Japanese paintings, which were in vogue in Paris at the time.

Impressionism in music was marked by a refusal to use traditional tonality, resulting in new sounds that composers used to capture different moods. Like impressionist art, tonal "color" was used, the Oriental five-tone scale was used, and nature was the dominant subject matter. Composers, such as Debussy, attempted to express the qualities of light.

Post-impressionism in art refers to a collection of personal styles, all inspired in some way by impressionism. The styles were as diverse as the artists, ranging from the emotional intensity of Van Gogh, to the precision of Seurat, to the allegory of Gauguin, to the structural integrity of the "father of modern art," Cezanne.

Twentieth Century, (1900-2000 A.D.)
The twentieth century arts are marked by vastness and diversity. Advances in communication technologies have condensed the world considerably, making cultural exchange an everyday occurrence. Increasing tolerance and interest in new ideas and information result in an even greater stylistic variety. While the following styles occur in the visual arts, some are reflected in the fields of architecture, music, literature, theater, and cinematography.

Expressionism refers to German art, literature, and film-making that elicits a specific emotional response from the viewer, mirroring the expression of the artist. Fauvism is closely related to expressionism, marked by bizarre use of color and wild distortion.

Cubism seeks to redefine space in relation to the subject matter and time, usually resulting in a fragmented image. Abstract art begins with a real subject or image, which is then distorted for any number of reasons, depending on the artist.

Non-objective or non-representational art does not begin with subject matter in the real world and is often the result of the artist experimenting with an artistic/intellectual problem or an aesthetic theory.

Dadaism and Surrealism are related styles that focus on disgust and satire of the arts, and the role of the subconscious in art, respectively. Absurdity, hostility, and the effects of a mechanical universe marked Dadaism during the early years of the century. Surrealism is characterized by intrigue with the intuitive mind. Mimicking the nightmarish quality of dreams by the juxtaposition of bizarre objects and using a panoramic, hazy backdrop to represent the human "mindscape" were favorite techniques of the surrealist artists.

Abstract expressionism is an umbrella-label for a collection of diverse artistic styles. All, however, are characterized by freedom of the artist from traditional subject matter and techniques, resulting in powerful, highly-personal expressions.
Pop and Op art, products mostly of the 1950s and 60s, stem from the words "popular" and "optical," respectively. Pop art deals with imagery from popular culture and often carries a message decrying the superficial quality of modern society. Optical art deals with illusionary art, most often utilizing non-representational designs to stimulate eye movement.

Photo-realism, a branch of Pop art, utilizes photographic images in complex ways to convey the messages of the artists. Conceptual art is an intellectual exercise, often using unorthodox materials and requiring the separation of aesthetics and creativity. The idea is basically anti-art in nature, claiming that art is not necessary if the mind is creative. Therefore, art objects can be minimal, temporary, or simply documented.

Twentieth-century music contrasts with prior music in several ways, including the elimination of meter, the inclusion of dissonance to a higher degree, and the refusal to use traditional tonality. A proliferation of styles marks modern music. Jazz centers around improvised variations on a theme, rendered with an emotional quality that is mimicked by the instruments. Offshoots emerged, such as ragtime, blues, swing, and bebop, as the century progressed.

In an attempt to control musical elements more tightly in a composition, surrealism as a musical style was developed. It involved the creation of the structure of the piece before the actual piece itself.

Aleatory music was an effort in the opposite direction, incorporating randomness in many aspects of the composition. The development of new technologies in instruments and recording has also significantly contributed to the changes in twentieth-century music, although not to changes in style itself.

Skill 17.2   Interpret and compare representations of works of art from different periods and cultures in terms of form, subject, theme, mood, or technique.

The field of the humanities is overflowing with examples of works of art that hold in common various themes, motifs, and symbols. Themes, motifs, and symbols effortlessly cross the lines between the visual arts, literature, music, theater, and dance. Listed below are a few examples culled from the immense heritage of the arts.

Examples of Works that Share Thematic and Symbolic Motifs

A popular symbol or motif of the fifteenth, sixteenth, and seventeenth centuries was David, the heroic second king of the Hebrews. The richness of the stories pertaining to David, and the opportunities for visual interpretation, made him a favorite among artists, all of whom cast him in different lights. Donatello's bronze statue of *David* is a classically proportioned nude, portrayed with Goliath's head between his feet. This David is not gloating over his kill, but instead seems to be viewing his own sensuous body with a Renaissance air of self-awareness. Verrocchio's bronze sculpture of *David*, also with the severed head of Goliath, represents a confident young man, proud of his accomplishment, and seemingly basking in praise. Michelangelo, always original, gives us a universal interpretation of the David theme. Weapon in hand, Michelangelo's marble *David* tenses muscles as he summons up the power to deal with his colossal enemy, symbolizing as he does so, every person or community who has had to do battle against overwhelming odds. Bernini's marble *David*, created as it was during the Baroque era, explodes with energy as it captures forever the most dramatic moment of David's action, the throwing of the stone that kills Goliath. Caravaggio's painting, *David and Goliath*, treats the theme in yet another way. Here David is shown as if in the glare of a spotlight, looking with revulsion at the bloodied, grotesque head of Goliath, leaving the viewer to speculate about the reason for disgust. Is David revolted at the ungodliness of Goliath, or is he sickened at his own murderous action?

Symbols related to the David theme include David, Goliath's head, and the stone and slingshot.

Another popular religious motif, especially during the medieval and renaissance periods, was the Annunciation. This event was the announcement by the archangel Gabriel to the Virgin Mary that she would bear a son and name him Jesus. It is also believed that this signified the moment of Incarnation. Anonymous medieval artists treated this theme in altarpieces, murals, and illuminated manuscripts. During the thirteenth century, both Nicola Pisano and his son, Giovanni, carved reliefs of the Annunciation theme. Both men included the Annunciation and the Nativity theme into a single panel. Martini's painted rendition of *the Annunciation* owes something to the court etiquette of the day in the use of the heraldic devises of the symbolic colorings and stilted manner of the Virgin. Della Francesca's fresco of the Annunciation borders on the abstract, with its simplified gestures and lack of emotion, the ionic column providing a barrier between Gabriel and Mary. Fra Angelico's *Annunciation* is a lyrical painting, combining soft, harmonious coloring with simplicity of form and gesture.

Symbols related to the Annunciation theme are Gabriel, Mary, the dove of the Holy Spirit, the lily, an olive branch, a garden, a basket of wool, a closed book, and various inscriptions.

During the 1800s, a new viewpoint surfaced in Europe. Intellectuals from several countries became painfully aware of the consequences of social conditions and abuses of the day and set out to expose them. The English social satirist Hogarth created a series of paintings entitled *Marriage a-la-Mode*, which honed in on the absurdity of arranged marriages. Other works by Hogarth explored conditions which led to prostitution and the poorhouse.

In France, Voltaire was working on the play *Candide*, which recounted the misfortunes of a young man, while providing biting commentary on the social abuses of the period.

In the field of music, Mozart's *Marriage of Figaro*, based on a play by Beaumarchais, explores the emotion of love as experienced by people from all ages and walks of life. At the same time, it portrays the follies of convention in society.

Attitudes toward universal themes are reflected in the humanities.

Each artist and author brings to his work his own personal view of the world, based on his own experiences. Those of us who view the works and read the books also bring our own biases to the experience. Therefore, the universal themes that are reflected in artistic works are colored both by the hands that create the works and the eyes that perceive them. Is it any wonder, then, that every work in the arts and humanities is open to so many varied interpretations?

Universal themes are themes that reflect the human experience, regardless of time period, location, social standing or economic considerations, religious or cultural beliefs. However, individuals or societies may condone or object to the particular manner in which a theme is approached.

For example, during the Renaissance, Michelangelo painted the ceiling of the Sistine Chapel with glowing frescoes, the theme of which is the creation of the universe and man. Although the frescoes are based on stories from the Old Testament, the theme is universal in that mankind has always sought to understand its origins. During Michelangelo's own time, controversy surrounded the ceiling frescoes, due in large measure to the manner in which Michelangelo portrayed the theme. Church scholars were divided over whether Michelangelo had departed too far from the classical notions of beauty advocated by the ancient Greeks or whether he had followed the Greek conventions (including nudity) too closely! Michelangelo contended that his style was a personal one, derived in part from observation of classical sculpture and in part from his observations from life. He expressed a desire to paint differently from the Greeks because the society he was painting for was dramatically different from the Greek society.

The most obvious way in which attitudes toward universal themes are reflected in the humanities is the ability of the artist to express his opinions through his work. For example, the English satirist, William Hogarth, addressed the universal themes of social cruelty through his paintings. Because of his dramatic portrayals and biting satire, Hogarth's works reflect his own humanitarian viewpoints regarding his 18th century English society. The fact that his paintings aroused similar emotions among the general public is evidenced by the fact that his series of paintings were made into engravings so that they would be more affordable to the masses of people who sought to buy them. The wide distribution of these prints indicates the extent to which the public sought social change.

(See Skill 17.1 for information on universal themes throughout history.)

The history of the humanities is replete with examples of how history has, in one way or another, influenced various areas of the humanities.

History provides a common frame of reference (subject matter) in which artists and audiences may express dialogue and viewpoints about various topics. Displeasure over a tyrannical government, for example, may find expression in a play based on a historical incident of tyranny. Therefore, history influences the humanities by providing specific subject matter, as evidenced by the many references to historical characters in great literature or the many paintings of important events in the history of art.

History also influences the humanities in a more subtle way. Throughout the centuries, the humanities have served as a mirror, reflecting the ideas, mores, people, and events of the passing years. In this way, we gain more than simply subject matter from the past. We also gain the benefit (or liability!) of the experience of our forbearers.

History also provides the knowledge and foundation, technical and otherwise, for contemporary humanities. Since most of the arts are expressed in some traditional format, historical conventions are bound to play a role, even in the most contemporary of works. In other words, artists do not create in a vacuum. They base their work on a foundation already laid, a foundation reaching far back into the past.

Examples of Historical Influence on the Arts

In 1937, Pablo Picasso painted a large mural, entitled *Guernica*, for the Spanish pavilion in the Paris International Exposition. He chose an allegorical representation to show how the small town of Guernica had been sacrificed by Spanish leader Franco to the brutality of Germany's "blitzkrieg" during the Spanish Civil War. Using distortion and stark colors, Picasso created a personal, and public, symbol for the horrors of war. Although the inspiration and technique of the painting was contemporary, the historical events on which the painting is based, as well as Picasso's moral indictment of the brutality of a totalitarian government, live on in the minds of people who view the painting today.

In 1928, novelist Virginia Woolf wrote a feminist work entitled *A Room of One's Own*. In this piece, Woolf puts forward the views that although the right to vote is an important step in the autonomy of women, equal opportunities for education and life experiences are even more vital. To illustrate the point, she compares experiences in colleges for men with those in colleges for women. Later in the book, she contemplates the various changes in society that the war initiated. In this way, readers today gain insight into some of the views and realities that comprised the gender bias in the early twentieth century.

A study of Roman art clearly shows the preoccupation of the Romans with Greek ideals, even to the point where early Roman artists simply copied sculptures and claimed them as their own. Later, Roman artists and authors created original works based on the format and ideals of the Greeks. Eventually, these works evolved into even more original styles. The point is that the Romans served as transmitters of Greek culture, an example of how history influenced the art, not only of the Romans, but of future civilizations who looked to both the Greeks and the Romans for inspiration.

It is often said that the arts are a mirror of society, reflecting the morals, attitudes and concerns of people in any given culture. Because the humanities deal with the expression of the human experience, it stands to reason that society's views of what is appropriate to reveal about that experience plays a major role in what artists express. At any time in history, political, social, and religious powers have influenced what artists feel comfortable expressing.

(In contrast to this is the view of "art for art's sake," a slogan touted by Oscar Wilde and Samuel Coleridge, among others. This opinion holds that the arts, out of necessity, are outside the realm of these forces and that art can and should exist solely for its own benefit and because of its intrinsic beauty.)

Political influence can be seen in the monumental sculpture of the Roman Empire, constructed to glorify the state. An example is the 6'8" sculpture of *Augustus in Armor*, depicting the emperor as a consul, confidently striding forward to deliver an inspiring speech to his legions. The bare feet denote courage, while the staff symbolizes the power of the emperor over the Roman Senate. The bronze *Equestrian Statue of Marcus Aurelius* serves as a second example, illustrating the "philosopher-king" concept of the emperor as a man of learning, ruling over Rome with wisdom and justice instead of brute force.

A recent example of how governmental powers affect the humanities can be viewed in the early twentieth-century in the Soviet Union. The communist regime feared artists might encourage the onset of capitalism and democracy and, accordingly, took actions to repress freedom of expression in favor of rhetoric favorable to the cause of communism, including persecution of artists and authors. The result was an outpouring of state-produced, stilted graphic art and literature, while meaningful expressions in the arts had to be smuggled out of the country to receive acclaim. Aleksandr Solzhenitsyn, author of *One Day in the Life of Ivan Denisovich* and *The Gulag Archipelago*, was forced to live in exile for several years.

The influence of religion on art can most clearly be viewed in the works of the medieval European period. During this era, the Roman Catholic Church ruled as a state government and, as such, was the major patron of the arts. As a result, much of the art from this period was religious in nature. Examples are Duccio's *Christ Entering Jerusalem* and Master Honore's *David and Goliath*.

Skill 17.3   Analyze ways in which the content of a given work of art reflects or influences a specific social or historical context.

Although the elements of design have remained consistent throughout history, the emphasis on specific aesthetic principles has periodically shifted. Aesthetic standards or principles vary from time period to time period, and from society to society.

An obvious difference in aesthetic principles occurs between works created by eastern and western cultures. Eastern works of art are more often based on spiritual considerations, while much western art is secular in nature. In attempting to convey reality, eastern artists generally prefer to use line, local color, and a simplistic view. Western artists tend toward a literal use of line, shape, color, and texture to convey a concise, detailed, complicated view. Eastern artists portray the human figure with symbolic meanings and little regard for muscle structure, resulting in a mystical view of the human experience. Western artists use the "principle of ponderation," which requires the knowledge of both human anatomy and an expression of the human spirit.

In attempts to convey the illusion of depth or visual space in a work of art, eastern and western artists use different techniques. Eastern artists prefer a diagonal projection of eye movement into the picture plane and often leave large areas of the surface untouched by detail. The result is the illusion of vast space, an infinite view that coincides with the spiritual philosophies of the Orient. Western artists rely on several techniques, such as overlapping planes, variation of object size, object position on the picture plane, linear and aerial perspective, color change, and various points of perspective to convey the illusion of depth. The result is space that is limited and closed.

In the application of color, eastern artists use arbitrary choices of color. Western artists generally rely on literal color usage or emotional choices of color. The end result is that eastern art tends to be more universal in nature, while western art is more individualized.

An interesting change in aesthetic principles occurred between the Renaissance period (1400-1630 A.D.) and the Baroque period (1630-1700 A.D.) in Europe. The shift is easy to understand when viewed in the light of Wolfflin's categories of stylistic development (see 5.3).

The Renaissance period was concerned with the rediscovery of the works of classical Greece and Rome. The art, literature, and architecture was inspired by classical orders, which tended to be formal, simple, and concerned with the ideal human proportions. This means that the painting, sculpture, and architecture was of a teutonic, or closed nature, composed of forms that were restrained and compact. For example, consider the visual masterpieces of the period: Raphael's painting, *The School of Athens*, with its highly-precisioned use of space, Michelangelo's sculpture, *David*, with its compact mass, and the facade of the *Palazzo Strozzi*, with its defined use of the rectangle, arches, and rustication of the masonry.

The word "baroque" means "grotesque," which was the contemporary criticism of the new style. In comparison to the styles of the Renaissance, the Baroque was concerned with the imaginative flights of human fancy. The painting, sculpture, and architecture were of an ateutonic, or open nature, composed of forms that were whimsical and free flowing. Consider again the masterpieces of the period: Ruben's painting, *The Elevation of the Cross*, with its turbulent forms of light and dark tumbling diagonally through space, Puget's sculpture, *Milo of Crotona*, with its use of open space and twisted forms, and Borromini's, *Chapel of St.Ivo*, with a facade that plays convex forms against concave ones.

In the 1920s and 30s, the German art historian, Professor Wolfflin outlined these shifts in aesthetic principles in his influential book *Principles of Art History*. He arranged these changes into five categories of "visual analysis," sometimes referred to as the "categories of stylistic development." Wolfflin was careful to point out that no style is inherently superior to any other. They are simply indicators of the phase of development of that particular time or society.

However, Wolfflin goes on to state, correctly or not, that once the evolution occurs, it is impossible to regress. These modes of perception apply to drawing, painting, sculpture, and architecture. They are as follows:

1. From a linear mode to a painterly mode.
This shift refers to stylistic changes that occur when perception or expression evolves from a linear form that is concerned with the contours and boundaries of objects, to perception or expression that stresses the masses and volumes of objects. From viewing objects in isolation, to seeing the relationships between objects, is an important change in perception. Linear mode implies that objects are stationary and unchanging, while the painterly mode implies that objects and their relationships to other objects is always in a state of flux.

2. From plane to recession.

This shift refers to perception or expression that evolves from a planar style, when the artist views movement in the work in an "up and down" and "side to side" manner, to a recessional style, when the artist views the balance of a work in an "in and out" manner. The illusion of depth may be achieved through either style, but only the recessional style uses an angular movement forward and backward through the visual plane.

3. From closed to open form.

This shift refers to perception or expression that evolves from a sense of enclosure, or limited space, in "closed form," to a sense of freedom in "open form." The concept is obvious in architecture, as in buildings that clearly differentiate between "outside" and "inside" space and buildings that open up the space to allow the outside to interact with the inside.

4. From multiplicity to unity.

This shift refers to an evolution from expressing unity through the use of balancing many individual parts, to expressing unity by subordinating some individual parts to others. Multiplicity stresses the balance between existing elements, whereas unity stresses emphasis, domination, and accent of some elements over other elements.

5. From absolute to relative clarity.

This shift refers to an evolution from works that clearly and thoroughly express everything there is to know about the object, to works that express only part of what there is to know and leave the viewer to fill in the rest from his own experiences. Relative clarity, then, is a sophisticated mode because it requires the viewer to actively participate in the "artistic dialogue." Each of the previous four categories is reflected in this, as linearity is considered to be concise, while painterliness is more subject to interpretation. Planarity is more factual, while recessional movement is an illusion, and so on.

COMPETENCY 18.0   UNDERSTAND, INTERPRET, AND COMPARE EXAMPLES OF LITERATURE FROM DIFFERENT PERIODS AND CULTURES, AND UNDERSTAND THE RELATIONSHIP OF WORKS OF LITERATURE TO THEIR SOCIAL AND HISTORICAL CONTEXTS.

Skill 18.1   Identify and evaluate major historical and contemporary developments and movements in world literature.

The major literary genres include allegory, ballad, drama, epic, epistle, essay, fable, novel, poem, romance, and the short story.

Allegory: A story in verse or prose with characters representing virtues and vices. There are two meanings, symbolic and literal. John Bunyan's *The Pilgrim's Progress* is the most renowned of this genre.

Autobiography: A form of biography, but it is written by the subject himself or herself. Autobiographies can range from the very formal to intimate writings made during one's life that were not intended for publication. These include letters, diaries, journals, memoirs, and reminiscences. Autobiography, generally speaking, began in the 15th century; one of the first examples is one written in England by Margery Kempe. There are four kinds of autobiography: thematic, religious, intellectual, and fictionalized. Some "novels" may be thinly-disguised autobiography, such as the novels of Thomas Wolfe.

Ballad: An *in medias res* story told or sung, usually in verse and accompanied by music. Literary devices found in ballads include the refrain, or repeated section, and incremental repetition, or anaphora, for effect. Earliest forms were anonymous folk ballads. Later forms include Coleridge's Romantic masterpiece, *The Rime of the Ancient Mariner*.

Biography: A form of nonfiction literature, the subject of which is the life of an individual. The earliest biographical writings were probably funeral speeches and inscriptions, usually praising the life and example of the deceased. Early biographies evolved from this and were almost invariably uncritical, even distorted, and always laudatory.

Beginning in the 18th century, this form of literature saw major development; an eminent example is James Boswell's *Life of Johnson*, which is very detailed and even records conversations. Eventually, the antithesis of the grossly-exaggerated tomes praising an individual, usually a person of circumstance, developed. This form is denunciatory, debunking, and often inflammatory. A famous modern example is Lytton Strachey's *Eminent Victorians* (1918).

Drama: Plays – comedy, modern, or tragedy – typically in five acts. Traditionalists and neoclassicists adhere to Aristotle's unities of time, place, and action. Plot development is advanced via dialogue. Literary devices include asides, soliloquies, and the chorus representing public opinion. Greatest of all dramatists/playwrights is William Shakespeare. Other dramaturges include Ibsen, Williams, Miller, Shaw, Stoppard, Racine, Moliére, Sophocles, Aeschylus, Euripides, and Aristophanes.

Epic: Long poems, usually of book length, reflecting values inherent in the generative society. Epic devices include an invocation to a Muse for inspiration, purpose for writing, universal setting, protagonist and antagonist who possess supernatural strength and acumen, and interventions of a God or the gods. Understandably, there are very few epics: Homer's *Iliad* and *Odyssey*, Virgil's *Aeneid*, Milton's *Paradise Lost*, Spenser's *The Fairie Queene*, Barrett Browning's *Aurora Leigh*, and Pope's mock-epic, *The Rape of the Lock*.

Epistle: A letter that is not always originally intended for public distribution, but due to the fame of the sender and/or recipient, becomes public domain. Paul wrote epistles that were later placed in the Bible.

Essay: Typically a limited-length prose work focusing on a topic and propounding a definite point of view and authoritative tone. Great essayists include Carlyle, Lamb, DeQuincy, Emerson, and Montaigne, who is credited with defining this genre.

Fable: Terse tale offering up a moral or exemplum. Chaucer's *The Nun's Priest's Tale* is a fine example of a *bete fabliau*, or beast fable, in which animals speak and act characteristically human, illustrating human foibles.

Informational books and articles: These make up much of the reading of modern Americans. Magazines began to be popular in the 19th century in this country, and while many of the contributors to those publications intended to influence the political/social/religious convictions of their readers, many also simply intended to pass on information. A book or article whose purpose is simply to be informative, that is, not to persuade, is called exposition (adjectival form: expository). An example of an expository book is the *MLA Style Manual*. The writers do not intend to persuade their readers to use the recommended stylistic features in their writing; they are simply making them available in case a reader needs such a guide.

Articles in magazines, such as *Time*, may be persuasive in purpose, such as Joe Klein's regular column, but for the most part, they are expository, giving information that television coverage of a news story might not have time to include.

Legend: A traditional narrative, or a collection of related narratives, popularly regarded as historically factual but actually a mixture of fact and fiction.

Myth: Stories that are more or less universally shared within a culture to explain its history and traditions.

Newspaper accounts of events: Expository in nature, of course, a reporting of a happening. That happening might be a school board meeting, an automobile accident that sent several people to a hospital and accounted for the death of a passenger, or the election of the mayor. They are not intended to be persuasive although the bias of a reporter or of an editor must be factored in. A newspaper's editorial stance is often openly declared, and it may be reflected in such things as news reports. Reporters are expected to be unbiased in their coverage, and most of them will defend their disinterest fiercely, but what a writer *sees* in an event is inevitably shaped to some extent by the writer's beliefs and experiences.

Novel: The longest form of fictional prose, containing a variety of characterizations, settings, local color, and regionalism. Most have complex plots, expanded description, and attention to detail. Some of the great novelists include Austin, the Brontes, Twain, Tolstoy, Hugo, Hardy, Dickens, Hawthorne, Forster, and Flaubert.

Poem: The only requirement is rhythm. Sub-genres include fixed types of literature, such as the sonnet, elegy, ode, pastoral, and villanelle. Unfixed types of literature include blank verse and dramatic monologue.

Romance: A highly-imaginative tale set in a fantastical realm dealing with the conflicts between heroes, villains, and/or monsters. *The Knight's Tale* from Chaucer's *Canterbury Tales*, *Sir Gawain and the Green Knight*, and Keats' *The Eve of St. Agnes* are prime representatives.

Short Story: Typically a terse narrative, with less developmental background about characters. May include description, author's point of view, and tone. Poe emphasized that a successful short story should create one focused impact. Considered to be great short story writers are Hemingway, Faulkner, Twain, Joyce, Shirley Jackson, Flannery O'Connor, de Maupassant, Saki, Edgar Allen Poe, and Pushkin.

Dramatic Texts

Comedy: The comedic form of dramatic literature is meant to amuse and often ends happily. It uses techniques such as satire or parody and can take many forms, from farce to burlesque.

Examples include Dante Alighieri's *The Divine Comedy,* Noel Coward's play *Private Lives,* and some of Geoffrey Chaucer's *Canterbury Tales* and William Shakespeare's plays.

Tragedy: Tragedy is comedy's other half. It is defined as a work of drama written in either prose or poetry, telling the story of a brave, noble hero who, because of some tragic character flaw, brings ruin upon himself. It is characterized by serious, poetic language that evokes pity and fear. In modern times, dramatists have tried to update its image by drawing its main characters from the middle class and showing their nobility through their nature instead of their standing. The classic example of tragedy is Sophocles' *Oedipus Rex*, while Henrik Ibsen and Arthur Miller epitomize modern tragedy.

Drama: In its most general sense, a drama is any work that is designed to be performed by actors on stage. It can also refer to the broad literary genre that includes comedy and tragedy. Contemporary usage, however, denotes drama as a work that treats serious subjects and themes but does not aim for the same grandeur as tragedy. Drama usually deals with characters of a less stately nature than tragedy. A classical example is Sophocles' tragedy *Oedipus Rex,* while Eugene O'Neill's *The Iceman Cometh* represents modern drama.

Dramatic Monologue: A dramatic monologue is a speech given by an actor, usually intended for himself, but with the intended audience in mind. It reveals key aspects of the character's psyche and sheds insight on the situation at hand. The audience takes the part of the silent listener, passing judgment and giving sympathy at the same time. This form was invented and used predominantly by Victorian poet Robert Browning.

Prior to twentieth century, research on child development and child/adolescent literature's relationship to that development, books for adolescents were primarily didactic. They were designed to be instructive of history, manners, and morals.

Middle Ages

As early as the eleventh century, Anselm, the Archbishop of Canterbury, wrote an encyclopedia designed to instill in children the beliefs and principles of conduct acceptable to adults in medieval society. Early monastic translations of the *Bible* and other religious writings were written in Latin for the edification of the upper class. Fifteenth century hornbooks were designed to teach reading and religious lessons. William Caxton printed English versions of *Aesop's Fables*, Malory's *Le Morte d'Arthur*, and stories from Greek and Roman mythology. Though printed for adults, tales of adventures of Odysseus and the Arthurian knights were also popular with literate adolescents.

Renaissance

The Renaissance saw the introduction of the inexpensive chapbooks, small in size and 16-64 pages in length. Chapbooks were condensed versions of mythology and fairy tales. Designed for the common people, chapbooks were imperfect grammatically but were immensely popular because of their adventurous contents. Though most of the serious, educated adults frowned on the sometimes-vulgar little books, they received praise from Richard Steele of *Tatler* fame for inspiring his grandson's interest in reading and pursuing his other studies.

Meanwhile, the Puritans' three most popular reads were the *Bible*, John Foxe's *Book of Martyrs*, and John Bunyan's *Pilgrim's Progress*. Though venerating religious martyrs and preaching the moral propriety that was to lead to eternal happiness, the stories of the *Book of Martyrs* were often lurid in their descriptions of the fate of the damned. Not written for children, and difficult reading even for adults, *Pilgrim's Progress* was as attractive to adolescents for its adventurous plot as for its moral outcome. In Puritan America, the *New England Primer* set forth the prayers, catechisms, *Bible* verses, and illustrations meant to instruct children in the Puritan ethic. The seventeenth-century French fables and fairy tales were used to entertain adults, but children found them enjoyable as well.

Seventeenth century

The late seventeenth century brought the first concern with providing literature that specifically targeted the young. Pierre Perrault's *Fairy Tales*, Jean de la Fontaine's retellings of famous fables, Mme. d'Aulnoy's novels based on old folktales, and Mme. de Beaumont's *Beauty and the Beast* were written to delight, as well as instruct, young people. In England, publisher John Newbury was the first to publish a line for children. These include a translation of Perrault's *Tales of Mother Goose and A Little Pretty Pocket-Book*, "intended for instruction and amusement," but decidedly moralistic and bland in comparison to the previous century's chapbooks; and *The Renowned History of Little Goody Two Shoes*, allegedly written by Oliver Goldsmith for a juvenile audience.

Eighteenth century

By and large, however, into the eighteenth century adolescents were finding their reading pleasure in adult books: Daniel Defoe's *Robinson Crusoe*, Jonathan Swift's *Gulliver's Travels*, and Johann Wyss's *Swiss Family Robinson*. More books were being written for children, but the moral didacticism, though less religious, was nevertheless ever present. The short stories of Maria Edgeworth, the four-volume *The History of Sandford and Merton* by Thomas Day, and Martha Farquharson's twenty-six volume *Elsie Dinsmore* series dealt with pious protagonists who learned restraint, repentance, and rehabilitation from sin.

Two bright spots in this period of didacticism were Jean Jacques Rousseau's *Emile* and *The Tales of Shakespear*, Charles and Mary Lamb's simplified versions of Shakespeare's plays. Rousseau believed that a child's abilities were enhanced by a free, happy life, and the Lambs subscribed to the notion that children were entitled to more entertaining literature in language comprehensible to them.

Nineteenth century

Child/adolescent literature truly began its modern rise in nineteenth-century Europe. Hans Christian Andersen's *Fairy Tales* were fanciful adaptations of the somber revisions of the Grimm brothers in the previous century. Andrew Lang's series of colorful fairy books contain the folklores of many nations and are still part of the collections of many modern libraries. Clement Moore's *A Visit from St. Nicholas* is a cheery, non-threatening child's view of the "night before Christmas." The humor of Lewis Carroll's books about Alice's adventures, Edward Lear's poems with caricatures, and Lucretia Nole's stories of the Philadelphia Peterkin family, were full of fancy and not a smidgen of morality. Other popular Victorian novels introduced the modern fantasy and science fiction genres: William Makepeace Thackeray's *The Rose and the Ring*, Charles Dickens' *The Magic Fishbone*, and Jules Verne's *Twenty Thousand Leagues Under the Sea*. Adventure to exotic places became a popular topic: Rudyard Kipling's *Jungle Books*, Verne's *Around the World in Eighty Days*, and Robert Louis Stevenson's *Treasure Island* and *Kidnapped*. In 1884, the first English translation of Johanna Spyre's *Heidi* appeared.

North America was also finding its voices for adolescent readers. American Louisa May Alcott's *Little Women* and Canadian L.M. Montgomery's *Anne of Green Gables* ushered in the modern age of realistic fiction. American youth were enjoying the articles of Tom Sawyer and Huckleberry Finn. For the first time, children were able to read books about real people just like themselves.

Twentieth century

The literature of the twentieth century is extensive and diverse and, as in previous centuries, much influenced by the adults who write, edit, and select books for youth consumption. In the first third of the century, suitable adolescent literature dealt with children from good homes with large families. These books projected an image of a peaceful, rural existence. Though the characters and plots were more realistic, the stories maintained focus on topics that were considered emotionally and intellectually proper. Popular at this time were Laura Ingalls Wilder's *Little House on the Prairie* series and Carl Sandburg's biography, *Abe Lincoln Grows Up*. English author J.R.R. Tolkien's fantasy *The Hobbit* prefaced modern adolescent readers' fascination with the works of Piers Antony, Madelaine L'Engle, and Anne McCaffery.

Fiction and Nonfiction

Fiction is the opposite of fact, and, simple as that may seem, it's the major distinction between fictional works and nonfiction works. The earliest nonfiction came in the form of cave-paintings, the record of what prehistoric man caught on hunting trips. On the other hand, we don't know if some of it might be fiction—that is, what they would like to catch on future hunting trips. Cuneiform inscriptions, which hold the earliest writings, are probably nonfiction about conveying goods, such as oxen and barley, and dealing with the buying and selling of these items. It's easy to assume that nonfiction, then, is pretty boring since it simply serves the purpose of recording everyday facts. Fiction, on the other hand, is the result of imagination and is recorded for the purpose of entertainment. If a work of nonfiction endures beyond its original time, it tends to be viewed as either exceptionally well made or perfectly embodying the ideas, manners, and attitudes of the time when it was produced.

Some (not all) types of nonfiction:

- Almanac
- Autobiography
- Biography
- Blueprint
- Book report
- Diary
- Dictionary
- Documentary film
- Encyclopedia
- Essay
- History
- Journal
- Letter
- Philosophy
- Science book
- Textbook
- User manual

These can also be called genres of nonfiction—divisions of a particular art according to criteria particular to that form. How these divisions are formed is vague. There are actually no fixed boundaries for either fiction or nonfiction. They are formed by sets of conventions, and many works cross into multiple genres by way of borrowing and recombining these conventions.

Some genres of fiction (not all):

- Action-adventure
- Crime
- Detective
- Erotica
- Fantasy
- Horror
- Mystery
- Romance
- Science fiction
- Thriller
- Western

A *bildungsroman* (from the German) means a "novel of education" or a "novel of formation" and is a novel that traces the spiritual, moral, psychological, or social development and growth of the main character from childhood to maturity. Dickens' *David Copperfield* (1850) represents this genre, as does Thomas Wolfe's *Look Homeward Angel* (1929).

A work of fiction typically has a central character, called the protagonist, and a character that stands in opposition, called the antagonist. The antagonist might be something other than a person. In Stephen Crane's short story, *The Open Boat*, for example, the antagonist is a hostile environment—a stormy sea. Conflicts between protagonists and antagonists are typical of a work of fiction, and climax is the point at which those conflicts are resolved. The plot has to do with the form or shape that the conflicts take as they move toward resolution. A fiction writer artistically uses devices, labeled characterization, to reveal character. Characterization can depend on dialogue, description, or the attitude or attitudes of one or more characters toward another.

Enjoying fiction depends upon the ability of the reader to suspend belief, to some extent. The reader makes a deal with the writer that, for the time it takes to read the story, his/her own belief will be put aside, replaced by the convictions and reality that the writer has written into the story. This is not true in nonfiction. The writer of nonfiction declares in the choice of that genre that the work is reliably based upon reality. The *MLA Style Manual*, for instance, can be relied upon because it is not the result of someone's imagination.

Skill 18.2 **Interpret and compare works of literature from different periods and cultures in terms of form, subject, theme, mood, or technique.**

A piece of writing is an integrated whole. It's not enough to just look at the various parts; the total entity must be examined. It should be considered in two ways:

- As an emotional expression of the author
- As an artistic embodiment of a meaning or set of meanings

This is what is sometimes called "**tone**" in literary criticism.

It's important to remember that the writer is a human being with his/her own individual bents, prejudices, and emotions. A writer is telling the readers about the world as he/she sees it and will give voice to certain phases of his/her own personality. By reading a writer's works, we can know the personal qualities and emotions of the writer embodied in the work itself. However, it's important to remember that not all the writer's characteristics will be revealed in a single work. People change and may have very different attitudes at different times in their lives. Sometimes, a writer will be influenced by a desire to have a piece of work accepted or to appear to be current or by the interests and desires of the readers he/she hopes to attract. It can destroy a work or make it less than it might be. Sometimes the best works are not commercial successes in the generation when they were written, but are discovered at a later time and by another generation.

There are four places to look for tone:

- Choice of form: tragedy or comedy; melodrama or farce; parody or sober lyric.
- Choice of materials: characters that have human qualities that are attractive; others that are repugnant. What an author shows in a setting will often indicate what his/her interests are.
- The writer's interpretation: it may be explicit—telling us how he/she feels.
- The writer's implicit interpretations: the author's feelings for a character come through in the description. For example, the use of "smirked" instead of "laughed;" "minced," "stalked," "marched," instead of walked.

The reader is asked to join the writer in the feelings expressed about the world and the things that happen in it. The tone of a piece of writing is important in a critical review of it.

Style, in literature, means a distinctive manner of expression and applies to all levels of language, beginning at the phonemic level—word choices, alliteration, assonance, etc.; the syntactic level—length of sentences, choice of structure and phraseology, patterns, etc.; and extends even beyond the sentence to paragraphs and chapters. What is distinctive about this writer's use of these elements?

In Steinbeck's *Grapes of Wrath*, for instance, the style is quite simple in the narrative sections, and the dialogue is dialectal. Because the emphasis is on the story—the narrative—his style is straightforward, for the most part. He just tells the story.

However, there are inter chapters where he varies his style. He uses symbols and combines them with description that is realistic. He sometimes shifts to a crisp, repetitive pattern to underscore the beeping and speeding of cars. By contrast, some of those inter chapters are lyrical, almost poetic.

These shifts in style reflect the attitude of the author toward the subject matter. He intends to make a statement, and he uses a variety of styles to strengthen the point.

Skill 18.3 Analyze ways in which the content of a given work of literature reflects or influences a specific social or historical context.

See Skill 18.1.

COMPETENCY 19.0 UNDERSTAND AND ANALYZE THE MAJOR POLITICAL, SOCIAL, ECONOMIC, SCIENTIFIC, AND CULTURAL DEVELOPMENTS THAT SHAPED THE COURSE OF HISTORY.

Skill 19.1   Demonstrate an understanding of the principal characteristics and important cultural values of the major civilizations of Asia, Africa, Europe, and the Americas.

The earliest known civilizations developed in the Tigris-Euphrates valley of **Mesopotamia** (modern Iraq) and the Nile valley of Egypt between 4000 BCE and 3000 BCE. Because these civilizations arose in river valleys, they are known as fluvial civilizations. Geography and the physical environment played a critical role in the rise and the survival of both of these civilizations. The Fertile Crescent was bounded on the West by the Mediterranean, on the South by the Arabian Desert, on the north by the Taurus Mountains, and on the east by the Zagros Mountains. It included Mesopotamia, Syria, and Palestine. This region was marked by almost constant invasions and migrations. These invaders and migrants seemed to have destroyed the culture and civilization that existed. Upon taking a longer view, however, it becomes apparent that they actually absorbed and supplemented the civilization that existed before their arrival. This is one of the reasons the civilization developed so quickly and created such an advanced culture.

First, the **rivers** provided a source of water that would sustain life, including animal life. The hunters of the society had ample access to a variety of animals, initially for hunting to provide food, as well as hides, bones, antlers, etc. from which clothing, tools, and art could be made. Second the proximity to water provided a natural attraction to animals, which could be herded and husbanded to provide a stable supply of food and animal products. Third, the rivers of these regions overflowed their banks each year, leaving behind a deposit of very rich soil. As these early people began to experiment with growing crops rather than gathering food, the soil was fertile, and water was readily available to produce sizeable harvests. In time, the people developed systems of irrigation that channeled water to the crops, without significant human effort, on a continuing basis.

Ancient civilizations were able to thrive and flourish because human communities subsisted initially as gatherers – gathering berries, leaves, etc. With the invention of tools, it became possible to dig for roots, hunt small animals, and catch fish from **rivers** and **oceans**. Humans observed their environments and soon learned to plant seeds and harvest crops. As people migrated to areas in which game and fertile soil were abundant, communities began to develop. When people had the knowledge to grow crops and the skills to hunt game, they began to understand division of labor. Some of the people in the community tended to agricultural needs, while others hunted game.

As habitats attracted larger numbers of people, environments became crowded, and there was competition. The concept of division of labor and sharing of food soon came, in more heavily populated areas, to be managed. Camps soon became villages. Villages became year-round settlements. Animals were domesticated and gathered into herds that met the needs of the village. With the settled life, it was no longer necessary to "travel light." Pottery was developed for storing and cooking food.

By 8000 BCE, culture was beginning to evolve in these villages. Agriculture was developed for the production of grain crops, which led to a decreased reliance on wild plants. Domesticating animals for various purposes decreased the need to hunt wild game. Life became more settled. It was then possible to turn attention to such matters as managing water supplies, producing tools, making cloth, etc. There was both the social interaction and the opportunity to reflect upon existence. Mythologies and various kinds of belief systems arose. Rituals arose that re-enacted the mythologies that gave meaning to life. As farming and animal husbandry skills increased, the dependence upon wild game and food gathering declined. With this change, came the realization that a larger number of people could be supported on the produce of farming and animal husbandry.

Two things seem to have come together to produce cultures and civilizations: a society and culture based on agriculture and the development of centers of the community with literate social and religious structures. The members of these hierarchies then managed water supply and irrigation, ritual and religious life, and exerted their own right to use a portion of the goods produced by the community for their own subsistence in return for their management.

As **trade routes** developed and travel between cities became easier, trade led to specialization. Trade enables a people to obtain the goods they desire in exchange for the goods they are able to produce. This, in turn, leads to increased attention to refinements of technique and the sharing of ideas. The knowledge of a new discovery or invention provides knowledge and technology that increases the ability to produce goods for trade.

Mountains and **rivers** still formed formidable boundaries for countries and civilizations. This was the case everywhere around the world, except, of course, in the sands of sub-Saharan Africa, where struggles took the form of wars of attrition, the victors being those who weathered the sandstorms and lack of water the best. The Middle East, with its flat lands interrupted by only a few hills, rivers, and isolated mountains, saw more than its fair share of combat, as was the case in the early history, and continues to be the case today.

When Egypt came under the domination of the Hyksos, Kush reached its greatest power and cultural energy (1700-1500 BCE). When the Hyksos were eventually expelled from Egypt, the New Kingdom brought Kush back under Egyptian colonial control. The collapse of the New Kingdom in Egypt (ca. 1000 BCE) provided the second opportunity for Kush to develop independently of Egyptian control and to conquer the entire Nubian region. **Egypt** made numerous significant contributions, including construction of the great pyramids; development of hieroglyphic writing; preservation of bodies after death; making paper from papyrus; contributing to developments in arithmetic and geometry; the invention of the method of counting in groups of 1-10 (the decimal system); completion of a solar calendar; and the foundation for science and astronomy.

The ancient civilization of the **Sumerians** invented the wheel; developed irrigation through use of canals, dikes, and devices for raising water; devised the system of cuneiform writing; learned to divide time; and built large boats for trade. The Babylonians devised the famous **Code of Hammurabi**, a code of laws.

The ancient **Assyrians** were warlike and aggressive, due to a highly-organized military, and used horse-drawn chariots. The **Hebrews**, also known as the ancient Israelites, instituted "monotheism," which is the worship of one God, Yahweh, and combined the 66 books of the Hebrew and Christian Greek scriptures into the Bible we have today. The **Minoans** had a system of writing using symbols to represent syllables in words. They built palaces with multiple levels containing many rooms, water and sewage systems with flush toilets, bathtubs, hot and cold running water, and bright paintings on the walls.

The **Mycenaeans** changed the Minoan writing system to aid their own language and used symbols to represent syllables. The **Phoenicians** were sea traders well known for their manufacturing skills in glass and metals and the development of their famous purple dye. They became so proficient in the skill of navigation that they were able to sail by the stars at night. Further, they devised an alphabet using symbols to represent single sounds, which was an improved extension of the Egyptian principle and writing system.

In **India**, the caste system was developed, the principle of zero in mathematics was discovered, and the major religion of Hinduism was begun. Hinduism was a continuing influence, along with the rise of Buddhism. Industry and commerce developed, along with extensive trading with the Near East. Outstanding advances in the fields of science and medicine were made, and India was one of the first to be active in navigation and maritime enterprises during this time.

China is considered by some historians to be the oldest, uninterrupted civilization in the world and was in existence around the same time as the ancient civilizations founded in Egypt, Mesopotamia, and the Indus Valley. The Chinese studied nature and weather; stressed the importance of education, family, and a strong central government; followed the religions of Buddhism, Confucianism, and Taoism; and invented such things as gunpowder, paper, printing, and the magnetic compass. **China** began building the Great Wall; practiced crop rotation and terrace farming; increased the importance of the silk industry, and developed caravan routes across Central Asia for extensive trade. Also, they increased proficiency in rice cultivation and developed a written language based on drawings or pictographs (no alphabet symbolizing sounds, as each word or character had a form different from all others).

The ancient **Persians** developed an alphabet; contributed the philosophies of **Zoroastrianism**, **Mithraism**, and **Gnosticism**; and allowed conquered peoples to retain their own customs, laws, and religions.

The classical civilization of **Greece** reached the highest levels in man's achievements based on the foundations already laid by such ancient groups as the Egyptians, Phoenicians, Minoans, and Mycenaeans. Among the more important contributions of Greece were the Greek alphabet, derived from the Phoenician letters, which formed the basis for the Roman alphabet and our present-day alphabet. Extensive trading and colonization resulted in the spread of the Greek civilization. The love of sports, with emphasis on a sound body, led to the tradition of the Olympic Games. Greece was responsible for the rise of independent, strong city-states. Other important areas that the Greeks are credited with influencing include drama, epic and lyric poetry, fables, myths centered on the many gods and goddesses, science, astronomy, medicine, mathematics, philosophy, art, architecture, and recording historical events. The conquests of Alexander the Great spread Greek ideas to the areas he conquered and brought to the Greek world many ideas from Asia and the value of ideas, wisdom, curiosity, and the desire to learn as much about the world as possible.

The civilization in **Japan** appeared to, during this time, have borrowed much of their culture from China. It was the last of these classical civilizations to develop. Although they used, accepted, and copied Chinese art, law, architecture, dress, and writing, the Japanese refined these into their own unique way of life, including incorporating the religion of Buddhism into their culture.

The civilizations in **Africa** south of the Sahara were developing the refining and use of iron, especially for farm implements and later for weapons. Trading was over land, using camels, and at important seaports. The Arab influence was extremely important, as was their later contact with Indians, Christian Nubians, and Persians. Their trading activities were the most important factor in the spread of and assimilation of different ideas and stimulation of cultural growth.

In other parts of the world, were the **Byzantine** and **Saracen** (or Islamic) civilizations, both dominated by religion. The major contributions of the Saracens were in the areas of science and philosophy. Included were accomplishments in astronomy, mathematics, physics, chemistry, medicine, literature, art, trade and manufacturing, agriculture, and a marked influence on the Renaissance period of history. The **Byzantines** (Christians) made important contributions in art and the preservation of Greek and Roman achievements, including architecture (especially in Eastern Europe and Russia), the Code of Justinian, and Roman law.

The ancient civilization of **Rome** lasted approximately 1,000 years, including the periods of republic and empire, although its lasting influence on Europe and its history was for a much longer period. There was a very sharp contrast between the curious, imaginative, inquisitive Greeks and the practical, simple, down-to-earth, no-nonsense Romans, who spread and preserved the ideas of ancient Greece and other culture groups. The contributions and accomplishments of the Romans are numerous, but their greatest included language, engineering, building, law, government, roads, trade, and the "**Pax Romana**." Pax Romana was the long period of peace enabling free travel and trade, spreading people, cultures, goods, and ideas all over a vast area of the known world.

The ancient empire of **Ghana** occupied an area that is now known as Northern Senegal and Southern Mauritania. There is no absolute certainty regarding the origin of this empire. Oral history dates the rise of the empire to the seventh century BCE. Most believe, however, that the date should be placed much later. Many believe the nomads who were herding animals in the fringes of the desert posed a threat to the early Soninke people, who were an agricultural community. In times of drought, it is believed the nomads raided the agricultural villages for water and places to pasture their herds. To protect themselves, it is believed that these farming communities formed a loose confederation that eventually became the empire of ancient Ghana.

Skill 19.2   Evaluate the influence of varied ideas, movements, and historical developments on Western religious, artistic, scientific, and political ideas and beliefs (e.g., the Renaissance, the Reformation, the French Revolution).

Eight common religions are practiced today. Interestingly, all of these religions have divisions or smaller sects within them. Not one of them is completely unified.

Judaism: the oldest of the eight and was the first to teach and practice the belief in one God, Yahweh.

Christianity: came from Judaism, grew and spread in the First Century throughout the Roman Empire, despite persecution. A later schism resulted in the Western (Roman Catholic) and Eastern (Orthodox) parts. Protestant sects developed as part of the Protestant Revolution. The name "Christian" means one who is a follower of Jesus Christ, who started Christianity. Christians follow his teachings and examples, living by the laws and principles of the Bible.

Islam: founded in Arabia by Mohammed who preached about God, Allah. Islam spread through trade, travel, and conquest, and followers of it fought in the Crusades as well as in other wars against Christians and today against the Jewish nation of Israel. Followers of Islam, called Muslims, live by the teachings of the Koran, their holy book, and of their prophets.

Hinduism: a complex religion, centering around the belief that through many reincarnations of the soul, man will eventually be united with the universal soul, which assumes the three forms of Brahma (the creator), Vishnu (the preserver), and Siva (the destroyer). Hinduism was begun by people called Aryans around 1500 BCE and spread into India. The Aryans blended their culture with the culture of the Dravidians, natives they conquered. Today, it has many sects and promotes worship of hundreds of gods and goddesses and belief in reincarnation. Though forbidden today by law, a prominent feature of Hinduism in the past was a rigid adherence to and practice of the infamous caste system.

Buddhism: a religion similar to Hinduism, but which rejects the caste system in favor of all men following the "eightfold path" toward spiritual living. Nirvana (spiritual peace) may be reached even in one lifetime by righteous living. Buddhism was developed in India from the teachings of Prince Gautama and spread to most of Asia. Its beliefs opposed the worship of numerous deities, the Hindu caste system, and the supernatural. Worshippers must be free of attachment to all things worldly and devote themselves to finding release from life's suffering.

Confucianism: is a Chinese religion based on the teachings of the 5th century Chinese philosopher Confucius; noted for his teachings that reflect faith in mankind, he advocated living an active life of learning, participating in government, and devotion to family. There is no clergy, no organization, and no belief in a deity or in life after death. It emphasizes political and moral ideas with respect for authority and ancestors. Rulers were expected to govern according to high moral standards.

Taoism: 6th century B.C. philosopher Lao-tse taught that since laws cannot improve man's lot, government should be a minimal force in man's life. Man should live passively in harmony with Tao (nature). Lao-tse wrote a book known as *The Tao* virtue, a native Chinese religion with worship of more deities than almost any other religion. It teaches all followers to make the effort to achieve the two goals of happiness and immortality. Practices and ceremonies include meditation, prayer, magic, reciting scriptures, special diets, breath control, beliefs in witchcraft, fortune telling, astrology, and communicating with the spirits of the dead.

Shinto: ancient religious beliefs, known as the "Way of the Gods," incorporate nature and ancestor worship with shamanistic practices, such as belief in magic to control nature, heal sickness, and predict the future. The native religion of Japan developed from native folk beliefs worshipping spirits and demons in animals, trees, and mountains. According to its mythology, deities created Japan and its people, which resulted in worshipping the emperor as a god. Shinto was strongly influenced by Buddhism and Confucianism but never had strong doctrines on salvation or life after death.

*   *   *

The **Byzantine Empire**, which the Eastern Empire became, was closer to the Middle East and so better inherited the traditions of Mesopotamia and Persia. This was in stark contrast to the Western Empire, which inherited the traditions of Greece and Carthage. Byzantium was known for its exquisite artwork (including the famous church Hagia Sophia), something for which the West was never known. Perhaps the most wide-ranging success of the Byzantine Empire was in the area of trade. Uniquely situated at the gateway to both West and East, Byzantium could control trade going in both directions. Indeed, the Eastern Empire was much more centralized and rigid in its enforcement of its policies than the feudal West.

A few years after the death of the Emperor Justinian, **Mohammed** was born (570 CE) in a small Arabian town near the Red Sea. Before this time, Arabians played only an occasional role in history. Arabia was a vast desert of rock and sand, except the coastal areas on the Red Sea. It was populated by nomadic wanderers called **Bedouin**, who lived in scattered tribes near oases where they watered their herds. Tribal leaders engaged in frequent war with one another. The family or tribe was the social and political unit, under the authority of the head of the family, within which there was cruelty, infanticide, and suppression of women. Their religion was a crude and superstitious paganism and idolatry. Although there was regular contact with Christians and Jews through trading interactions, the idea of monotheism was foreign. What vague unity there was within the religion was based upon common veneration of certain sanctuaries. The most important of these was a small square temple called **the Kaaba** (cube), located in the town of **Mecca**. Arabs came from all parts of the country in annual pilgrimages to Mecca during the sacred months when warfare was prohibited. For this reason, Mecca was considered the center of Arab religion.

In about 610, a prophet named **Mohammed** came to some prominence. He called his new religion **Islam** (submission [to the will of God]), and his followers were called **Moslems** – those who had surrendered themselves. His first converts were members of his family and his friends. As the new faith began to grow, it remained a secret society. But when they began to make their faith public, they met with opposition and persecution from the pagan Arabians, who feared the new religion and the possible loss of the profitable trade with the pilgrims who came to the Kaaba every year.

Islam slowly gained ground, and the persecutions became more severe around Mecca. In 622, Mohammed and his close followers fled the city and found refuge in **Medina** to the North. His flight is called the **Hegira**. This event marks the beginning of the Moslem calendar. Mohammed took advantage of the ongoing feuds between Jews and Arabs in the city and became the ruler of Medina, making it the capital of a rapidly growing state.

In the years that followed, Islam changed significantly. It became a fighting religion, and Mohammed became a political leader. The group survived by raiding caravans on the road to Mecca and by plundering nearby Jewish tribes. This was a victorious religion that promised plunder and profit in this world and the blessings of paradise after death. It attracted many converts from the Bedouin tribes. By 630, Mohammed was strong enough to conquer Mecca and make it the religious center of Islam, toward which all Moslems turned to pray, and the *Kaaba,* the most sacred **Mosque** or temple. Medina remained the political capital.

Mohammed left behind a collection of divine revelations (**surahs***)* he believed were delivered by the angel Gabriel. These were collected and published in a book called the **Koran** (reading), which has since been the holy scripture of Islam. The revelations were never dated or kept in any kind of chronological order. After the prophet's death, they were organized by length (in diminishing order). The *Koran* contains Mohammed's teachings on moral and theological questions, his legislation on political matters, and his comments on current events.

Origins and development of imperialism and its consequences for both colonizers and colonized

Europe, Italy, and Germany were each totally united into one nation from many smaller states. There were revolutions in Austria and Hungary, the Franco-Prussian War, the dividing of Africa among the strong European nations, interference and intervention of Western nations in Asia, and the breakup of Turkish dominance in the Balkans.

France, Great Britain, Italy, Portugal, Spain, Germany, and Belgium controlled the entire continent of Africa, except Liberia and Ethiopia. In Asia and the Pacific Islands, only China, Japan, and present-day Thailand (Siam) kept their independence. The others were controlled by the strong European nations.

An additional reason for **European imperialism** was the harsh, urgent demand for the raw materials needed to fuel and feed the great Industrial Revolution. These resources were not available in the huge quantity so desperately needed, which necessitated (and rationalized) the partitioning of the continent of Africa and parts of Asia. In turn, these colonial areas would purchase the finished manufactured goods. Nineteenth-century Europe was a crowded place. Populations were growing, but resources were not. The peoples of many European countries were also agitating for rights as never before. To address these concerns, European powers began to look elsewhere for relief.
One of the main places for European imperialist expansion was Africa. Britain, France, Germany, and Belgium took over countries in Africa and claimed them as their own. The resources (including people) were then shipped back to the mainland and claimed as colonial gains. The Europeans made a big deal about "civilizing the savages," reasoning that their technological superiority gave them the right to rule and "educate" the peoples of Africa.

Southeast Asia was another area of European expansion at this time, mainly by France. So, too, was India, which was colonized by Great Britain. These two nations combined with Spain to occupy countries in Latin America. Spain also seized the rich lands of the Philippines.

As a result of all this activity, a whole new flood of goods, people, and ideas began to come back to Europe, and a whole group of people began to travel to these colonies to oversee the colonization and to "help bring the people up" to the European level. European leaders could also assert their authority in these colonies as they could not back home.

In the United States, **territorial expansion** occurred in the expansion westward under the banner of "**Manifest Destiny**." In addition, the U.S. was involved in the War with Mexico, the Spanish-American War, and support of the Latin American colonies of Spain in their revolt for independence. In Latin America, the Spanish colonies were successful in their fight for independence and self-government.

The time from 1830 to 1914 is characterized by the extraordinary growth and spread of patriotic pride in a nation, along with intense, widespread imperialism. Loyalty to one's nation included national pride; extension and maintenance of sovereign political boundaries; unification of smaller states with common language, history, and culture into a more powerful nation; or smaller national groups who, as part of a larger multi-cultural empire, wished to separate into smaller, political, cultural nations.

Skill 19.3   Analyze the major causes of varied historical developments (e.g., the Industrial Revolution, Colonialism) and evaluate their impact on the politics and culture of the modern world.

Westward Expansion

Westward expansion occurred for a number of reasons, most important being economic. Cotton had become extremely important to most of the people who lived in the southern states. The effects of the Industrial Revolution, which began in England, were now being felt in the United States. With the invention of power-driven machines, the demand for cotton fiber greatly increased for the yarn needed in spinning and weaving. Eli Whitney's cotton gin made the separation of the seeds from the cotton much more efficient and faster. This, in turn, increased the demand, and more and more farmers became involved in the growing and selling of cotton.

The innovations and developments of better methods of long-distance transportation moved the cotton in greater quantities to textile mills in England, as well as the areas of New England and the Middle Atlantic States in the U.S. As prices increased, along with increased demand, Southern farmers began expanding by clearing increasingly more land to grow more cotton. Movement, settlement, and farming headed west to utilize the fertile soils. This, in turn, demanded increased need for a large supply of cheap labor. The system of slavery expanded, both in numbers and in the movement to lands "west" of the South.

All of this was started on an optimistic and scientific note. After the U.S. purchased the Louisiana Territory, Jefferson appointed **Captains Meriwether Lewis and William Clark** to explore it and to find out exactly what had been bought. The expedition went all the way to the Pacific Ocean, returning two years later with maps, journals, and artifacts. This led the way for future explorers to make available more knowledge about the territory and resulted in the Westward Movement and the later belief in the doctrine of Manifest Destiny.

Cotton farmers and slave owners were not the only ones heading west. Many in other fields of economic endeavor began the migration: trappers, miners, merchants, ranchers, and others were all seeking their fortunes. Fur companies hired men, known as "Mountain Men," to go westward, searching for the animal pelts to supply the market and meet the demands of the East and Europe. These men, in their own way, explored and discovered the many passes and trails that would eventually be used by settlers in their trek to the West. The California gold rush also had a very large influence on the movement west.

As the nation extended its borders into the lands west of the Mississippi, thousands of settlers streamed into this part of the country, bringing with them ideas and concepts and adapting them to the development of the unique characteristics of the region. Equality for everyone, as stated in the Declaration of Independence, did not yet apply to minority groups, black Americans, or American Indians. Voting rights and the right to hold public office were restricted in varying degrees in each state. All of these factors decidedly affected the political, economic, and social life of the country, and all three were focused in the attitudes of the three sections of the country on slavery.

There were also religious reasons for westward expansion. Increased settlement was encouraged by missionaries who traveled west with the fur traders. They sent word back East for more settlers, and the results were tremendous. By the 1840s, the population increases in the Oregon country alone were at a rate of about a thousand people a year. People of many different religions and cultures, as well as Southerners with black slaves, made their way west, which leads to a third reason: political.

It was the belief of many that the United States was destined to control all of the land between the two oceans, or as one newspaper editor termed it, "Manifest Destiny." This mass migration westward put the U.S. government on a collision course with the Indians, Great Britain, Spain, and Mexico. The fur traders and missionaries ran up against the Indians in the Northwest and the claims of Great Britain for the Oregon country. The U.S. and Britain had shared the Oregon country, but by the 1840s, with increases in the free and slave populations and the demand of the settlers for control and government by the U.S., the conflict had to be resolved. In a treaty, signed in 1846, by both nations, a peaceful resolution occurred, with Britain giving up its claims south of the 49th parallel.

In the American Southwest, the results were exactly the opposite. Spain had claimed this area since the 1540s, had spread northward from Mexico City, and, in the 1700s, had established missions, forts, villages, towns, and very large ranches. After the purchase of the Louisiana Territory in 1803, Americans began moving into Spanish territory. A few hundred American families in what is now Texas were allowed to live there but had to agree to become loyal subjects to Spain. In 1821, Mexico successfully revolted against Spanish rule, won independence, and chose to be more tolerant towards the American settlers and traders. The Mexican government encouraged and allowed extensive trade and settlement, especially in Texas. Many of the new settlers were Southerners and brought with them their slaves. Slavery was outlawed in Mexico and technically illegal in Texas although the Mexican government rather looked the other way.

With the influx of so many Americans and the liberal policies of the Mexican government, there came to be concern over the possible growth and development of an American state within Mexico. Settlement restrictions, cancellation of land grants, the forbidding of slavery, and increased military activity brought everything to a head. The order of events included the fight for Texas independence, the brief Republic of Texas, the eventual annexation of Texas, statehood, and finally war with Mexico. The Texas controversy was not the sole reason for war. Since American settlers had begun pouring into the Southwest, the cultural differences played a prominent part. Language, religion, law, customs, and government were totally different and opposite between the two groups. A clash was bound to occur.

The impact of the entire westward movement resulted in the completion of the borders of the present-day conterminous United States. These events included the bloody war with Mexico; the ever-growing controversy over slave versus free states affecting the balance of power or influence in the U.S. Congress, especially the Senate; and finally, the Civil War itself.

General patterns of frontier life and the impact of the frontier on U.S. society

In the West, restless pioneers moved into new frontiers, seeking land, wealth, and opportunity. Many were from the South and were slave owners, bringing their slaves with them. Life on the frontier had marked differences. All facets of daily living--clothing, food, housing, economic and social activities--were all connected to what was needed to sustain life and to survive in the wilderness. Everything was produced practically by themselves. They were self-sufficient and extremely individualistic and independent. There were little, if any, levels of society or class distinctions, as they considered themselves to be the equal to all others, regardless of station in life. The roots of equality, independence, individual rights, and freedoms were strong and well developed. People were not judged by their fancy dress, expensive house, eloquent language, or titles following their names.

American Revolution

By the 1750s in Europe, Spain was "out of the picture," no longer the most powerful nation and not a contender. The remaining rivalry was between Britain and France. For nearly 25 years, between 1689 and 1748, a series of "armed conflicts" involving these two powers had been taking place. These conflicts had spilled over into North America. The War of the League of Augsburg in Europe, 1689 to 1697, had been King William's War. The War of the Spanish Succession, 1702 to 1713, had been Queen Anne's War. The War of the Austrian Succession, 1740 to 1748, was called King George's War in the colonies. The two nations fought for possession of colonies, especially in Asia and North America, and for control of the seas, but none of these conflicts was decisive.

The final conflict, which decided who was the most powerful, began in North America in 1754, in the Ohio River Valley. It was known in America as the French and Indian War and in Europe as the Seven Years War, since it began there in 1756. In America, both sides had advantages and disadvantages. The British colonies were well established and consolidated in a smaller area. British colonists outnumbered French colonists 23 to 1.

Both sides had stunning victories and humiliating defeats. If there were one person who could be given the credit for British victory, it would have to be William Pitt. He was a strong leader, enormously energetic, supremely self-confident, and determined on a complete British victory. Despite the advantages and military victories of the French, Pitt succeeded. In the army, he got rid of the incompetents and replaced them with men who could do the job. He sent more troops to America, strengthened the British navy, gave to the officers of the colonial militia equal rank to the British officers - in short, he saw to it that Britain took the offensive and kept it to victory. Of all the British victories, perhaps the most crucial and important was winning Canada.

The French depended on the St. Lawrence River for transporting supplies, soldiers, and messages—the link between New France and the Mother Country. Tied into this waterway system was the connecting links of the Great Lakes, Mississippi River, and its tributaries, along which were scattered French forts, trading posts, and small settlements. When, in 1758, the British captured Louisburg on Cape Breton Island, New France was doomed. Louisburg gave the British navy a base of operations, preventing French reinforcements and supplies from getting to their troops. Other forts fell to the British: Frontenac, Duquesne, Crown Point, Ticonderoga, and Niagara, those in the upper Ohio Valley, and, most importantly, Quebec and finally Montreal. Spain entered the war in 1762 to aid France, but it was too late. British victories occurred all around the world: in India, in the Mediterranean, and in Europe.

In 1763, Paris, Spain, France, and Britain met to draw up the Treaty of Paris. Great Britain got most of India and all of North America east of the Mississippi River, except for New Orleans. Britain received from Spain control of Florida and returned to Spain Cuba and the islands of the Philippines, which were taken during the war. France lost nearly all of its possessions in America and India and was allowed to keep four islands, Guadeloupe, Martinique, Haiti on Hispaniola, and Miquelon and St. Pierre. France gave Spain New Orleans and the vast territory of Louisiana, west of the Mississippi River. Britain was now the most powerful nation--period.

Delegates from seven of the thirteen colonies met at Albany, New York, along with the representatives from the Iroquois Confederation and British officials. Franklin's proposal, known as the Albany Plan of Union, was totally rejected by the colonists, along with a similar proposal from the British. They simply did not want each of the colonies to lose its right to act independently. However, the seed was planted.

The war for independence occurred due to a number of changes, the two most important ones being economic and political. By the end of the French and Indian War in 1763, Britain's American colonies were thirteen out of a total of thirty-three scattered around the Earth. Like all other countries, Britain strove for having a strong economy and a favorable balance of trade. To have that delicate balance, a nation needs wealth, self-sufficiency, and a powerful army and navy. This is where the overseas colonies appeared. The colonies would provide raw materials for the industries in the Mother Country. The colonies were a market for the finished products, buying them and assisting the Mother Country in becoming powerful and strong (as in the case of Great Britain). They had a strong merchant fleet, which would be a school for training for the Royal Navy and provide places as bases of operation for the Royal Navy.

The foregoing explained the major reason for British encouragement and support of colonization, especially in North America. So between 1607 and 1763, at various times and for various reasons, the British Parliament enacted different laws to assist the government in getting and keeping this trade balance. One series of laws required that most of the manufacturing be done only in England, such as prohibition of exporting any wool or woolen cloth from the colonies and no manufacture of beaver hats or iron products. The colonists weren't concerned, as they had no money and no highly skilled labor to set up any industries, anyway.

The **Navigation Acts of 1651** put restrictions on shipping and trade within the British Empire by requiring that it was allowed only on British ships. This increased the strength of the British merchant fleet and greatly benefited the American colonists. Since they were British citizens, they could have their own vessels, building and operating them as well. By the end of the war in 1763, the shipyards in the colonies were building one third of the merchant ships under the British flag. There were quite a number of wealthy American colonial merchants.

The **Navigation Act of 1660** restricted the shipment and sale of colonial products to England only. In 1663, another Navigation Act stipulated that the colonies had to buy manufactured products only from England and that any European goods going to the colonies had to go to England first. These acts were a protection from enemy ships and pirates and from competition from European rivals.

The New England and Middle Atlantic colonies at first felt threatened by these laws, as they had started producing many of the products already being produced in Britain. They soon found new markets for their goods and began what was known as a "triangular trade." Colonial vessels started the first part of the triangle by sailing for Africa, loaded with kegs of rum from colonial distilleries. On Africa's West Coast, the rum was traded for either gold or slaves. The second part of the triangle was from Africa to the West Indies, where slaves were traded for molasses, sugar, or money. The third part of the triangle was home, bringing sugar or molasses (to make more rum), gold, and silver.

In 1763, after the war, money was needed to pay the British war debt, for the defense of the empire, and to pay for the governing of 33 colonies scattered around the Earth. It was decided to adopt a new colonial policy and to pass laws to raise revenue. It was reasoned that the colonists were subjects of the king. Since the king and his ministers had spent a great deal of money defending and protecting them, especially for the American colonists, it was only right and fair that the colonists should help pay the costs of defense, especially theirs. The earlier laws passed had been for the purposes of regulating production and trade, which generally put money into colonial pockets. These new laws would take some of that rather hard-earned money out of their pockets, and it would be done, in colonial eyes, unjustly and illegally.

In fact, there was a far greater degree of independence and self-government in the British colonies in America than could be found in Britain or the major countries on the Continent or any other colonies anywhere. There were a number of reasons for this:

1. The religious and scriptural teachings of previous centuries put forth the worth of the individual and equality in God's sight. Keep in mind that freedom of worship and freedom from religious persecution were major reasons to live in the New World.
2. European Protestants, especially Calvinists, believed and taught the idea that government originates from those governed, that rulers are required to protect individual rights, and that the governed have the right and privilege to choose their rulers.
3. Trading companies put into practice the principle that their members had the right to make the decisions and to shape the policies affecting their lives.
4. The colonists believed and supported the idea that a person's property should not be taken without his consent, based on that treasured English document, Magna Carta, and English common law.
5. From about 1700 to 1750, population increases in America came about through immigration and generations of descendants of the original settlers. The immigrants were mainly Scots-Irish, who hated the English, Germans who cared nothing about England, and black slaves who knew nothing about England. The descendants of the original settlers had never been out of America at any time.
6. In America, as new towns and counties were formed, there began the practice of representation in government. Representatives to the colonial legislative assemblies were elected from the district in which they lived, chosen by qualified property-owning male voters, and representing the interests of the political district from which they were elected. Each of the 13 colonies had a royal governor appointed by the king, representing his interests in the colonies. Nevertheless, the colonial legislative assemblies controlled the purse strings, having the power to vote on all issues involving money to be spent by the colonial governments.

Contrary to this was the governmental set-up in England. Members of Parliament were not elected to represent their own districts. They were considered representative of classes, not individuals. If some members of a professional or commercial class or some land interests were able to elect representatives, then those classes or special interests were represented. It had nothing at all to do with numbers or territories. Some large population centers had no direct representation at all, yet the people there considered themselves represented by men elected from their particular class or interest somewhere else.

Consequently, it was extremely difficult for the English to understand why American merchants and landowners claimed they were not represented. They did not vote for a Member of Parliament.

The colonists' protest of "**no taxation without representation**" was meaningless to the English. Parliament represented the entire nation, was completely unlimited in legislation, and had become supreme; and the colonists were incensed at the English attitude of, "Of course you have representation-- everyone does." The colonists considered their colonial legislative assemblies equal to Parliament, which was totally unacceptable in England, of course. There were two different environments of the older traditional British system in the Mother Country and in America. There were new ideas and different ways of doing things. In a new country, a new environment has little or no traditions, institutions, or vested interests. New ideas and traditions grew extremely fast, pushing aside what was left of the old ideas and old traditions. By 1763, Britain had changed its perception of its American colonies to their being a "territorial" empire. The stage was set, and the conditions were right for a showdown.

It all began in 1763, when Parliament decided to have a standing army in North America to reinforce British control. In 1765, the Quartering Act was passed, requiring the colonists to provide supplies and living quarters for the British troops. In addition, efforts by the British were made to keep the peace by establishing good relations with the Indians. Consequently, a proclamation was issued that prohibited any American colonists from making any settlements west of the Appalachians until provided for through treaties with the Indians. The Sugar Act of 1764 required efficient collection of taxes on any molasses that were brought into the colonies. The Act gave British officials free license to conduct searches of the premises of anyone suspected of violating the law. The colonists were taxed on newspapers, legal documents, and other printed matter under the Stamp Act of 1765. Although a stamp tax was already in use in England, the colonists would have none of it, and after the ensuing uproar of rioting and mob violence, Parliament repealed the tax. Other acts leading up to armed conflict included the Townshend Acts, passed in 1767, which taxed lead, paint, paper, and tea brought into the colonies. This really increased anger and tension, resulting in the British sending troops to New York City and Boston.

In Boston, mob violence provoked retaliation by the troops, thus bringing about the deaths of five people and the wounding of eight others. The so-called Boston Massacre shocked Americans and British alike. Subsequently, in 1770, Parliament voted to repeal all the provisions of the Townshend Acts, with the exception of the tea tax. In 1773, the tax on tea sold by the British East India Company was substantially reduced, fueling colonial anger once more. This gave the company an unfair trade advantage and forcibly reminded the colonists of the British right to tax them. Merchants refused to sell the tea; colonists refused to buy and drink it; and a shipload of it was dumped into Boston Harbor--a most violent Tea Party.

In 1774, the passage of the Quebec Act extended the limits of that Canadian colony's boundary southward to include territory located north of the Ohio River. However, the punishment for Boston's Tea Party came in the same year with the Intolerable Acts. Boston's port was closed; the royal governor of the colony of Massachusetts was given increased power, and the colonists were compelled to house and feed the British soldiers. The propaganda activities of the patriot organizations Sons of Liberty and Committees of Correspondence kept the opposition and resistance before everyone. Delegates from twelve colonies met in Philadelphia on September 5, 1774, in the First Continental Congress. They definitely opposed acts of lawlessness and wanted some form of peaceful settlement with Britain. They maintained American loyalty to the Mother Country and affirmed Parliament's power over colonial foreign affairs.

They insisted on the repeal of the Intolerable Acts and demanded ending all trade with Britain until this took place. The reply from George III, the last king of America, was an insistence of colonial submission to British rule or to be crushed. With the start of the Revolutionary War on April 19, 1775, the Second Continental Congress began meeting in Philadelphia on May 10 that year to conduct the business of war and government for the next six years.

Interestingly, one historian explains that the British were interested only in raising money to pay war debts, regulate the trade and commerce of the colonies, and look after business and financial interests between the Mother Country and the rest of her empire. The establishment of overseas colonies was first and foremost a commercial enterprise, not a political one. The political aspect was secondary and assumed. The British took it for granted that Parliament was supreme, was recognized so by the colonists, and were very resentful of the colonial challenge to Parliament's authority. They were contemptuously indifferent to politics in America and had no wish to exert any control over it. As resistance and disobedience swelled and increased in America, the British increased their efforts to punish them and put them in their place.

The British had been extremely lax and totally inconsistent in enforcement of the mercantile or trade laws passed in the years before 1754. The government itself was not particularly stable, so actions against the colonies occurred in anger, and their attitude was one of a moral superiority—they knew how to manage America better than the Americans did themselves. This of course points to a lack of sufficient knowledge of conditions and opinions in America. The colonists had been left on their own for nearly 150 years. By the time the Revolutionary War began, they were quite adept at self-government and adequately handling the affairs of their daily lives, with no one looking over their shoulders telling them how and what to do. The Americans equated ownership of land or property with the right to vote. Property was considered the foundation of life and liberty and, in the colonial mind and tradition, these went together.

Therefore, when an indirect tax on tea was made, the British felt that since it wasn't a direct tax, there should be no objection to it. The colonists viewed any tax, direct or indirect, as an attack on their property. They felt that, as a representative body, the British Parliament should protect British citizens, including the colonists, from arbitrary taxation. Since they felt they were not represented, Parliament, in their eyes, gave them no protection. So, war began. August 23, 1775, George III declared that the colonies were in rebellion and warned them to stop or else.

By 1776, the colonists and their representatives in the Second Continental Congress realized that things were past the point of no return. The Declaration of Independence was drafted and declared July 4, 1776. George Washington labored against tremendous odds to wage a victorious war. The turning point in the Americans' favor occurred in 1777 with the American victory at Saratoga. This victory encourage the French to align themselves with the Americans against the British. With the aid of Admiral deGrasse and French warships blocking the entrance to Chesapeake Bay, British General Cornwallis, who was trapped at Yorktown, Virginia, surrendered in 1781, and the war was over. The Treaty of Paris officially ended the war and was signed in 1783.

During the war, and after independence was declared, the former colonies now found themselves independent states. The Second Continental Congress was conducting a war with representation by delegates from thirteen separate states. The Congress had no power to act for the states or to require them to accept and follow its wishes. A permanent united government was desperately needed. On November 15, 1777, the Articles of Confederation were adopted, creating a league of free and independent states.

The central government of the new United States of America consisted of a Congress of two to seven delegates from each state, with each state having just one vote. The government under the Articles solved some of the postwar problems but had serious weaknesses. Some of its powers included: borrowing and coining money, directing foreign affairs, declaring war and making peace, building and equipping a navy, regulating weights and measures, and asking the states to supply men and money for an army. The delegates to Congress had no real authority, as each state carefully and jealously guarded its own interests and limited powers under the Articles. Also, the delegates to Congress were paid by their states and had to vote as directed by their state legislatures. The serious weaknesses were the lack of power to regulate finances, over interstate trade, over foreign trade, to enforce treaties, and military power. Something better and more efficient was needed. In May of 1787, delegates from all states, except Rhode Island, began meeting in Philadelphia. At first, they met to revise the Articles of Confederation, as instructed by Congress, but they soon realized that much more was needed. Abandoning the instructions, they set out to write a new Constitution, a new document, the foundation of all government in the United States and a model for representative government throughout the world.

The first order of business was the agreement among all the delegates that the convention would be kept secret. No discussion of the convention outside of the meeting room would be allowed. They wanted to be able to discuss, argue, and agree among themselves before presenting the completed document to the American people. They were afraid that if the people were aware of what was taking place before it was completed, the entire country would be plunged into argument and dissension. It would be extremely difficult to settle differences and come to an agreement. Between the official notes kept and the complete notes of future President James Madison, an accurate picture of the events of the Convention is part of the historical record.

The delegates went to Philadelphia representing different areas and different interests. They all agreed on a strong central government but not one with unlimited powers. They also agreed that no one section or part of government could control the rest. It would be a republican form of government (sometimes referred to as representative democracy), in which the supreme power was in the hands of the voters, who would elect the men who would govern for them.

One of the first serious controversies involved the small states versus the large states over representation in Congress. Virginia's Governor, Edmund Randolph, proposed that state population determine the number of representatives sent to Congress, also known as the Virginia Plan. New Jersey delegate William Paterson countered with what is known as the New Jersey Plan, in which each state would have equal representation.

After much argument and debate, the **Great Compromise** was devised, known also as the Connecticut Compromise, as proposed by Roger Sherman. It was agreed that Congress would have two houses. The Senate would have two Senators, giving equal powers in the Senate. The House of Representatives would have its members elected based on each state's population. Both houses could draft bills to debate and vote on, with the exception of bills pertaining to money, which must originate in the House of Representatives.

Another major controversy involved economic differences between the North and the South. One concerned the counting of the African slaves for determining representation in the House of Representatives. The Southern delegates wanted this but didn't want it to apply to determining taxes to be paid. The Northern delegates argued the opposite: count the slaves for taxes but not for representation. The resulting agreement was known as the "three-fifths" compromise. Three-fifths of the slaves would be counted for both taxes and determining representation in the House.

The last major compromise, also between North and South, was the Commerce Compromise. The economic interests of the northern part of the country were ones of industry and business, whereas the South's economic interests were primarily in farming. The Northern merchants wanted the government to regulate and control commerce with foreign nations and with the states. Of course, Southern planters opposed this idea, as they felt that any tariff laws passed would be unfavorable to them. The acceptable compromise to this dispute was that Congress was given the power to regulate commerce with other nations and the states, including levying tariffs on imports. However, Congress did not have the power to levy tariffs on any exports. This increased Southern concerns about the effects that the compromise would have on the slave trade. The delegates finally agreed that the importation of slaves would continue for 20 more years with no interference from Congress. Any import tax could not exceed 10 dollars per person. After 1808, Congress would be able to decide whether to prohibit or regulate any further importation of slaves.

Of course, when work was completed, and the document was presented, nine states needed to approve it for it to go into effect. There was a great amount of discussion, arguing, debating, and haranguing. The opposition had three major objections. The states seemed as if they were being asked to surrender too much power to the national government. The voters did not have enough control and influence over the men who would be elected by them to run the government, and there was also a lack of a "bill of rights" guaranteeing hard-won individual freedoms and liberties.

Eleven states finally ratified the document, and the new national government went into effect. It was no small feat that the delegates were able to produce a workable document that satisfied all opinions, feelings, and viewpoints. The separation of powers of the three branches of government, and the built-in system of checks and balances to keep power balanced, were a stroke of genius. It provided for the individuals and the states, as well as an organized central authority, to keep a new inexperienced young nation on track. They created a system of government so flexible that it has continued in its basic form to this day. In 1789, the Electoral College unanimously elected George Washington as the first President, and the new nation was on its way.

The causes and effects of the Industrial Revolution

The **Industrial Revolution**, which began in Great Britain and spread elsewhere, was the development of power-driven machinery (fueled by coal and steam) leading to the accelerated growth of industry, with large factories replacing homes and small workshops as work centers. The lives of people changed drastically, and a largely agricultural society changed to an industrial one. In Western Europe, the period of empire and colonialism began. The industrialized nations seized and claimed parts of Africa and Asia in an effort to control and provide the raw materials needed to feed the industries and machines in the "mother country." Later developments included power based on electricity and internal combustion, replacing coal and steam.

There was a marked degree of industrialization before and during the Civil War, but at war's end, industry in America was small. After the war, dramatic changes took place. Machines replaced hand labor, and extensive nationwide railroad service made possible the wider distribution of goods, invention of new products made available in large quantities, and large amounts of money from bankers and investors for expansion of business operations. American life was definitely affected by this phenomenal industrial growth. Cities became the centers of this new business activity, resulting in mass population movements there and tremendous growth. This new boom in business resulted in huge fortunes for some Americans and extreme poverty for many others. The discontent this caused resulted in a number of new reform movements, from which came measures controlling the power and size of big business and helping the poor.

The use of machines in industry enabled workers to produce a large quantity of goods much faster than by hand. With the increase in business, hundreds of workers were hired, assigned to perform a certain job in the production process. This was a method of organization called "**division of labor**," and by its increasing the rate of production, businesses lowered prices for their products, making the products affordable for more people. As a result, sales and businesses were increasingly successful and profitable.

A great variety of new products or inventions became available, such as the typewriter, the telephone, barbed wire, the electric light, the phonograph, and the gasoline automobile. The increase in business and industry was greatly affected by the many rich natural resources that were found throughout the nation. The industrial machines were powered by the abundant water supply. The construction industry, as well as products made from wood, depended heavily on lumber from the forests. Coal and iron ore in abundance were needed for the steel industry, which profited and increased from the use of steel in such things as skyscrapers, automobiles, bridges, railroad tracks, and machines. Other minerals, such as silver, copper, and petroleum played a large role in industrial growth, especially petroleum, from which gasoline was refined as fuel for the increasingly popular automobile.

Between 1870 and 1916, more than 25 million immigrants came into the United States, adding to the phenomenal population growth taking place. This tremendous growth aided business and industry in two ways: (1) The number of consumers increased, creating a greater demand for products and thus enlarging the markets for the products, and (2) with increased production and expanding business, more workers were available for newly created jobs. The completion of the nation's transcontinental railroad in 1869 contributed greatly to the nation's economic and industrial growth. Some examples of the benefits of using the railroads included the quick shipping of raw materials by the mining companies, and the finished products were sent to all parts of the country. Many wealthy industrialists and railroad owners saw tremendous profits steadily increasing due to this improved method of transportation.

The late 1800s and early 1900s were a period of the efforts of many to make significant reforms and changes in the areas of politics, society, and the economy. There was a need to reduce the levels of poverty and to improve the living conditions of those affected by it. Regulations of big business and ridding governmental corruption and making it more responsive to the needs of the people were also on the list of reforms to be accomplished. Until 1890, there was very little success, but from 1890 on, the reformers gained increased public support and were able to achieve some influence in government. Since some of these individuals referred to themselves as "**progressives**," the period of 1890 to 1917 is referred to by historians as the Progressive Era.

Skilled laborers were organized into a labor union called the American Federation of Labor in an effort to gain better working conditions and wages for its members. Farmers joined organizations, such as the National Grange and Farmers Alliances. Farmers were producing more food than people could afford to buy. This was the result of (1) new farmlands rapidly sprouting on the plains and prairies, and (2) development and availability of new farm machinery and newer and better methods of farming. They tried selling their surplus abroad but faced stiff competition from other nations selling the same farm products. Other problems contributed significantly to their situation. Items they needed for daily life were priced exorbitantly high. Having to borrow money to carry on farming activities kept them constantly in debt. Higher interest rates, shortage of money, falling farm prices, dealing with the so-called middlemen, and the increasingly high charges by the railroads to haul farm products to large markets all contributed to the desperate need for reform to relieve the plight of American farmers.

The nation witnessed significant industrial growth during the Civil War. This continued after the war. Steam power generation, sophisticated manufacturing equipment, the ability to move about the country quickly by railroad, and the invention of the steam-powered tractor resulted in a phenomenal growth in industrial output. The new steel and oil industries provided a significant impetus to industrial growth and added thousands of new jobs.

The "inventive spirit" of the time was a major force propelling the industrial revolution forward. This spirit led to improvement in products, development of new production processes and equipment, and even to the creation of entirely new industries. During the last 40 years of the nineteenth century, inventors registered almost 700,000 new patents.

The industrial boom produced several very wealthy and powerful "captains of industry" (Andrew Carnegie, John D. Rockefeller, Jay Gould, J.P Morgan, and Philip Armour). While they were envied and respected for their business acumen and success, they were condemned for exploitation of workers and questionable business practices, and they were feared because of their power.

While these "captains of industry" were becoming wealthy, the average worker enjoyed some increase in the standard of living. Most workers were required to put in long hours, in dangerous conditions, doing monotonous work, for low wages. Most were not able to afford to participate in the new comforts and forms of entertainment that were becoming available. Farmers believed they were also being exploited by the bankers, suppliers, and the railroads. This produced enough instability to fuel several recessions and two severe depressions.

One result of industrialization was the growth of the Labor Movement. There were numerous boycotts and strikes, which often became violent when the police or the militia were called in to stop the strikes. Labor and farmer organizations were created and became a political force. Industrialization also brought an influx of immigrants from Asia (particularly Chinese and Japanese) and from Europe (particularly European Jews, the Irish, and Russians). High rates of immigration led to the creation of communities in various cities, like "little Russia" or "little Italy." Industrialization also led to overwhelming growth of cities, as workers moved closer to their places of work. The economy was booming, but that economy was based on basic needs and luxury goods, for which there was to be only limited demand, especially during times of economic recession or depression.

Skill 19.4   **Demonstrate knowledge of the major political movements of the twentieth century and analyze their influence on contemporary societies.**

World War I - 1914 to 1918

The origins of World War I are complex and drawn mainly along the lines of various alliances and treaties that existed between the world powers. Imperialism, nationalism, and economic conditions of the time led to a series of sometimes shaky alliances among the powerful nations, each wishing to protect its holdings and to provide mutual defense from smaller powers.

On June 28, 1914, Serbian Gavrilo Princip assassinated Archduke Ferdinand of Austria-Hungary while he was on a visit to Sarajevo, Serbia. Serbian nationalism had led the country to seek dominance on the Balkan Peninsula, a movement that had been opposed by Austria-Hungary.

Seeing an opportunity to move on Serbia, Austria-Hungary issued an ultimatum after the assassination, demanding that they be allowed to perform a complete investigation. Serbia refused, and in July, Austria-Hungary, with the backing of its ally Germany, declared war on Serbia. Serbia called on its ally Russia to come to its defense, and Russia began to move troops into the area.

Germany, allied with Austria-Hungary, viewed the Russian mobilization as an act of war and declared war on Russia. A few days afterwards, Germany declared war of France, which was allied with Russia by treaty. Germany invaded Belgium, a neutral country, to be closer to Paris. Britain, bound by treaty to defend both Belgium and France, subsequently declared war on Germany. The United States, under President Woodrow Wilson, declared neutrality in the affair and did not enter the war immediately. Not until Germany threatened commercial shipping with submarine warfare did the U.S. join the fray, in 1917. Fighting continued until November 1918, when Germany petitioned for armistice. Peace negotiations began in early 1919, and the Treaty of Versailles was signed in June of that year. Also growing out of the peace negotiations was the League of Nations, a group of countries agreeing to avoid armed conflict through disarmament and diplomacy.

During the period of 1823 to the 1890s, the major interests and efforts of the American people were concentrated on expansion, settlement, and development of the continental United States. The Civil War, 1861-1865, preserved the Union and eliminated the system of slavery, and from 1865 onward, the focus was on taming the West and developing industry. During this time, travel and trade between the United States and Europe were continuous. By the 1890s, American interests turned to areas outside the boundaries of the United States. The West was developing into a major industrial area, and people in the United States became very interested in selling their factory and farm surplus to overseas markets. In fact, some Americans desired getting and controlling land outside the U.S. boundaries. Before the 1890s, the U.S. had little, if anything, to do with foreign affairs. It was not a strong nation militarily and had inconsequential influence on international political affairs. In fact, the Europeans looked on the American diplomats as inept and bungling in their diplomatic efforts and activities. However, all of this changed, and the Spanish-American War of 1898 saw the entry of the United States as a world power.

During the 1890s, Spain controlled such overseas possessions as Puerto Rico, the Philippines, and Cuba. Cubans rebelled against Spanish rule, and the U.S. government found itself besieged by demands from Americans to assist the Cubans in their revolt. When the U.S. battleship Maine blew up off the coast of Havana, Cuba, Americans blamed the Spaniards for it and demanded American action against Spain. Two months later, Congress declared war on Spain, and the U.S. quickly defeated the Spaniards. The peace treaty gave the U.S. possession of Puerto Rico, the Philippines, Guam, and Hawaii, which was annexed during the war.

This success enlarged and expanded the U.S. role in foreign affairs. Under the administration of Theodore Roosevelt, the U.S. armed forces were built up, greatly increasing its strength. Roosevelt's foreign policy was summed up in the slogan of, "Speak softly, and carry a big stick," backing up the efforts in diplomacy with a strong military. During the years before the outbreak of World War I, evidence of U.S. emergence as a world power could be seen in a number of actions. Using the Monroe Doctrine of non-involvement of Europe in the affairs of the Western Hemisphere, President Roosevelt forced Italy, Germany, and Great Britain to remove their blockade of Venezuela.

He gained the rights to construct the Panama Canal by threatening force and assumed the finances of the Dominican Republic to stabilize it and prevent any intervention by Europeans. In 1916 under President Woodrow Wilson, U.S. troops were sent to the Dominican Republic to keep order.

War broke out in 1914 and ended in 1918 in Europe. Eventually, nearly 30 nations were involved. One of the major causes of the war was the tremendous surge of nationalism during the 1800s and early 1900s. People of the same nationality or ethnic group sharing a common history, language, or culture began uniting or demanding the right of unification, especially in the empires of Eastern Europe, such as the Russian Ottoman and Austrian-Hungarian Empires. Getting stronger and more intense were the beliefs of these peoples in loyalty to common political, social, and economic goals, considered to be before any loyalty to the controlling nation or empire.

Emotions ran high, and minor disputes magnified into major ones and sometimes quickly led to threats of war. Especially sensitive to these conditions was the area of the states on the Balkan Peninsula. Along with the imperialistic colonization for industrial raw materials, military build-up (especially by Germany), and diplomatic and military alliances, the conditions for one tiny spark to set off the explosion were in place. In July 1914, a Serbian national assassinated the Austrian heir to the throne and his wife, and war began a few weeks later. There were a few attempts to keep war from starting, but these efforts were futile.

World War I saw the introduction of such warfare as use of tanks, airplanes, machine guns, submarines, poison gas, and flame throwers. Fighting on the Western front was characterized by a series of trenches that were used throughout the war until 1918. U.S. involvement in the war did not occur until 1916. When it began in 1914, President Woodrow Wilson declared that the U.S. was neutral, and most Americans were opposed to any involvement anyway. In 1916, Wilson was reelected to a second term based on the slogan proclaiming his efforts at keeping America out of the war. For a few months after, he put forth most of his efforts to stopping the war, but German submarines began unlimited warfare against American merchant shipping.

At the same time, Great Britain intercepted and decoded a secret message from Germany to Mexico, urging Mexico to go to war against the U.S. The publishing of this information, along with continued German destruction of American ships, resulted in the eventual entry of the U.S. into the conflict, the first time the country prepared to fight in a conflict not on American soil. Though unprepared for war, governmental efforts and activities resulted in massive defense mobilization, with America's economy directed to the war effort. Though America made important contributions of war materials, its greatest contribution to the war was manpower, soldiers desperately needed by the Allies.

Some ten months before the war ended, President Wilson had proposed a program called the Fourteen Points as a method of bringing the war to an end with an equitable peace settlement. In these Points, he had five points setting out general ideals; there were eight pertaining to immediately working to resolve territorial and political problems; and the fourteenth point counseled establishing an organization of nations to help keep world peace.

When Germany agreed in 1918 to an armistice, it assumed that the peace settlement would be drawn up on the basis of these Fourteen Points. However, the peace conference in Paris ignored these points, and Wilson had to be content with efforts at establishing the League of Nations. Italy, France, and Great Britain, having suffered and sacrificed far more in the war than America, wanted retribution. The treaties punished severely the Central Powers, taking away arms and territories and requiring payment of reparations. Germany was punished more than the others and, according to one clause in the treaty, was forced to assume the responsibility for causing the war.

Pre-war empires lost tremendous amounts of territories, as well as the wealth of natural resources in them. New, independent nations were formed, and some predominately ethnic areas came under control of nations of different cultural backgrounds. Some national boundary changes overlapped and created tensions and hard feelings, as well as political and economic confusion. The wishes and desires of every national or cultural group could not possibly be realized and satisfied, resulting in disappointments for both: those who were victorious and those who were defeated. Germany received harsher terms than expected from the treaty. It weakened its post-war government and, along with the worldwide depression of the 1930s, set the stage for the rise of Adolf Hitler and his Nationalist Socialist Party and World War II.

President Wilson lost in his efforts to get the U.S. Senate to approve the peace treaty. The Senate at the time was a reflection of American public opinion, and its rejection of the treaty was a rejection of Wilson. The approval of the treaty would have made the U.S. a member of the League of Nations, but Americans had just come off a bloody war to ensure that democracy would exist throughout the world. Americans just did not want to accept any responsibility that resulted from its new position of power and were afraid that membership in the League of Nations would embroil the U.S. in future disputes in Europe.

World War II - 1939 to 1945

The Treaty of Versailles that ended the First World War was in part the cause of the second. Severely limited by the treaty, Germany grew to resent its terms, which required reparations and limited the size of its army, and worked constantly to revise them. This was done through diplomacy and negotiation through the 1920s. In 1933, Adolf Hitler became Chancellor of Germany and shortly thereafter was granted dictatorial powers. Hitler was determined to remove all restrictions imposed by the treaty and to unify the German speaking people of the surrounding countries into a single country. Toward this end, Hitler marched into Austria in 1938 and was welcomed. He later made claims on the Sudetenland, a German-speaking area of Czechoslovakia, a claim that was supported internationally. However, Hitler continued to march into the whole of Czechoslovakia, to which he had no claim.

France and Britain, who had followed a policy of appeasing Hitler in the hopes that he would be content with Austria, were now concerned, as Germany looked next to Poland. They pledged to fight Germany if Hitler invaded Poland, which he did in September 1939, after signing a pact with the Soviet Union. Days later, France and Britain declared war on Germany, and the fighting began.

Again, the United States stayed out of the fighting at first. Only when Japan, an ally of Germany, attacked a U.S. naval base in Pearl Harbor, Hawaii, did the U.S. enter the war.

The European theater of WWII ended in 1945, when Allied troops invaded Germany, and Hitler committed suicide. In the Pacific, the U.S. dropped two atomic bombs on Japan in August of that year, forcing the Japanese to surrender.

WWII left the British and European economies in ruins and established the United States and the Soviet Union as the two major powers of the world, laying the foundation for the Cold War. Dismayed at the failure of the League of Nations to prevent war, a stronger organization was created, the United Nations, with the ability to raise peacekeeping forces. Under the Marshall plan, the United States helped rebuild Europe into an industrial, reliable economy again.

The end of World War I and the decade of the 1920s saw tremendous changes in the United States, signifying the beginning of its development into its modern society of today. The shift from farm to city life was occurring in tremendous numbers. Social changes and problems were occurring at such a fast pace that it was extremely difficult and perplexing for many Americans to adjust to them. Politically, the 18th Amendment to the Constitution, the so-called prohibition amendment, prohibited selling alcoholic beverages throughout the U.S., resulting in problems affecting all aspects of society. The passage of the 19th Amendment gave women the right to vote in all elections. The decade of the 1920s also showed a marked change in roles and opportunities for women, with more and more of them seeking and finding careers outside the home. They began to think of themselves as the equals of men, and not as much as housewives and mothers. Racial attitudes began to shift slowly, as a literary movement among African Americans gained steam in the 1920s. This "Harlem Renaissance" was to pave the way for the Civil Rights movement forty years later.

The influence of the automobile, the entertainment industry, and the rejection of the morals and values of pre-World War I life resulted in the fast-paced "Roaring Twenties." It had significant effects on events leading to the depression-era 1930s and another world war. Many Americans greatly desired the pre-war life and supported political policies and candidates in favor of the return to what was considered normal. It was desired to end government's strong role and adopt a policy of isolating the country from world affairs, a result of the war.

Prohibition of the sale of alcohol had caused the increased activities of bootlegging and the rise of underworld gangs and the illegal speakeasies, the jazz music and dances they promoted. The customers of these clubs were considered "modern," reflected by extremes in clothing, hairstyles, and attitudes towards authority and life. Movies and, to a certain degree, other types of entertainment, along with increased interest in sports figures and the accomplishments of national heroes, such as Lindbergh, influenced Americans to admire, emulate, and support individual accomplishments.

As wild and uninhibited modern behavior became more prevalent, this decade witnessed an increase in a religious tradition known as "revivalism," emotional preaching. Although law and order were demanded by many Americans, the administration of President Warren G. Harding was marked by widespread corruption and scandal, not unlike the administration of Ulysses S. Grant, except Grant was honest and innocent. The decade of the 20s also saw the resurgence of such racist organizations as the Ku Klux Klan.

The U.S. economy experienced a tremendous period of boom. Restrictions on business because of war no longer existed, and the conservatives in control adopted policies that helped and encouraged big business. To keep foreign goods from competing with American goods, tariffs were raised to the highest level. New products were developed by American manufacturers, and many different items became readily available to the people. These included refrigerators, radios, washing machines, and, most importantly, the automobile.

Americans in the 1920s heavily invested in corporation stocks, providing companies with a large amount of capital for expanding their businesses. The more money investors put into the stock market, the more the value of the stocks increased. This, in turn, led to widespread speculation that increased stock value to a point beyond the level that was justified by earnings and dividends.

Much of the stock speculation involved paying a small part of the cost and borrowing the rest. This led eventually to the stock market crash of 1929, financial ruin for many investors, a weakening of the nation's economy, and the Great Depression of the 1930s. The depression hit the United States tremendously hard, resulting in bank failures; loss of jobs due to cut-backs in production; and a lack of money, leading to a sharp decline in spending, which, in turn, affected businesses, factories, and stores and resulted in higher unemployment. Farm products were not affordable, so the farmers suffered even more. Foreign trade sharply decreased, and in the early 1930s, the U.S. economy was effectively paralyzed. Europe was affected even more so.
The war had seriously damaged the economies of the European countries, both the victors and the defeated, leaving them deeply in debt. There was difficulty on both sides paying off war debts and loans. It was difficult to find jobs, and some countries, like Japan and Italy, found themselves without enough resources and too many people. Solving these problems by expanding the territory merely set up conditions for war later. Germany suffered horribly with runaway inflation ruining the value of its money and wiping out the savings of millions.

Even though the U.S. made loans to Germany, which helped the government to restore some order and provided a short existence of some economic stability in Europe, the Great Depression only served to undo any good that had been done. Mass unemployment, poverty, and despair greatly weakened the democratic governments that had been formed and greatly strengthened the increasing power and influence of extreme political movements, such as communism, fascism, and national-socialism. These movements promised to put an end to the economic problems.

Germany, Italy, and Japan initiated a policy of aggressive territorial expansion, with Japan being the first to conquer. In 1931, the Japanese forces seized control of Manchuria, a part of China containing rich natural resources, and in 1937, began an attack on China, occupying most of its eastern part by 1938. Italy invaded Ethiopia in Africa in 1935, having it totally under its control by 1936. The Soviet Union did not invade or take over any territory, but, along with Italy and Germany, actively participated in the Spanish Civil War, using it as a proving ground to test tactics and weapons, setting the stage for World War II.

In Germany, almost immediately after taking power, in direct violation of the World War I peace treaty, Hitler began the buildup of the armed forces. He sent troops into the Rhineland in 1936, invaded Austria in 1938, and united it with Germany. Then, he seized control of the Sudetenland in 1938 (part of western Czechoslovakia and containing mostly Germans), the rest of Czechoslovakia in March 1939, and, on September 1, 1939, began World War II in Europe by invading Poland. In 1940, Germany invaded and controlled Norway, Denmark, Belgium, Luxembourg, the Netherlands, and France.

After the war began in Europe, U.S. **President Franklin D. Roosevelt** announced that the United States was neutral. Most Americans, although hoping for an Allied victory, wanted the U.S. to stay out of the war. President Roosevelt and his supporters, called "interventionists," favored all aid except war to the Allied nations fighting Axis aggression. They were fearful that an Axis victory would seriously threaten and endanger all democracies. On the other hand, the "isolationists" were against any U.S. aid being given to the warring nations, accusing President Roosevelt of leading the U.S. into a war very much unprepared to fight. Roosevelt's plan was to defeat the Axis nations by sending the Allied nations the equipment needed to fight: ships, aircraft, tanks, and other war materials.

In Asia, the U.S. had opposed Japan's invasion of Southeast Asia, an effort to gain Japanese control of that region's rich resources. Consequently, the U.S. stopped all important exports to Japan, whose industries depended heavily on petroleum, scrap metal, and other raw materials. Later, Roosevelt refused the Japanese withdrawal of its funds from American banks. General Tojo became the Japanese premier in October 1941 and quickly realized that the U.S. Navy was powerful enough to block Japanese expansion into Asia. Deciding to cripple the Pacific Fleet, the Japanese aircraft, without warning, bombed the Fleet December 7, 1941, while at anchor in **Pearl Harbor** in Hawaii. Temporarily, it was a success. It destroyed many aircraft and disabled much of the U.S. Pacific Fleet. In the end, it was a costly mistake, as it quickly motivated the Americans to prepare for and wage war.

Military strategy in the European theater of war as developed by **Roosevelt, Churchill, and Stalin** was to concentrate on Germany's defeat first, then Japan's. The start was made in North Africa, pushing Germans and Italians off the continent, beginning in the summer of 1942 and ending successfully in May 1943. Before the war, Hitler and Stalin had signed a non-aggression pact in 1939, which Hitler violated in 1941 by invading the Soviet Union. The German defeat at Stalingrad, which marked a turning point in the war, was brought about by a combination of entrapment by Soviet troops and the death of German troops by starvation and freezing due to the horrendous winter conditions. This occurred at the same time that the Allies were driving them out of North Africa.

The liberation of Italy began in July 1943, and ended May 2, 1945. The third part of the strategy was **D-Day, June 6, 1944,** with the Allied invasion of France at Normandy. At the same time, starting in January 1943, the Soviets began pushing the German troops back into Europe, and they were greatly assisted by supplies from Britain and the United States. By April 1945, Allies occupied positions beyond the Rhine, and the Soviets moved on to Berlin, surrounding it by April 25. Germany surrendered on May 7, and the war in Europe was finally over.

Meanwhile, in the Pacific, in the six months after the attack on Pearl Harbor, Japanese forces moved across Southeast Asia and the western Pacific Ocean.

By August 1942, the Japanese Empire was at its largest size and stretched northeast to Alaska's Aleutian Islands, west to Burma, and south to what is now Indonesia. Invaded and controlled areas included Hong Kong, Guam, Wake Island, Thailand, part of Malaysia, Singapore, the Philippines, and Darwin on the north coast of Australia.

The raid of General Doolittle's bombers on Japanese cities and the American naval victory at Midway, along with the fighting in the Battle of the Coral Sea, helped turn the tide against Japan. Island-hopping by U.S. Seabees and Marines, and the grueling bloody battles fough,t resulted in gradually pushing the Japanese back towards Japan.

After victory was attained in Europe, concentrated efforts were made to secure Japan's surrender, but it took dropping two atomic bombs on the cities of Hiroshima and Nagasaki to finally end the war in the Pacific. Japan formally surrendered on September 2, 1945, aboard the U.S. battleship Missouri, anchored in Tokyo Bay. The war was finally ended.

Again, after a major world war came efforts to prevent war from occurring again throughout the world. Preliminary work began in 1943, when the U.S., Great Britain, the Soviet Union, and China sent representatives to Moscow, where they agreed to set up an international organization that would work to promote peace around the Earth. In 1944, the four Allied powers met again and made the decision to name the organization the **United Nations**. In 1945, a charter for the U.N. was drawn up and signed, taking effect in October of that year.

Major consequences of the war included horrendous death and destruction, millions of displaced persons, and the gaining of strength and spread of Communism and Cold War tensions as a result of the beginning of the nuclear age. World War II ended more lives and caused more devastation than any other war.. Besides the losses of millions of military personnel, the devastation and destruction directly affected civilians, reducing cities, houses, and factories to ruin and rubble and totally wrecking communication and transportation systems. Millions of civilian deaths, especially in China and the Soviet Union, were the results of famine.

More than twelve million people were uprooted by war's end, having no place to live. They were prisoners of war, those that survived Nazi concentration camps and slave labor camps, orphans, and people who escaped war-torn areas and invading armies. Changing national boundary lines also caused the mass movement of displaced persons.

Germany and Japan were completely defeated; Great Britain and France were seriously weakened; and the Soviet Union and the United States became the world's leading powers. Although allied during the war, the alliance fell apart as the Soviets pushed Communism in Europe and Asia. In spite of the tremendous destruction it suffered, the Soviet Union was stronger than ever. During the war, it took control of Lithuania, Estonia, and Latvia, and by mid-1945, parts of Poland, Czechoslovakia, Finland, and Romania. It helped Communist governments gain power in Bulgaria, Romania, Hungary, Czechoslovakia, Poland, and North Korea. China fell to **Mao Zedong's** Communist forces in 1949. Before the fall of the Berlin Wall in 1989, and the dissolution of Communist governments in Eastern Europe and the Soviet Union, the United States and the Soviet Union faced off in what was called a "Cold War."

Korean War - 1950 to 1953

Korea was under Japan's control from 1895 to the end of the Second World War in 1945. At war's end, the Soviet and U.S. military troops moved into Korea, with the U.S. troops in the southern half and the Soviet troops in the northern half, and with the 38 degree North Latitude line as the boundary.

The General Assembly of the U.N. in 1947 ordered elections throughout all of Korea to select one government for the entire country. The Soviet Union would not allow the North Koreans to vote, so they set up a Communist government there. The South Koreans set up a democratic government, but both claimed the entire country. At times, there were clashes between the troops from 1948 to 1950. After the U.S. removed its remaining troops in 1949 and announced in early 1950 that Korea was not part of its defense line in Asia, the Communists decided to act and invaded the south.

Participants were: North and South Korea, United States of America, Australia, New Zealand, China, Canada, France, Great Britain, Turkey, Belgium, Ethiopia, Colombia, Greece, South Africa, Luxembourg, Thailand, the Netherlands, and the Philippines. It was the first war in which a world organization played a major military role, and it presented quite a challenge to the U.N., which had only been in existence five years.

The war began June 25, 1950, and ended July 27, 1953. A truce was drawn up, and an armistice agreement was signed, ending the fighting. A permanent treaty of peace has never been signed, and the country remains divided between the Communist North and the Democratic South. It was a very costly and bloody war, destroying villages and homes and displacing and killing millions of people.

The Vietnam War - 1957 to 1973 (U.S. Involvement)

U.S. involvement was the second phase of three in Vietnam's history. The first phase began in 1946 when the Vietnamese fought French troops for control of the country. Vietnam, prior to 1946, had been part of the French colony of Indochina (since 1861, along with Laos and Kampuchea or Cambodia). In 1954, the defeated French left, and the country became divided into Communist North and Democratic South. United States' aid and influence continued as part of the U.S. "Cold War" foreign policy to help any nation threatened by Communism.

The second phase involved the U.S. commitment. The Communist Vietnamese considered the war one of national liberation, a struggle to avoid continual dominance and influence of a foreign power. A cease-fire was arranged in January 1973, and a few months later, U.S. troops left for good. The third and final phase consisted of fighting between the Vietnamese but ended April 30, 1975, with the surrender of South Vietnam, the entire country being united under a Communist ruler.

Participants were the United States of America, Australia, New Zealand, South and North Vietnam, South Korea, Thailand, and the Philippines. With active U.S. involvement from 1957 to 1973, it was the longest war participated in by the U.S.; was tremendously destructive; and completely divided the American public in their opinions and feelings about the war. Many were frustrated and angered by the fact that it was the first war fought on foreign soil in which U.S. combat forces were totally unable to achieve their goals and objectives.

Returning **Vietnam veterans** faced not only readjustment to normal civilian life, but also bitterness, anger, rejection, and no heroes' welcomes. Many suffered severe physical and deep psychological problems. The war set a precedent with Congress, and the American people actively challenged U.S. military and foreign policy. The conflict, though tempered markedly by time, still exists and still has a definite effect on people.

The struggle between the Communist world under Soviet Union leadership and the non-Communist world under Anglo-American leadership resulted in what became known as the **Cold War**.

The United States experienced success in its space program by successfully landing space crews on the moon. In the late 1980s and early 1990s, the Berlin Wall was torn down, and Communism fell in the Soviet Union and Eastern Europe. The 15 republics of the former USSR became independent nations, with varying degrees of freedom and democracy in government, and together formed the Commonwealth of Independent States (CIS). The former Communist nations of Eastern Europe also emphasized their independence with democratic forms of government.

Tremendous progress in communication and transportation has tied all parts of the Earth and drawn them closer. There are still vast areas of the former Soviet Union that have unproductive land, extreme poverty, food shortages, rampant diseases, violent friction between cultures, the ever-present nuclear threat, environmental pollution, rapid reduction of natural resources, urban over-crowding, acceleration in global terrorism and violent crimes, and a diminishing middle class.

Skill 19.5   Demonstrate an understanding of significant individuals, movements, ideas, and conflicts that have shaped U.S. history and culture (e.g., the Civil War, the New Deal).

Civil War and Reconstruction from 1860 to 1877

It is ironic that South Carolina was the first state to secede from the Union, and the first shots of the war were fired on Fort Sumter in Charleston Harbor. Both sides quickly prepared for war. The North had more in its favor: a larger population; superiority in finances and transportation facilities; and manufacturing, agricultural, and natural resources. The North possessed most of the nation's gold, had about 92% of all industries, and almost all known supplies of copper, coal, iron, and various other minerals. Most of the nation's railroads were in the North and mid-West, and men and supplies could be moved wherever needed; food could be transported from the farms of the mid-West to workers in the East and to soldiers on the battlefields. Trade with nations overseas could go on as usual due to control of the navy and the merchant fleet. The Northern states numbered 24 and included Western (California and Oregon) and border (Maryland, Delaware, Kentucky, Missouri, and West Virginia) states.

The Southern states numbered 11 and included South Carolina, Georgia, Florida, Alabama, Mississippi, Louisiana, Texas, Virginia, North Carolina, Tennessee, and Arkansas, making up the Confederacy. Although outnumbered in population, the South was completely confident of victory. They knew that all they had to do was fight a defensive war and protect their own territory, until the North, who had to invade and defeat an area almost the size of Western Europe, tired of the struggle and gave up. Another advantage of the South was that a number of its best officers had graduated from the U.S. Military Academy at West Point and had had long years of army experience. Some exercised varying degrees of command in the Indian Wars and the War with Mexico. Men from the South were conditioned to living outdoors and were more familiar with horses and firearms than many men from northeastern cities. Since cotton was such an important crop, Southerners felt that British and French textile mills were so dependent on raw cotton that they would be forced to help the Confederacy in the war.

The South had specific reasons and goals for fighting the war, more so than the North. The major aim of the Confederacy never wavered: to win independence, the right to govern themselves as they wished, and to preserve slavery. The Northerners were not as clear in their reasons for conducting war. At the beginning, most believed, along with Lincoln, that preservation of the Union was paramount. Only a few extremely fanatical abolitionists looked on the war as a way to end slavery. However, by war's end, more and more Northerners had come to believe that freeing the slaves was just as important as restoring the Union.

The war strategies for both sides were relatively clear and simple. The South planned a defensive war, wearing down the North until it agreed to peace on Southern terms. One exception was to gain control of Washington, D.C., go North through the Shenandoah Valley into Maryland and Pennsylvania and drive a wedge between the Northeast and mid-West, interrupt the lines of communication, and end the war quickly. The North had three basic strategies:

1. Blockade the Confederate coastline in order to cripple the South;
2. Seize control of the Mississippi River and interior railroad lines to split the Confederacy in two; and
3. Seize the Confederate capital of Richmond, Virginia, driving southward and joining up with Union forces coming east from the Mississippi Valley.

The South won decisively until the Battle of Gettysburg, July 1 - 3, 1863. Until Gettysburg, Lincoln's commanders, McDowell and McClellan, were less than desirable, and Burnside and Hooker, not what were needed. Lee, on the other hand, had many able officers, including Jackson and Stuart, who were depended on heavily by him. Jackson died at Chancellorsville and was replaced by Longstreet. Lee decided to invade the North and depended on J.E.B. Stuart and his cavalry to keep him informed of the location of Union troops and their strengths. Four things worked against Lee at Gettysburg:

1. The Union troops gained the best positions and the best ground first, making it easier to make a stand there.
2. Lee's move into Northern territory put him and his army a long way from food and supply lines. They were more or less on their own.
3. Lee thought that his Army of Northern Virginia was invincible and could fight and win under any conditions or circumstances.
4. Stuart and his men did not arrive at Gettysburg until the end of the second day of fighting, and by then, it was too little too late. He and the men had had to detour around Union soldiers, and he was delayed in getting the information Lee needed.

Consequently, he made the mistake of failing to listen to Longstreet and following the strategy of regrouping back into Southern territory to the supply lines. Lee felt that regrouping was retreating and almost an admission of defeat. He was convinced the army would be victorious. Longstreet was concerned about the Union troops occupying the best positions and felt that regrouping to a better position would be an advantage. He was also very concerned about the distance from supply lines.

It was not the intention of either side to fight there, but the fighting began when a Confederate brigade stumbled into a unit of Union cavalry while looking for shoes. The third and last day Lee launched the final attempt to break Union lines. General George Pickett sent his division of three brigades under Generals Garnet, Kemper, and Armistead against Union troops on Cemetery Ridge under command of General Winfield Scott Hancock. Union lines held, and Lee and the defeated Army of Northern Virginia made their way back to Virginia. Although Lincoln's commander, George Meade, successfully turned back a Confederate charge, he and the Union troops failed to pursue Lee and the Confederates. This battle was the turning point for the North. After this, Lee never again had the troop strength to launch a major offensive.

The day after Gettysburg, on July 4, Vicksburg, Mississippi surrendered to Union General Ulysses Grant, thus severing the Western Confederacy from the Eastern part. In September 1863, the Confederacy won its last important victory at Chickamauga. In November, the Union victory at Chattanooga made it possible for Union troops to go into Alabama and Georgia, splitting the Eastern Confederacy in two. Lincoln gave Grant command of all Northern armies in March of 1864. Grant led his armies into battles in Virginia, while Phil Sheridan and his cavalry did as much damage as possible. In a skirmish at a place called Yellow Tavern, Virginia, Sheridan's and Stuart's forces met, with Stuart being fatally wounded. The Union won the Battle of Mobile Bay, and in May 1864, William Tecumseh Sherman began his march to successfully demolish Atlanta, and then went on to Savannah. He and his troops turned northward through the Carolinas to Grant in Virginia. On April 9, 1865, Lee formally surrendered to Grant at Appamattox Courthouse, Virginia.

The Civil War took more American lives than any other war in history, the South losing one-third of its soldiers in battle, compared to about one-sixth for the North. More than half of the deaths were caused by disease and the horrendous conditions of field hospitals. Both sides paid a tremendous economic price, but the South suffered more severely from direct damages. Destruction was pervasive, with towns, farms, trade, industry, lives and homes of men, women, children all destroyed, and an entire Southern way of life was lost. The deep resentment, bitterness, and hatred that remained for generations gradually lessened as the years went by, but legacies of it surface and remain to this day. The South had no voice in the political, social, and cultural affairs of the nation, lessening to a great degree the influence of the more traditional Southern ideals. The Northern Yankee Protestant ideals of hard work, education, and economic freedom became the standard of the United States and helped influence the development of the nation into a modem, industrial power.

The effects of the Civil War were tremendous. It changed the methods of waging war and has been called the first modern war. It introduced weapons and tactics that, when improved later, were used extensively in the wars of the late 1800s and 1900s. Civil War soldiers were the first to fight in trenches, the first to fight under a unified command, and the first to wage a defense called "major cordon defense," a strategy of advance on all fronts. They were also the first to use repeating and breech loading weapons. Observation balloons were first used during the war, along with submarines, ironclad ships, and mines. Telegraphy and railroads were put to use first in the Civil War. It was considered a modern war because of the vast destruction and was "total war," involving the use of all resources of the opposing sides. There was probably no way it could have ended other than total defeat and unconditional surrender of one side or the other.

By executive proclamation and constitutional amendment, slavery was officially and finally ended. Although there remained deep prejudice and racism, which still raises its ugly head today. Also, the Union was preserved, and the states were finally truly united. Sectionalism, especially in the area of politics, remained strong for another 100 years, but not to the degree and with the violence as existed before 1861. It has been noted that the Civil War may have been American democracy's greatest failure, for, from 1861 to 1865, calm reason, basic to democracy, fell to human passion. Yet, democracy did survive. The victory of the North established that no state has the right to end or leave the Union. Because of unity, the U.S. became a major global power. Lincoln never proposed to punish the South. He was most concerned with restoring the South to the Union in a program that was flexible and practical, rather than rigid and unbending. In fact, he never really felt that the states had succeeded in leaving the Union but that they had left the "family circle" for a short time. His plans consisted of two major steps:

All Southerners taking an oath of allegiance to the Union, promising to accept all federal laws and proclamations dealing with slavery, would receive a full pardon. The exceptions were men who had resigned from civil and military positions in the federal government to serve in the Confederacy, those who were part of the Confederate government, those in the Confederate army above the rank of lieutenant, and Confederates who were guilty of mistreating prisoners of war and blacks.

A state would be able to write a new constitution, elect new officials, and return to the Union fully equal to all other states on certain conditions. First, a minimum number of persons (at least 10% of those who were qualified voters in their states before secession from the Union who had voted in the 1860 election) must take an oath of allegiance.

As the war dragged on to its bloody, destructive conclusion, Lincoln was very concerned and anxious to get the states restored to the Union. He showed flexibility in his thinking as he made changes to his Reconstruction program to make it as easy and painless as possible. Of course, Congress had final approval of many actions, and it would be interesting to know how differently things might have turned out if Lincoln had lived to see some or all of his kind policies, supported by fellow moderates, put into action. Unfortunately, it didn't turn out that way. After Andrew Johnson became President and the radical Republicans gained control of Congress, the harsh measures of radical Reconstruction were implemented.

The economic and social chaos in the South after the war was unbelievable, with starvation and disease rampant, especially in the cities. The U.S. Army provided some relief of food and clothing for both white and blacks, but the major responsibility fell to the Freedmen's Bureau. Though the bureau agents, to a certain extent, helped Southern whites, their main responsibility was to the freed slaves. They were to assist the freedmen to become self-supporting and to protect them from being taken advantage of by others. Northerners looked on it as a real, honest effort to help the South out of the chaos it was in. Most white Southerners charged the bureau with causing racial friction, deliberately encouraging the freedmen to consider former owners as enemies.

As a result, as Southern leaders began to be able to restore life as it had once been, they adopted a set of laws known as "black codes," containing many of the provisions of the prewar "slave codes." There were certain improvements in the lives of freedmen, but the codes denied the freedmen their basic civil rights. In short, except for the condition of freedom and a few civil rights, white Southerners made every effort to keep the freedmen in a way of life subordinate to theirs.

Radicals in Congress pointed out these illegal actions by white Southerners as evidence that they were unwilling to recognize, accept, and support the complete freedom of black Americans and could not be trusted. Therefore, Congress drafted its own program of Reconstruction, including laws that would protect and further the rights of blacks. Three amendments were added to the Constitution. The 13th Amendment of 1865 outlawed slavery throughout the entire United States. The 14th Amendment of 1868 made blacks American citizens. The 15th Amendment of 1870 gave black Americans the right to vote and made it illegal to deny anyone the right to vote based on race.

Federal troops were stationed throughout the South and protected Republicans who took control of Southern governments. Bitterly resentful, white Southerners fought the new political system by joining a secret society called the Ku Klux Klan, using violence to keep black Americans from voting and getting equality. However, before being allowed to rejoin the Union, the Confederate states were required to agree to all federal laws. Between 1866 and 1870, all of them had returned to the Union, but Northern interest in Reconstruction was fading.

Reconstruction officially ended when the last Federal troops left the South in 1877. It can be said that Reconstruction had a limited success, as it set up public school systems and expanded legal rights of black Americans. Nevertheless, white supremacy came to be in control again, and its bitter fruitage is still with us today.

Lincoln and Johnson had considered the conflict of Civil War as a "rebellion of individuals," but Congressional Radicals, such as Charles Sumner in the Senate, considered the Southern states as complete political organizations. He considered them in the same position as any unorganized Territory and thought they should be treated as such. Radical House leader Thaddeus Stevens considered the Confederate States not as Territories, but as conquered provinces, and felt they should be treated that way. President Johnson refused to work with congressional moderates, insisting on having his own way. As a result, the Radicals gained control of both houses of Congress, and when Johnson opposed their harsh measures, they came within one vote of impeaching him.

General Grant was elected President in 1868, serving two scandal-ridden terms. He was himself an honest, upright person, but he greatly lacked political experience, and his greatest weakness was a blind loyalty to his friends. He absolutely refused to believe that his friends were not honest and stubbornly would not admit to their using him to further their own interests. One of the sad results of the war was the rapid growth of business and industry with large corporations controlled by unscrupulous men. However, after 1877, some degree of normalcy returned, and there was time for rebuilding, expansion, and growth.

Post-Reconstruction industrialization and reform

There was a marked degree of **industrialization** before and during the Civil War, but at war's end, industry in America was small. After the war, dramatic changes took place: machines replaced hand labor, extensive nationwide railroad service made possible the wider distribution of goods, the invention of new products were made available in large quantities, and there were large amounts of money from bankers and investors for expansion of business operations. American life was definitely affected by this phenomenal industrial growth. Cities became the centers of this new business activity, resulting in mass population movements there and tremendous growth. This new boom in business resulted in huge fortunes for some Americans and extreme poverty for many others. The discontent this caused resulted in a number of new reform movements from which came measures controlling the power and size of big business and helping the poor.

Of course, industry before, during, and after the Civil War was centered mainly in the North, especially the tremendous industrial growth after. The late 1800s and early 1900s saw the increasing buildup of military strength and the U.S. becoming a world power.

The use of machines in industry enabled workers to produce a large quantity of goods much faster than by hand. With the increase in business, hundreds of workers were hired, assigned to perform a certain job in the production process. This was a method of organization called "**division of labor,**" and by its increasing the rate of production, businesses lowered prices for their products, making the products affordable for more people. As a result, sales and businesses were increasingly successful and profitable.

A great variety of new products or inventions became available, such as the typewriter, the telephone, barbed wire, the electric light, the phonograph, and the gasoline automobile. From this list, the one that had the greatest effect on America's economy was the automobile.

The increase in business and industry was greatly affected by the many rich natural resources that were found throughout the nation. The industrial machines were powered by the abundant water supply. The construction industry, as well as products made from wood, depended heavily on lumber from the forests. Coal and iron ore in abundance were needed for the steel industry, which profited and increased from the use of steel in such things as skyscrapers, automobiles, bridges, railroad tracks, and machines. Other minerals, such as silver, copper, and petroleum, played a large role in industrial growth, especially petroleum, from which gasoline was refined as fuel for the increasingly popular automobile.

Between 1870 and 1916, more than 25 million immigrants came into the United States, adding to the phenomenal population growth taking place. This tremendous growth aided business and industry in two ways: (1) The number of consumers increased, creating a greater demand for products and thus enlarging the markets for the products. (2) With increased production and expanding business, more workers were available for newly created jobs. The completion of the nation's transcontinental railroad in 1869 contributed greatly to the nation's economic and industrial growth. Some examples of the benefits of using the railroads included raw materials were shipped quickly by the mining companies and finished products were sent to all parts of the country. Many wealthy industrialists and railroad owners saw tremendous profits steadily increasing due to this improved method of transportation.

The Industrial Revolution

The Industrial Revolution had spread from Great Britain to the United States. Before 1800, most manufacturing activities were done in small shops or in homes. However, starting in the early 1800s, factories with modern machines were built, making it easier to produce goods faster. The Eastern part of the country became a major industrial area although some developed in the West. At about the same time, improvements began to be made in building roads, railroads, canals, and steamboats. The increased ease of travel facilitated the westward movement, as well as boosted the economy with faster and cheaper shipment of goods and products, covering larger and larger areas. Some of the innovations included the Erie Canal, connecting the interior and Great Lakes with the Hudson River, and the coastal port of New York. Many other natural waterways were connected by canals.

Robert Fulton's "**Clermont**," the first commercially successful steamboat, led the way in the fastest method of shipping goods, making it the most important way to do so. Later, steam-powered railroads soon became the biggest rival of the steamboat as a means of shipping, eventually being the most important transportation method, opening the West. With expansion into the interior of the country, the United States became the leading agricultural nation in the world. The hardy pioneer farmers produced a vast surplus, and emphasis went to producing products with a high-sale value. Such implements as the cotton gin and reaper aided in this.

More industries and factories required more and more labor. Women, children, and, at times, entire families worked the long hours and days until the 1830s. By that time, the factories were getting even larger, and employers began hiring immigrants who were coming to America in huge numbers. Before then, efforts were made to organize a labor movement to improve working conditions and increase wages. It never really caught on until after the Civil War, but the seed had been sown.

The Great Depression and the New Deal

The 1929 Stock Market Crash was the powerful event that is generally interpreted as the beginning of the Great Depression in America. Although the crash of the Stock Market was unexpected, it was not without identifiable causes. The 1920s had been a decade of social and economic growth and hope. But the attitudes and actions of the 1920s regarding wealth, production, and investment created several trends that quietly set the stage for the 1929 disaster.

The other factor contributing to the Great Depression was the economic condition of Europe. The U.S. was lending money to European nations to rebuild. Many of these countries used this money to purchase U.S. food and manufactured goods. But they were not able to pay off their debts. While the U.S. was providing money, food, and goods to Europe, however, it was not willing to buy European goods. Trade barriers were enacted to maintain a favorable trade balance.

Several other factors are cited by some scholars as contributing to the Great Depression. First, in 1929, the Federal Reserve increased interest rates. Second, some believe that as interest rates rose, and the stock market began to decline, people began to hoard money. This was certainly the case after the crash. There is a question as to whether it was a cause of the crash.

In September 1929, stock prices began to slip somewhat, yet people remained optimistic. On Monday, October 21, prices began to fall quickly. The volume traded was so high that the tickers were unable to keep up. Investors were frightened, and they started selling very quickly. This caused further collapse. For the next two days, prices stabilized somewhat. On **Black Thursday**, October 24, prices plummeted again. By this time, investors had lost confidence. On Friday and Saturday, an attempt to stop the crash was made by some leading bankers. But on Monday the 28th, prices began to fall again, declining by 13% in one day. The next day, **Black Tuesday, October 29**, saw 16.4 million shares traded. Stock prices fell so far that, at many times, no one was willing to buy at any price.

Unemployment quickly reached 25% nationwide. People thrown out of their homes created makeshift domiciles of cardboard, scraps of wood, and tents. With unmasked reference to President Hoover, who was quite obviously overwhelmed by the situation and incompetent to deal with it, these communities were called "**Hoovervilles**." Families stood in bread lines, rural workers left the dust bowl of the plains to search for work in California, and banks failed. More than 100,000 businesses failed between 1929 and 1932. The despair that swept the nation left an indelible scar on all who endured the Depression.

When the stock market crashed, businesses collapsed. Without demand for products, other businesses and industries collapsed. This set in motion a domino effect, bringing down the businesses and industries that provided raw materials or components to these industries. Hundreds of thousands became jobless. Then, the jobless often became homeless. Desperation prevailed. Little had been done to assess the toll hunger, inadequate nutrition, or starvation took on the health of those who were children during this time. Indeed, food was cheap, relatively speaking, but there was little money to buy it.

Hoover's bid for re-election in 1932 failed. The new president, Franklin D. Roosevelt, won the White House on his promise to the American people of a "new deal." Upon assuming the office, Roosevelt and his advisers immediately launched a massive program of innovation and experimentation to try to bring the Depression to an end and to get the nation back on track. Congress gave the President unprecedented power to act to save the nation. During the next eight years, the most extensive and broadly-based legislation in the nation's history was enacted. The legislation was intended to accomplish three goals: relief, recovery, and reform.

The first step in the "**New Deal**" was to relieve suffering. This was accomplished through a number of job-creation projects. The second step, the recovery aspect, was to stimulate the economy. The third step was to create social and economic change through innovative legislation.

To provide economic stability and to prevent another crash, Congress passed the **Glass-Steagall Act**, which separated banking and investing. The Securities and Exchange Commission was created to regulate dangerous speculative practices on Wall Street. The Wagner Act guaranteed a number of rights to workers and unions in an effort to improve worker-employer relations. The **Social Security Act of 1935** established pensions for the aged and infirm, as well as a system of unemployment insurance.

Many of the steps taken by the Roosevelt administration have had far-reaching effects. They alleviated the economic disaster of the Great Depression, they enacted controls that would mitigate the risk of another stock market crash, and they provided greater security for workers. The nation's economy, however, did not fully recover until America entered World War II.

By far the worst natural disaster of the decade came to be known as the **Dust Bowl.** Due to severe and prolonged drought in the Great Plains, and previous reliance on inappropriate farming techniques, a series of devastating dust storms occurred in the 1930s that resulted in destruction, economic ruin for many, and dramatic ecological change.

Crops were ruined, the land was destroyed, and people either lost or abandoned homes and farms. Fifteen percent of Oklahoma's population left. Because so many of the migrants were from Oklahoma, the migrants came to be called "**Okies**," no matter where they came from. Estimates of the number of people displaced by this disaster range from 300,000 or 400,000 to 2.5 million.

COMPETENCY 20.0   UNDERSTAND AND ANALYZE THE CONCEPTS OF FREEDOM, DIVERSITY, AND TOLERANCE, THEIR HISTORICAL DEVELOPMENT, AND THEIR INFLUENCE IN HUMAN HISTORY.

Skill 20.1   Demonstrate an understanding of the democratic principles embodied in the Declaration of Independence and the United States Constitution.

The three most basic rights guaranteed by the Declaration of Independence are "life, liberty, and the pursuit of happiness." The first one is self-explanatory: Americans are guaranteed the right to live their lives in America. The second one is basic as well: Americans are guaranteed the right to live their lives *free* in America. (This principle has been violated for many people throughout history, most notably African-Americans, violently, and women, politically and sometimes violently.) The last basic right is more esoteric but no less important: Americans are guaranteed the right to pursue a happy life. First and foremost, they are allowed the ability to make a life for themselves in America, "the Land of Opportunity." That happiness also extends to the pursuit of life free from oppression or discrimination, two things that, again, African-Americans, women, and non-white Americans have suffered from, to varying degrees, throughout the history of the country.

The **Declaration of Independence** is an outgrowth of both ancient Greek ideas of democracy and individual rights and the ideas of the European Enlightenment and the Renaissance, especially the ideology of the political thinker **John Locke**. Thomas Jefferson (1743-1826), the principle author of the Declaration, borrowed much from Locke's theories and writings. John Locke was one of the most influential political writers of the seventeenth century; he put great emphasis on human rights and put forth the belief that when governments violate those rights, people should rebel. He wrote the book *Two Treatises of Government* in 1690, which had tremendous influence on political thought in the American colonies and helped to shape the U.S. Constitution and Declaration of Independence.

The Declaration of Independence was the founding document of the United States of America. The Articles of Confederation were the first attempt of the newly independent states to reach a new understanding amongst themselves. The Declaration was intended to demonstrate the reasons that the colonies were seeking separation from Great Britain. Conceived by and written for the most part by **Thomas Jefferson,** it is not only important for what it says, but also for how it says it. The Declaration is, in many respects, a poetic document. Instead of a simple recitation of the colonists' grievances, it set out clearly the reasons why the colonists were seeking their freedom from Great Britain. They had tried all means to resolve the dispute peacefully. It was the right of a people, when all other methods of addressing their grievances have been tried and failed, to separate themselves from that power that was keeping them from fully expressing their rights to "**life, liberty, and the pursuit of happiness.**"

A convention met under the presidency of George Washington, with fifty-five of the sixty-five appointed members present. A constitution was written in four months. The Constitution of the United States is the fundamental law of the republic. It is a precise, formal, written document of the *extraordinary*, or *supreme*, type of constitution. The founders of the Union established it as the highest governmental authority. There is no national power superior to it. The foundations were so broadly laid as to provide for the expansion of national life and to make it an instrument that would last for all time. To maintain its stability, the framers created a difficult process for making any changes to it. No amendment can become valid until it is ratified by three-fourths of all of the states. The British system of government was part of the basis of the final document; however, significant changes were necessary to meet the needs of a partnership of states that were tied together as a single federation, yet sovereign in their own local affairs. This constitution established a system of government that was unique and advanced far beyond other systems of its day.

The constitution binds the states in a governmental unity in everything that affects the welfare of all. At the same time, it recognizes the right of the people of each state to independence of action in matters that relate only to them. Since the Federal Constitution is the law of the land, all other laws must conform to it.

The debates conducted during the Constitutional Congress represent the issues and the arguments that led to the compromises in the final document. The debates also reflect the concerns of the Founding Fathers that the rights of the people be protected from abrogation by the government itself and the determination that no branch of government should have enough power to continually dominate the others. There is a **system of checks and balances.**

Bill Of Rights - The first ten amendments to the United States Constitution, dealing with civil liberties and civil rights. James Madison was credited with writing a majority of them. They are in brief:

1.   Freedom of Religion.
2.   Right To Bear Arms.
3.   Security from the quartering of troops in homes.
4.   Right against unreasonable search and seizures.
5.   Right against self-incrimination.
6.   Right to trial by jury; right to legal council.
7.   Right to jury trial for civil actions.
8.   No cruel or unusual punishment allowed.
9.   These rights shall not deny other rights the people enjoy.
10.   Powers not mentioned in the Constitution shall be retained by the states or the people.

The American nation was founded very much with the idea that the people would have a large degree of autonomy and liberty. The famous maxim, "no taxation without representation," was a rallying cry for the Revolution, not only because the people didn't want to suffer the increasingly oppressive series of taxes imposed on them by the British Parliament, but also because the people could not in any way influence the lawmakers in Parliament in regard to those taxes. No American colonist had a seat in Parliament, and no American colonist could vote for members of Parliament.

One of the most famous words in the Declaration of Independence is "liberty," the pursuit of which all people should be free to attempt. That idea, that a people should be free to pursue their own course, even to the extent of making their own mistakes, has dominated political thought in the 200-plus years of the American republic.

Representation, the idea that a people can vote—or even replace—their lawmakers, was not a new idea, except in America. Residents of other British colonies did not have these rights, of course, and America was only a colony, according to the conventional wisdom of the British Government at the time. What the Sons of Liberty and other revolutionaries were asking for was to stand on an equal footing with the Mother Country. Along with the idea or representation, comes the idea that key ideas and concepts can be deliberated and discussed, with theoretically everyone having a chance to voice their views. This applied to both lawmakers and to the people who elected them. Lawmakers wouldn't just pass bills that became laws; rather, they would debate the particulars and go back and forth on the strengths and weaknesses of proposed laws before voting on them. Members of both houses of Congress had the opportunity to speak out on the issues, as did the people at large, who could contact their lawmakers and express their views.

This idea ran very much counter to the experience that the Founding Fathers had before the Revolution—that of taxation without representation. The different branches of government were designed to serve as a mechanism of checks and balances on each other so that no one branch could become over powerful. They each have their own specific powers.

Another key concept in the American ideal is **equality**, the idea that every person has the same rights and responsibilities under the law. The Great Britain that the American colonists knew was one of a stratified society, with social classes firmly in place. Not everyone was equal under the law or in the coffers, and it was clear for all to see that the more money and power a person had, the easier it was for that person to avoid things like serving in the army and being charged with a crime. The goal of the Declaration of Independence and the Constitution was to provide equality for all who read those documents. The reality, though, was vastly different for large sectors of society, including women and non-white Americans.

Due process under law was also a big concern of the founders. Various amendments protect the rights of people. Amendments five through eight protect citizens who are accused of crimes and are brought to trial. Every citizen has the right to due process of law (due process as defined earlier being that the government must follow the same fair rules for everyone brought to trial). These rules include the right to a trial by an impartial jury, the right to be defended by a lawyer, and the right to a speedy trial. The last two amendments limit the powers of the federal government to those that are expressly granted in the Constitution; any rights not expressly mentioned in the Constitution, thus, belong to the states or to the people. This feeds into the idea of **opportunity**. The "American Dream" is that every individual has an equal chance to make his or her fortune in a new land and that the United States welcomes and encourages that initiative. The history of the country is filled with stories of people who ventured to America and made their fortunes in the Land of Opportunity. Unfortunately, for anyone who wasn't a white male, that basic opportunity was sometimes a difficult thing to achieve.

Skill 20.2 **Analyze ways in which the evolution of democracy reflects a specific social or historical context.**

A person who lives in a democratic society theoretically has a list of rights guaranteed to him or her by the government. In the United States, this is the Constitution and its Amendments. Among these very important rights are:

- the right to speak out in public;
- the right to pursue any religion;
- the right for a group of people to gather in public for *any* reason that doesn't fall under a national security cloud;
- the right *not* to have soldiers stationed in your home;
- the right *not* to be forced to testify against yourself in a court of law;
- the right to a speedy and public trial by a jury of your peers;
- the right *not* to the victim of cruel and unusual punishment;
- and the right to avoid unreasonable search and seizure of your person, your house, and your vehicle.

The average citizen of an authoritarian country has little, if any, of these rights and must watch his or her words, actions, and even magazine subscriptions and Internet visits in order to avoid *the appearance* of disobeying one of the many oppressive laws that help the government govern its people.

Both the democratic-society and the authoritarian-society citizens can serve in government. They can even run for election and can be voted in by their peers. One large difference exists, however: In an authoritarian society, the members of government will most likely be of the same political party. A country with this setup, like China, will have a government that includes representatives elected by the Chinese people, but all of those elected representatives will belong to the Communist Party, which runs the government and the country. When the voters cast their ballots, only Communist Party members are listed. In fact, in many cases, only one candidate is on the ballot for each office. China, in fact, chooses its head of government through a meeting of the Party leaders. In effect, the Party is higher in the governmental hierarchy than the leader of the country. Efforts to change this governmental structure and practice are discouraged.

On the other side of this spectrum is the citizen of the democratic society, who can vote for whomever he or she wants to and can run for any office he or she wants to. On those ballots will appear names and political parties that run the spectrum, including the Communist Party. Theoretically, *any* political party can get its candidates on ballots locally, statewide, or nationwide; varying degrees of effort have to be put in to do this, of course. Building on the First Amendment freedom to peacefully assemble, American citizens can have political party meetings, fund-raisers, and even conventions without fearing reprisals from the Government.

In a civil society, people are certainly free to pursue both private and public business interests. Private activities are less regulated than public ones, but public activities are not discouraged or dissuaded, as long as they don't violate laws or other people's rights.

In America, and in other countries as well, a person has the right to pursue any kind of business strategy he or she wants. The age of Internet advertising and marketing has created opportunities abound for new and different businesses. Rather than discourage people from starting businesses, the American government and its various associated entities actually encourage such endeavors. Prospective business owners can find whole libraries of information encouraging them and guiding them through the sometimes rigorous practice of starting a business. Entire organizations exist just to answer questions about this process.

America is a land full of groups—religious groups, political groups, social groups, and business and economic groups. All these groups meet in public and in private, and the people who belong to these groups are free to associate with any groups that they choose, again as long as the practices of those groups are not illegal or harmful to other people.

Freedom to practice the faith of your choice finds extraordinary protection under U.S. law. The First Amendment guarantees every American the right to worship as he or she sees fit, without fear of reprisal by the government. Religious organizations, however, do not, for the most part, receive funding from governments to support their efforts. The First Amendment also denies the government the right to establish a religion, meaning that it can favor no one religion over others. Entities like parochial schools, which provide both education and religious training, routinely have to seek funding in places other than the federal or state governments.

Social groups are encouraged as well. The First Amendment gives the American people the right to peaceable assembly. Social organizations are made up of people with similar interests or experiences who come together on a regular basis to discuss those interests and experiences and to pursue a joint appreciation.

Public officials have an overwhelming need to communicate. They want other people to know what they're doing and why. They want to make sure that the voters who elected them know what great jobs they're doing pursuing the agendas that are closest to their hearts. Ultimately, they want to do as much as they can to get themselves re-elected or, if term limits won't allow such re-election, to leaving a memorable public legacy.

In the court of **public opinion**, the newspaper or radio offers politicians a fairly easy way to get noticed. Television began to change all that with its visual record of events. The proliferation of cable and satellite television channels has made it very difficult for a lawmaker *not* to get noticed if her or she does something remarkable these days. The Internet offers a vast, heterogeneous world of opportunities. Internet opportunities include not just news websites, but personal websites and the eponymous blogs, public opinion pieces that may or may not contain factual information, contrasted with the scrutiny that major media outlets, such as newspapers, radio, and television undergo.

Public officials will hire people or an agency to conduct **public relations**, which are efforts intended to make the lawmakers look good in the eyes of their constituents. A public relations person or firm will have as its overreaching goal the happiness of the lawmaker who hired her or them and will gladly write press releases, arrange media events (like tours of schools or soup kitchens), and basically do everything else to keep their employer's name in the public eye in a positive way. This includes making the lawmaker's position on important issues known to the public. Especially controversial issues will be embraced on the other side by lawmakers, and those lawmakers will want their constituents to know how they intend to vote on those issues. It's also a good idea to find out what your constituents think about these issues of the day, since the fastest way to get yourself bad publicity or thrown out at re-election time is to ignore the weight of public opinion.

Skill 20.3   Analyze movements that have influenced the concepts of freedom, diversity, and tolerance.

Civil Rights Movement

The phrase, "Civil Rights Movement," generally refers to the nationwide effort made by black people and those who supported them to gain equal rights to whites and to eliminate segregation. Discussion of this movement is generally understood in terms of the period of the 1950s and 1960s.

The **key people** in the civil rights movement are:

Rosa Parks—A black seamstress from Montgomery, Alabama who, in 1955, refused to give up her seat on the bus to a white man. This event is generally understood as the spark that lit the fire of the Civil Rights Movement. She has been generally regarded as the "mother of the Civil Rights Movement."

Martin Luther King, Jr.—The most prominent member of the Civil Rights Movement. King promoted nonviolent methods of opposition to segregation. The "Letter from Birmingham Jail" explained the purpose of nonviolent action as a way to make people notice injustice. He led the march on Washington in 1963, at which he delivered his "I Have a Dream" speech. He received the 1968 Nobel Prize for Peace.

James Meredith—The first African American to enroll at the University of Mississippi.

Emmett Till—A teenage boy who was murdered in Mississippi while visiting from Chicago. The crime of which he was accused was "whistling at a white woman in a store." He was beaten and murdered, and his body was dumped in a river. His two white abductors were apprehended and tried. They were acquitted by an all-white jury. After the acquittal, they admitted their guilt, but remained free because of double jeopardy laws.

Ralph Abernathy—A major figure in the Civil Rights Movement who succeeded Martin Luther King, Jr. as head of the Southern Christian Leadership Conference

Malcolm X—A political leader and part of the Civil Rights Movement. He was a prominent Black Muslim.

Stokely Carmichael—One of the leaders of the Black Power movement that called for independent development of political and social institutions for blacks. Carmichael called for black pride and maintenance of black culture. He was head of the Student Nonviolent Coordinating Committee.

Key events of the Civil Rights Movement include:

Rosa Parks and the Montgomery Bus Boycott, 1955-56 – After refusing to give up her seat on a bus in Montgomery, Alabama, Parks was arrested, tried, and convicted of disorderly conduct and violating a local ordinance. When word reached the black community, a bus boycott was organized to protest the segregation of blacks and whites on public buses. The boycott lasted 381 days until the ordinance was lifted.

Strategy shift to "direct action," 1955-1965 – This was nonviolent resistance and civil disobedience. This action consisted mostly of bus boycotts, sit-ins, and freedom rides.

The Desegregation of Little Rock, 1957 – Following up on the decision of the Supreme Court in Brown vs. Board of Education, the Arkansas school board voted to integrate the school system. The NAACP chose Arkansas as the place to push integration because it was considered a relatively progressive Southern state. However, the governor called up the National Guard to prevent nine black students from attending Little Rock's Central High School.

Sit-ins – In 1960, students began to stage "sit-ins" at local lunch counters and stores as a means of protesting the refusal of those businesses to desegregate. The first was in Greensboro, NC. This led to a rash of similar campaigns throughout the South. Demonstrators began to protest parks, beaches, theaters, museums, and libraries. When arrested, the protesters made "jail-no-bail" pledges. This called attention to their cause and put the financial burden of providing jail space and food on the cities.

Freedom Rides – Activists traveled by bus throughout the Deep South to desegregate bus terminals (required by federal law). These protesters undertook extremely dangerous protests. Many buses were firebombed, and many protesters were attacked by the KKK and beaten. They were crammed into small, airless jail cells and mistreated in many ways. Key figures in this effort included John Lewis, James Lawson, Diane Nash, Bob Moses, James Bevel, Charles McDew, Bernard Lafayette, Charles Jones, Lonnie King, Julian Bond, Hosea Williams, and Stokely Carmichael.

The Birmingham Campaign, 1963-64 – A campaign was planned to use sit-ins, kneel-ins in churches, and a march to the county building to launch a voter registration campaign. The City obtained an injunction forbidding all such protests. The protesters, including Martin Luther King, Jr., believed the injunction was unconstitutional and defied it. They were arrested. While in jail, King wrote his famous "Letter from Birmingham Jail." When the campaign began to falter, the "Children's Crusade" called students to leave school and join the protests. The events became news when more than 600 students were jailed. The next day, more students joined the protest. The media was present and broadcast to the nation vivid pictures of fire hoses being used to knock down children and dogs attacking some of the children. The resulting public outrage led the Kennedy administration to intervene. About a month later, a committee was formed to end hiring discrimination, arrange for the release of jailed protesters, and establish normative communication between blacks and whites. Four months later, the KKK bombed the Sixteenth Street Baptist Church, killing 4 girls.

The March on Washington, 1963 – This was a march on Washington for jobs and freedom. It was a combined effort of all major civil rights organizations. The goals of the march were: meaningful civil rights laws, a massive federal works program, full and fair employment, decent housing, the right to vote, and adequate integrated education. It was at this march that Martin Luther King, Jr. made the famous "I Have a Dream" speech.

Selma to Montgomery marches, 1965 – Attempts to obtain voter registration in Selma, Alabama had been largely unsuccessful due to opposition from the city's sheriff. M.L. King came to the city to lead a series of marches. He and over 200 demonstrators were arrested and jailed. Each successive march was met with violent resistance by police. In March, a group of over 600 intended to walk from Selma to Montgomery (54 miles). News media were on hand when, 6 blocks into the march, state and local law enforcement officials attacked the marchers with billy clubs, tear gas, rubber tubes wrapped in barbed wire, and bull ships. They were driven back to Selma. National broadcast of the footage provoked a nationwide response. President Johnson again used public sentiment to achieve passage of the Voting Rights Act of 1965. This law changed the political landscape of the South irrevocably.

The **Women's Rights Movement** is concerned with the freedoms of women as differentiated from broader ideas of human rights. These issues are generally different from those that affect men and boys because of biological conditions or social constructs. The rights the movement has sought to protect throughout history include:

- The right to vote
- The right to work
- The right to fair wages
- The right to bodily integrity and autonomy
- The right to own property
- The right to an education
- The right to hold public office
- Marital rights
- Parental rights
- Religious rights
- The right to serve in the military
- The right to enter into legal contracts

Some of the most famous leaders in the women's movement throughout American history are:

- Abigail Adams
- Susan B. Anthony
- Gloria E. Anzaldua
- Betty Friedan
- Olympe de Gouges
- Gloria Steinem
- Harriet Tubman
- Mary Wollstonecraft
- Virginia Woolf
- Germaine Greer

Minority rights encompass two ideas: the first is the normal individual rights of members of ethnic, racial, class, religious, or sexual minorities; the second is the collective rights of minority groups. Various civil rights movements have sought to guarantee that the individual rights of persons are not denied on the basis of being part of a minority group. The effects of these movements may be seen in guarantees of minority representation, affirmative action quotas, etc.

The **disability rights** movement was a successful effort to guarantee access to public buildings and transportation, equal access to education and employment, and equal protection under the law in terms of access to insurance, and other basic rights of American citizens. As a result of these efforts, public buildings and public transportation must be accessible to persons with disabilities, and discrimination in hiring or housing on the basis of disability is also illegal.

A **prisoners' rights** movement has been working for many years to ensure the basic human rights of persons incarcerated for crimes. **Immigrant rights** movements have provided for employment and housing rights, as well as preventing abuse of immigrants through hate crimes. In some states, immigrant rights movements have led to bi-lingual education and public information access. Another group movement to obtain equal rights is the **lesbian, gay, bisexual and transgender** social movement. This movement seeks equal housing, freedom from social and employment discrimination, and equal recognition of relationships under the law.

Skill 20.3 Evaluate movements that have influenced the concepts of freedom, diversity, and tolerance.

See Skill 20.2.

Sample Test: Liberal Studies

1. **In an experiment, the scientist states that he believes a change in the color of a liquid is due to a change of pH. This is an example of _____ .**

   A. observing
   B. inferring
   C. measuring
   D. classifying

2. **When is a hypothesis formed?**

   A. Before the data is taken.
   B. After the data is taken.
   C. After the data is analyzed.
   D. Concurrent with graphing the data.

3. **If one inch equals 2.54 cm, how many mm is in 1.5 feet? (APPROXIMATELY)**

   A. 18 mm
   B. 1800 mm
   C. 460 mm
   D. 4,600 mm

4. **For her first project of the year, a student is designing a science experiment to test the effects of light and water on plant growth. You should recommend that she _____ .**

   A. manipulate the temperature also
   B. manipulate the water pH also
   C. determine the relationship between light and water unrelated to plant growth
   D. omit either water or light as a variable

5. **In an experiment measuring the growth of bacteria at different temperatures, what is the independent variable?**

   A. Number of bacteria
   B. Growth rate of bacteria
   C. Temperature
   D. Size of bacteria

6. **Which is the correct order of methodology?**

   1. collecting data
   2. planning a controlled experiment
   3. drawing a conclusion
   4. hypothesizing a result
   5. re-visiting a hypothesis to answer a question

   A. 1,2,3,4,5
   B. 4,2,1,3,5
   C. 4,5,1,3,2
   D. 1,3,4,5,2

7. A scientist exposes mice to cigarette smoke and notes that their lungs develop tumors. Mice that were not exposed to the smoke do not develop as many tumors. Which of the following conclusions may be drawn from these results?

    I.   Cigarette smoke causes lung tumors.
    II. Cigarette smoke exposure has a positive correlation with lung tumors in mice.
    III. Some mice are predisposed to develop lung tumors.
    IV. Mice are often a good model for humans in scientific research.

    A. I and II only
    B. II only
    C. I , II, and III only
    D. II and IV only

8. The world religion that includes a caste system, is:

    A.   Buddhism
    B.   Hinduism
    C.   Sikhism
    D.   Jainism

9. The following is not a good activity to encourage fifth graders' artistic creativity:

    A. Ask them to make a decorative card for a family member.
    B. Have them work as a team to decorate a large wall display.
    C. Ask them to copy a drawing from a book, with the higher grades being awarded to those students who come closest to the model.
    D. Have each student try to create an outdoor scene with crayons, giving them a choice of scenery.

10. The history of theatre is important. Describe how theatre has evolved over time. Which of the following is not a vital part of the many time periods of theatre history?

    A. Roman theatre
    B. American theatre
    C. Medieval drama
    D. Renaissance theatre

11. In the visual arts, a genre may refer to:

    A. scenes of everyday life
    B. a type of tempra paint
    C. the choice of medium
    D. opera

12. **Classicism in music and literature:**

    A. was designed to appeal to the masse.
    B. originated in the Medieval Period in Europe.
    C. was based on linear perspective.
    D. was formal, quiet, and restrained.

13. **The guiding principle of the Italian Renaissance was:**

    A. Humanis
    B. Manneris
    C. Neoclassicis
    D. Sfumato

14. **Impressionism in art and music was an attempt to:**

    A. capture the transitory aspects of the world.
    B. impress the audience with a photographic-like view of the world.
    C. express heart-felt emotions about nature.
    D. portray the common people in a heroic light.

15. **In the religion of Hinduism, the three aspects of the God-head are:**

    A. Brahma, Vishnu, and Shiva
    B. Nirvana, Vishnu, and Buddha
    C. Veda, Ramayana, and Buddha
    D. Rig-Veda, Rama, and Shiva

16. **The Japanese religion of Zen Buddhism emphasizes:**

    A. belief in reincarnation
    B. adherence to the caste system
    C. ancestor worship
    D. spirituality through meditation

17. **The contribution to Western civilization not associated with Judaism is the:**

    A. belief in ethical treatment of others
    B. belief in polytheism
    C. belief in monotheism
    D. belief in the supremacy of law

18. **The main contribution of Christianity to Western civilization is the:**

    A. advocating of ethical treatment of others
    B. belief in saints
    C. spirituality found in church art and architecture
    D. transmission of Hebraic history

19. **Universal themes are those which:**

    A. explain how the universe was created.
    B. explain the nature of the universe.
    C. can be experienced by all people.
    D. belong to specific groups of people.

20. **Twentieth century themes are marked by:**

    A. practicality
    B. idealism
    C. realism
    D. diversity

21. **The philosophy best associated with Lao-tse is:**

    A. Government should be a strong force in society.
    B. Mankind should live in fear of the gods.
    C. Mankind should live in harmony with nature.
    D. Mankind should strive toward intellectual perfection.

22. **Which one of the following would not be considered a result of World War II?**

    A. Economic depressions and slow resumption of trade financial aid
    B. Western Europe was no longer the center of world power.
    C. The beginnings of new power struggles, not only in Europe, but in Asia as well
    D. Territorial and boundary changes for many nations, especially in Europe

23. **The belief that the United States should control all of North America was called:**

    A. Westward Expansion
    B. Pan Americanism
    C. Manifest Destiny
    D. Nationalism

24. **Of all the major causes of both World Wars I and II, the most significant one is considered to be:**

    A. Extreme nationalism
    B. Military buildup and aggression
    C. Political unrest
    D. Agreements and alliances

25. **Which one of the following was not a reason why the United States went to war with Great Britain in 1812?**

    A. Resentment by Spain over the sale, exploration, and settlement of the Louisiana Territory
    B. The westward movement of farmers because of the need for more land
    C. Canadian fur traders were agitating the Northwestern Indians to fight American Expansion.
    D. Britain continued to seize American ships on the high seas and force American seamen to serve aboard British ships.

26. It can be reasonably stated that the change in the United States from primarily an agricultural country into an industrial power was due to all of the following except:

A. Tariffs on foreign imports
B. Millions of hardworking immigrants
C. An increase in technological developments
D. The change from steam to electricity for powering industrial machinery

27. From about 1870 to 1900, the settlement of America's "last frontier," the West, was completed. One attraction for settlers was free land, but it would have been to no avail without:

A. Better farming methods and technology
B. Surveying to set boundaries
C. Immigrants and others to seek new land
D. The railroad to get them there

28. Historians state that the West helped to speed up the Industrial Revolution. Which one of the following statements was not a reason for this?

A. Food supplies for the ever-increasing urban populations came from farms in the West.
B. A tremendous supply of gold and silver from Western mines provided the capital needed to build industries.
C. Descendants of Western settlers, educated as engineers, geologists, and metallurgists in the East, returned to the West to mine the mineral resources needed for industry.
D. Iron, copper, and other minerals from Western mines were important resources in manufacturing.

29. The post-Civil War years were a time of low public morality, greed, graft, and dishonesty. Which one of the following reasons for this would not be accurate?

A. The war itself because of the money and materials needed to carry on the War
B. The very rapid growth of industry and big business after the War
C. The personal example set by President Grant
D. Unscrupulous heads of large impersonal corporations

30. **After the Civil War, the U.S. adapted an attitude of isolation from foreign affairs. But the turning point marking the beginning of the U.S. becoming a world power was:**

    A. World War I
    B. Expansion of business and trade overseas
    C. The Spanish-American War
    D. The building and financial benefit of the Panama Canal

31. **A number of women worked hard in the first half of the 19th century for women's rights, but decisive gains did not come until after 1850. The earliest accomplishments were in:**

    A. Medicine
    B. Education
    C. Writing
    D. Temperance

32. **Which of the following lists elements usually considered to be responsibilities of citizenship under the American system of government?**

    A. Serving in public office, voluntary government service, military duty
    B. Paying taxes, jury duty, upholding the Constitution
    C. Maintaining a job, giving to charity, turning in fugitives
    D. Quartering of soldiers, bearing arms, government service

33. **Why is the system of government in the United States referred to as a federal system?**

    A. There are different levels of government.
    B. There is one central authority in which all governmental power is vested.
    C. The national government cannot operate without the consent of the governed.
    D. Elections are held at stated periodic times, rather than as called by the head of the government.

34. **Slavery arose in the Southern Colonies partly as a perceived economical way to:**

    A. Increase the owner's wealth through human beings used as a source of exchange
    B. Cultivate large plantations of cotton, tobacco, rice, indigo, and other crops
    C. Provide Africans with humanitarian aid, such as health care, Christianity, and literacy
    D. Keep ships' holds full of cargo on two out of three legs of the "triangular trade" voyage

35. A major quarrel between colonial Americans and the British concerned a series of British Acts of Parliament dealing with:

A. Taxes
B. Slavery
C. Native Americans
D. Shipbuilding

Answer Key: Liberal Studies

1.	B	19.	C.
2.	A	20.	D.
3.	C	21.	C.
4.	D	22.	A
5.	C	23.	C
6.	B	24.	A
7.	B	25.	A
8.	B.	26.	A
9.	C.	27.	D
10.	B.	28.	C
11.	A.	29.	C
12.	D.	30.	C
13.	A.	31.	B
14.	A.	32.	B
15.	A.	33.	A
16.	D.	34.	B
17.	B.	35.	A
18.	A.		

Answers with Rationale: Liberal Studies

1. B. To answer this question, note that the scientist has observed a change in color and has then made a guess as to its reason. This is an example of inferring. The scientist has not measured or classified in this case. Although s/he has observed [the color change], the explanation of this observation is inferring (B).

2. A. A hypothesis is an educated guess, made before undertaking an experiment. The hypothesis is then evaluated based on the observed data. Therefore, the hypothesis must be formed before the data is taken, not during or after the experiment. This is consistent only with answer (A).

3. C. To solve this problem, note that if one inch is 2.54 centimeters, then 1.5 feet (which is 18 inches), must be (18)(2.54) centimeters, i.e., approximately 46 centimeters. Because there are ten millimeters in a centimeter, this is approximately 460 millimeters:

(1.5 ft) (12 in/ft) (2.54 cm/in) (10 mm/cm) = (1.5) (12) (2.54) (10) mm = 457.2 mm

This is consistent only with answer (C).

4. D. As a science teacher for middle-school-aged kids, it is important to reinforce the idea of 'constant' vs. 'variable' in science experiments. At this level, it is wisest to have only one variable examined in each science experiment. (Later, students can hold different variables constant while investigating others.) Therefore, it is counterproductive to add in other variables (answers (A) or (B)). It is also irrelevant to determine the light-water interactions aside (A) from plant growth (C). So the only possible answer is (D).

5. C. To answer this question, recall that the independent variable in an experiment is the entity that is changed by the scientist in order to observe the effects (the dependent variable(s)). In this experiment, temperature is changed in order to measure growth of bacteria, so (C) is the answer. Note that answer (A) is the dependent variable, and neither (B) nor (D) is directly relevant to the question.

6. B. The correct methodology for the scientific method is first to make a meaningful hypothesis (educated guess), and then to plan and execute a controlled experiment to test that hypothesis. Using the data collected in that experiment, the scientist then draws conclusions and attempts to answer the original question related to the hypothesis. This is consistent only with answer (B).

7. B. Although cigarette smoke has been found to cause lung tumors (and many other problems), this particular experiment shows only that there is a positive correlation between smoke exposure and tumor development in these mice. It may be true that some mice are more likely to develop tumors than others, which is why a control group of identical mice should have been used for comparison. Mice are often used to model human reactions, but this is as much due to their low financial and emotional cost as it is due to their being a "good model" for humans. Therefore, the answer must be (B).

8.   B.
9.   C.
10. B.
11. A.
12. D.
13. A.
14. A.
15. A.
16. D.
17. B.
18. A.
19. C.
20. D.
21. C.

22. A. Following World War II, the economy was vibrant and flourished from the stimulant of war and an increased dependence of the world on United States' industries. Therefore, World War II didn't result in economic depressions and slow resumption of trade and financial aid. Western Europe was no longer the center of world power. New power struggles arose in Europe and Asia, and many European nations underwent changing territories and boundaries.

23. C. The belief that the United States should control all of North America was called (B) Manifest Destiny. This idea fueled much of the violence and aggression towards those already occupying the lands, such as the Native Americans. Manifest Destiny was certainly driven by sentiments of (D) nationalism and gave rise to (A) westward expansion.

24. A. Although military buildup and aggression, political unrest, and agreements and alliances were all characteristic of the world climate before and during World War I and World War II, the most significant cause of both wars was extreme nationalism. Nationalism is the idea that the interests and needs of a particular nation are of the utmost and primary importance, above all else. Some nationalist movements could be liberation movements, while others were oppressive regimes, much depends on their degree of nationalism. The nationalism that sparked WWI included a rejection of German, Austro-Hungarian, and Ottoman imperialism by Serbs, Slavs, and others, culminating in the assassination of Archduke Ferdinand by a Serb nationalist in 1914. Following WWI and the Treaty of Versailles, many Germans and others in the Central Alliance Nations who felt malcontent at the concessions and reparations of the treaty started a new form of nationalism. Adolf Hitler and the Nazi regime led this extreme nationalism. Hitler's ideas were an example of extreme, oppressive nationalism combined with political, social and economic scapegoating and was the primary cause of WWII.

25. A. The United States went to war with Great Britain in 1812 for a number of reasons, including the expansion of settlers westward and the need for more land, the agitation of Indians by Canadian fur traders in Eastern Canada, and the continued seizures of American ships by the British on the high seas. Therefore, the only statement given that was not a reason for the War of 1812 was the resentment by Spain over the sale, exploration, and settlement of the Louisiana Territory. In fact, the Spanish continually held more hostility towards the British than towards the United States. The War of 1812 is often considered to be the second American war for independence.

26. A. It can be reasonably stated that the change in the United States from primarily an agricultural country into an industrial power was due to a great degree because of three of the reasons listed above. It was a combination of millions of hard-working immigrants, an increase in technological developments, and the change from steam to electricity for powering industrial machinery. The only reason given that really had little effect was the tariffs on foreign imports.

27. D. From about 1870 to 1900, the settlement for America's "last frontier" in the West was made possible by the building of the railroad. Without the railroad, the settlers never could have traveled such distances in an efficient manner.

28. C. The West helped to speed up the Industrial Revolution in a number of important and significant ways. First, the land yielded crops for the growing urban populations. Second, the gold and silver supplies coming out of the Western mines provided the capital needed to build industries. Also, resources such as iron and copper were extracted from the mines in the West and provided natural resources for manufacturing. The descendants of Western settlers typically didn't become educated and then returned to the West as miners. The miners were typically working class with little or no education.

29. C. The post-Civil War years were a particularly difficult time for the nation, and public morale was especially low. The war had plunged the country into debt and ultimately into a recession by the 1890s. Racism was rampant throughout the South and the North, where freed Blacks were taking jobs for low wages. The rapid growth of industry and big business caused a polarization of rich and poor, workers and owners. Many people moved into the urban centers to find work in the new industrial sector, and jobs were typically low-wage, long hours, and poor working conditions. The heads of large impersonal corporations were arrogant in treating their workers inhumanely and letting morale drop to a record low. The heads of corporations showed their greed and malice towards the workingman by trying to prevent and disband labor unions.

30. C. The turning point marking the beginning of the United States becoming a super power was the Spanish-American War. This was seen as an extension of the Monroe doctrine, calling for United States' dominance in the Western Hemisphere and removal of European powers in the region. The United States' relatively easy defeat of Spain in the Spanish-American War marked the beginning of a continuing era of dominance for the United States. In addition, in the post-Civil War era, Spain was the largest land owner in the Americas. Their easy defeat at the hands of the United States in Cuba, the Philippines, and elsewhere showed the strength of the United States across the globe.

31. B. Although women worked hard in the early nineteenth century to make gains in medicine, writing, and temperance movements, the most prestigious accomplishments of the early women's movement were in the field of education. Women such as Mary Wollstonecraft (1759-1797), Alice Palmer (1855-1902), and, of course, Elizabeth Blackwell (1821-1910), led the way for women, particularly in the area of higher education.

32. B. Only paying taxes, jury duty, and upholding the Constitution are responsibilities of citizens as a result of rights and commitments outlined in the Constitution – for example, the right of citizens to a jury trial in the Sixth and Seventh Amendments and the right of the federal government to collect taxes in Article 1, Section 8. (A) Serving in public office, voluntary government service, military duty and (C) maintaining a job, giving to charity, and turning in fugitives are all highly admirable actions undertaken by many exemplary citizens, but they are considered purely voluntary actions, even when officially recognized and compensated. The United States has none of the compulsory military or civil service requirements of many other countries. (D) The quartering of soldiers is an act, which, according to Amendment III of the Bill of Rights, requires a citizen's consent. Bearing arms is a right guaranteed under Amendment II of the Bill of Rights.

33. A. The United States is composed of fifty states, each responsible for its own affairs but united under a federal government. (B) A centralized system is the opposite of a federal system. (C) That national government cannot operate except with the consent of the governed is a founding principle of American politics. It is not a political system like federalism. A centralized democracy could still be consensual but would not be federal. (D) This is a description of electoral procedure, not a political system like federalism.

34. B. The Southern states, with their smaller populations, were heavily dependent on slave labor as a means of being able to fulfill their role and remain competitive in the greater U.S. economy. (A) When slaves arrived in the South, the vast majority would become permanent fixtures on plantations, intended for work, not as a source of exchange. (C) While some slave owners instructed their slaves in Christianity, provided health care or some level of education, such attention was not their primary reason for owning slaves – a cheap and ready labor force was. (D) Whether or not ships' holds were full on two or three legs of the triangular journey was not the concern of Southerners as the final purchasers of slaves. Such details would have concerned the slave traders.

35. **A.** Acts of Parliament imposing taxes on the colonists always provoked resentment. Because the colonies had no direct representation in Parliament, they felt it unjust that that body should impose taxes on them, with so little knowledge of their very different situation in America and no real concern for the consequences of such taxes. (B) While slavery continued to exist in the colonies long after it had been completely abolished in Britain, it never was a source of serious debate between Britain and the colonies. By the time Britain outlawed slavery in its colonies in 1833, the American Revolution had already taken place, and the United States was free of British control. (C) There was no series of British Acts of Parliament passed concerning Native Americans. (D) Colonial shipbuilding was an industry that received little interference from the British.

SUBAREA VI.   WRITING

COMPETENCY 21.0   PREPARE AN ORGANIZED, DEVELOPED
                   COMPOSITION IN EDITED ENGLISH IN RESPONSE
                   TO INSTRUCTIONS REGARDING CONTENT,
                   PURPOSE, AND AUDIENCE.

Skill 21.1   Demonstrate the ability to prepare a unified and focused piece
              of writing on a given topic using language and style
              appropriate to a specified audience, purpose, and occasion.

❖

Skill 21.2   Demonstrate the ability to take a position on a contemporary,
              social, or political issue and defend that position with
              reasoned arguments and supporting examples.

❖

Skill 21.3   Demonstrate the ability to use effective sentence structure and
              apply the standards of edited English.

❖

Skill 21.4   Demonstrate the ability to spell, capitalize, and punctuate
              according to the standards of edited English.

❖

❋ *For Skills 21.1 - 21.4, see information contained throughout the
   following pages.*

ESSAY GUIDELINES

Even before you select a topic, determine what each prompt is asking you to discuss. This first decision is crucial. If you pick a topic you don't really understand or about which you have little to say, you'll have difficulty developing your essay. So take a few moments to analyze each topic carefully *before* you begin to write.

Topic A: A modern invention that can be considered a wonder of the world

In general, the topic prompts have two parts:
- the *SUBJECT* of the topic and
- an *ASSERTION* about the subject.

The **subject** is *a modern invention*. In this prompt, the word *modern* indicates you should discuss something invented recently, at least in this century. The word *invention* indicates you're to write about something created by humans (not natural phenomena such as mountains or volcanoes). You may discuss an invention that has potential for harm, such as chemical warfare or the atomic bomb; or you may discuss an invention that has the potential for good, such as the computer, DNA testing, television, antibiotics, and so on.

The **assertion** (a statement of point of view) is that *the invention has such powerful or amazing qualities that it should be considered a wonder of the world.* The assertion states your point of view about the subject, and it limits the range for discussion. In other words, you would discuss particular qualities or uses of the invention, not just discuss how it was invented or whether it should have been invented at all.

Note also that this particular topic encourages you to use examples to show the reader that a particular invention is a modern wonder. Some topic prompts lend themselves to essays with an argumentative edge, one in which you take a stand on a particular issue and persuasively prove your point. Here, you undoubtedly could offer examples or illustrations of the many "wonders" and uses of the particular invention you chose.

Be aware that misreading or misinterpreting the topic prompt can lead to serious problems. Papers that do not address the topic occur when one reads too quickly or only half understands the topic. This may happen if you misread or misinterpret words. Misreading can also lead to a paper that addresses only part of the topic prompt rather than the entire topic.

To develop a complete essay, spend a few minutes planning. Jot down your ideas, and quickly sketch an outline. Although you may feel under pressure to begin writing, you will write more effectively if you plan out your major points.

Prewriting

Before actually writing, you'll need to generate content and to develop a writing plan. Three prewriting techniques that can be helpful are:

Brainstorming

When brainstorming, quickly create a list of words and ideas that are connected to the topic. Let your mind roam free to generate as many relevant ideas as possible in a few minutes. For example, on the topic of computers, you may write:

computer—modern invention
types—personal computers, micro-chips in calculators and watches
wonder—acts like an electronic brain
uses—science, medicine, offices, homes, schools
problems—too much reliance; the machines aren't perfect

This list could help you focus on the topic and states the points you could develop in the body paragraphs. The brainstorming list keeps you on track and is well worth the few minutes it takes to jot down the ideas. While you haven't ordered the ideas, seeing them on paper is an important step.

Questioning
Questioning helps you focus as you mentally ask a series of exploratory questions about the topic. You may use the most basic questions: **who, what, where, when, why, and how.**

"**What** is my subject?"
    [computers]

"**What** types of computers are there?"
    [personal computers, micro-chip computers]

"**Why** have computers been a positive invention?"
    [acts like an electronic brain in machinery and equipment; helps solve complex scientific problems]

"**How** have computers been a positive invention?"
    [used to make improvements in:
    • science (space exploration, moon landings)
    • medicine (MRIs, CAT scans, surgical tools, research models)
    • business (PCs, FAX, telephone equipment)
    • education (computer programs for math, languages, science, social studies), and
    • personal use (family budgets, tax programs, healthy diet plans)]

"How can I show that computers are good?"
[citing numerous examples]

"**What** problems do I see with computers?"
[too much reliance; not yet perfect]

"**What** personal experiences would help me develop examples to respond to this topic? [my own experiences using computers]

Of course, you may not have time to write out the questions completely. You might just write the words *who, what, where, why, how* and the major points next to each. An abbreviated list might look as follows:

What — computers/modern wonder/making life better
How — through technological improvements: lasers, calculators, CAT scans, MUs.
Where — in science and space exploration, medicine, schools, offices

In a few moments, your questions should help you to focus on the topic and to generate interesting ideas and points to make in the essay. Later in the writing process, you can look back at the list to be sure you've made the key points you intended.

Clustering

Some visual thinkers find clustering to be an effective prewriting method. When clustering, you draw a box in the center of your paper, and write your topic within that box. Then, you draw lines from the center box ,and connect it to small satellite boxes that contain related ideas. Note the cluster below on computers:

SAMPLE CLUSTER

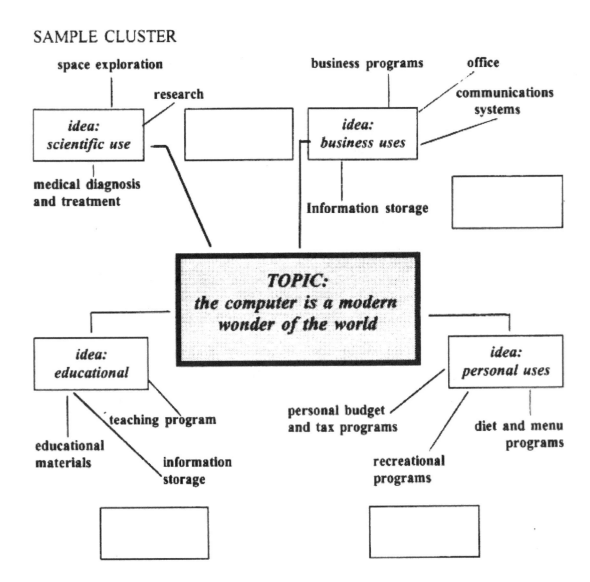

Writing the Thesis

After focusing on the topic and generating your ideas, form your thesis, the controlling idea of your essay. The thesis is your general statement to the reader that expresses your point of view and guides your essay's purpose and scope. The thesis should allow you either to explain your subject or to take an arguable position about it. A strong thesis statement is neither too narrow nor too broad.

Subject and Assertion of the Thesis

From the analysis of the general topic, you saw the topic in terms of its two parts: *subject* and *assertion*. On the exam, your thesis or viewpoint on a particular topic is stated in two important points:

1.   The *SUBJECT* of the paper
2.   The *ASSERTION* about the subject

The **subject of the thesis** relates directly to the topic prompt but expresses the specific area you have chosen to discuss. (Remember, the exam topic will be general and will allow you to choose a particular subject related to the topic.) For example, the computer is one modern invention.

The **assertion of the thesis** is your viewpoint, or opinion, about the subject. The assertion provides the motive or purpose for your essay, and it may be an arguable point or one that explains or illustrates a point of view.

For example, you may present an argument for or against a particular issue. You may contrast two people, objects, or methods to show that one is better than the other. You may analyze a situation in all aspects and make recommendations for improvement. You may assert that a law or policy should be adopted, changed, or abandoned. You may also, as in the computer example, explain to your reader that a situation or condition exists; rather than argue a viewpoint, you would use examples to illustrate your assertion about the essay's subject.

Specifically, the **subject** of Topic A is *the computer*. The **assertion** is that *it is a modern wonder that has improved our lives and that we rely on*. Now you quickly have created a workable thesis in a few moments:

> *The computer is a modern wonder of the world that has improved our lives and that we have come to rely on.*

Guidelines for Writing Thesis Statements

The following guidelines are not a formula for writing thesis statements, but rather are general strategies for making your thesis statement clearer and more effective.

1.   State a *particular point* of *view* about the topic with both a *subject* and an *assertion.* The thesis should give the essay purpose and scope and thus provide the reader with a guide. If the thesis is vague, your essay may be undeveloped because you do not have an idea to assert or a point to explain. Weak thesis statements are often framed as facts, questions, or announcements:

      a.   Avoid a fact statement as a thesis. While a fact statement may provide a subject, it generally does not include a point of view about the subject that provides the basis for an extended discussion. Example: *Recycling saved our community over $10,000 last year.* This fact statement provides a detail, *not* a point of view. Such a detail might be found within an essay, but it does not state a point of view.

      b.   Avoid framing the thesis as a vague question. In many cases, rhetorical questions do not provide a clear point of view for an extended essay. Example: *How do people recycle?* This question neither asserts a point of view nor helpfully guides the reader to understand the essay's purpose and scope.

      c.   Avoid the "announcer" topic sentence that merely states the topic you will discuss. Example: I *will discuss ways to recycle.* This sentence states the subject, but the scope of the essay is only suggested. Again, this statement does not assert a viewpoint that guides the essay's purpose. It merely "announces" that the writer will write about the topic.

2.   Start with a workable thesis. You might revise your thesis as you begin writing and discover your own point of view.

3.   If feasible and appropriate, perhaps state the thesis in multi-point form, expressing the scope of the essay. By stating the points in parallel form, you clearly lay out the essay's plan for the reader.
Example: *To improve the environment, we can recycle our trash, elect politicians who see the environment as a priority, and support lobbying groups who work for environmental protection.*

4.   Because of the exam time limit, place your thesis in the first paragraph to key the reader to the essay's main idea.

Creating a working outline

A good thesis gives structure to your essay and helps focus your thoughts. When forming your thesis, look at your prewriting strategy – clustering, questioning, or brainstorming. Then, decide quickly which two or three major areas you'll discuss. Remember, you must limit *the scope* of the paper because of the time factor.

The **outline** lists those main areas or points as topics for each paragraph. Looking at the prewriting cluster on computers, you might choose several areas in which computers help us, e.g., in science and medicine, business, and education. You might also consider people's reliance on this "wonder" and include at least one paragraph about this reliance. A formal outline for this essay might look like the one below:

I. Introduction and thesis
II. Computers used in science and medicine
II. Computers used in business
IV. Computers used in education
V. People's reliance on computers
VI. Conclusion

Under time pressure, however, you may use a shorter organizational plan, such as abbreviated key words in a list. For example:

1. intro: wonders of the computer -OR-
2. science
3. med
4. schools
5. business
6. conclusion

a. intro: wonders of computers - science
b. in the space industry
c. in medical technology
d. conclusion

Developing the essay

With a working thesis and outline, you can begin writing the essay. The essay should be in three main sections:

1) The **introduction** sets up the essay and leads to the thesis statement.
2) The **body paragraphs** are developed with concrete information leading from the **topic sentences**.
3) The **conclusion** ties the essay together.

Introduction

Put your thesis statement into a clear, coherent opening paragraph. One effective device is to use a funnel approach, in which you begin with a brief description of the broader issue and then move to a clearly-focused, specific thesis statement.

Consider the following introductions to the essay on computers. The length of each is an obvious difference. Read each and consider the other differences:

> Does each introduce the subject generally?
> Does each lead to a stated thesis?
> Does each relate to the topic prompt?

Introduction 1: *Computers are used every day. They have many uses. Some people who use them are workers, teachers, and doctors.*

Analysis: This introduction does give the general topic, computers used every day, but it does not explain what those uses are. This introduction does not offer a point of view in a clearly-stated thesis, nor does it convey the idea that computers are a modern wonder.

Introduction 2: *Computers are used just about everywhere these days. I don't think there's an office around that doesn't use computers, and we use them a lot in all kinds of jobs. Computers are great for making life easier and work better. I don't think we'd get along without the computer.*

Analysis: This introduction gives the general topic about computers and mentions one area that uses computers. The thesis states that people couldn't get along without computers, but it does not state the specific areas the essay discusses. Note, too, the meaning is not helped by vague diction, such as *a lot* or *great.*

Introduction 3: *Each day we either use computers or see them being used around us. We wake to the sound of a digital alarm operated by a micro-chip. Our cars run by computerized machinery. We use computers to help us learn. We receive phone calls and letters transferred from computers across continents. Our astronauts walked on the moon, and returned safely, all because of computer technology. The computer is a wonderful electronic brain that we have come to rely on, and it has changed our world through advances in science, business, and education.*

Analysis: This introduction is the most thorough and fluent because it provides interest in the general topic and offers specific information about computers as a modern wonder. It also leads to a thesis that directs the reader to the scope of the discussion—advances in science, business, and education.

Topic Sentences

Just as the essay must have an overall focus reflected in the thesis statement, each paragraph must also have a central idea reflected in the topic sentence. A good topic sentence also provides transition from the previous paragraph and relates to the essay's thesis. Good topic sentences, therefore, provide unity throughout the essay.

Consider the following potential topic sentences. Be sure that each provides transition and clearly states the subject of the paragraph.

Topic Sentence 1: *Computers are used in science.*

Analysis: This sentence simply states the topic—computers used in science. It does not relate to the thesis or provide transition from the introduction. The reader still does not know how computers are used.

Topic Sentence 2: *Now I will talk about computers used in science.*

Analysis: Like the faulty "announcer" thesis statement, this "announcer" topic sentence is vague and merely names the topic.

Topic Sentence 3: *First, computers used in science have improved our lives.*

Analysis: The transition word *First* helps link the introduction and this paragraph. It adds unity to the essay. It does not, however, give specifics about the improvement computers have made in our lives.

Topic Sentence 4: *First used in scientific research and spaceflights, computers are now used extensively in the diagnosis and treatment of disease.*

Analysis: This sentence is the most thorough and fluent. It provides specific areas that will be discussed in the paragraph and offers more than an announcement of the topic. The writer gives concrete information about the content of the paragraph that will follow.

Summary Guidelines for Writing Topic Sentences
1. Specifically relate the topic to the thesis statement.
2. State clearly and concretely the subject of the paragraph.
3. Provide some transition from the previous paragraph.
4. Avoid topic sentences that are facts, questions, or announcers.

Supporting Details

If you have a good thesis and a good outline, you should be able to construct a complete essay. Your paragraphs should contain concrete, interesting information and supporting details to support your point of view. As often as possible, create images in your reader's mind. Fact statements also add weight to your opinions, especially when you are trying to convince the reader of your viewpoint. Because every good thesis has an assertion, you should offer specifics, facts, data, anecdotes, expert opinions, and other details to *show* or *prove* that assertion. While *you* know what you mean, your *reader* does not. On the exam, you must explain and develop ideas as fully as possible in the time allowed.

In the following paragraph, the sentences in **bold print** provide a skeleton of a paragraph on the benefits of recycling. The sentences in bold are generalizations that by themselves do not explain the need to recycle. The sentences in *italics* add details to SHOW the general points in bold. Notice how the supporting details help you understand the necessity for recycling.

While one day recycling may become mandatory in all states, right now it is voluntary in many communities. *Those of us who participate in recycling are amazed by how much material is recycled.* **For many communities, the blue-box recycling program has had an immediate effect.** *By just recycling glass, aluminum cans, and plastic bottles, we have reduced the volume of disposable trash by one third, thus extending the useful life of local landfills by over a decade. Imagine the difference if those dramatic results were achieved nationwide.* **The amount of reusable items we thoughtlessly dispose of is staggering.** *For example, Americans dispose of enough steel everyday to supply Detroit car manufacturers for three months. Additionally, we dispose of enough aluminum annually to rebuild the nation's airfleet. These statistics, available from the Environmental Protection Agency (EPA), should encourage all of us to watch what we throw away.* **Clearly, recycling in our homes and in our communities directly improves the environment.**

Notice how the author's supporting examples enhance the message of the paragraph and relate to the author's thesis noted above. If you only read the boldface sentences, you have a glimpse at the topic. This paragraph of illustration, however, is developed through numerous details creating specific images: *reduced the volume of disposable trash by one-third; extended the useful life of local landfills by over a decade; enough steel everyday to supply Detroit car manufacturers for three months; enough aluminum to rebuild the nation's airfleet.* If the writer had merely written a few general sentences, as those shown in bold print, you would not fully understand the vast amount of trash involved in recycling or the positive results of current recycling efforts.

End your essay with a brief, straightforward **concluding paragraph** that ties together the essay's content and leaves the reader with a sense of its completion. The conclusion should: reinforce the main points and offer some insight into the topic, provide a sense of unity for the essay by relating it to the thesis, and signal clear closure of the essay.

On the next page is **sample strong response** to the prompt:

A problem people recognize and should do something about

Sample Strong Response

Does the introduction help orient the reader to the topic?

Is there a thesis? Does it clearly state the main idea of the essay?

Time magazine, which typically selects a person of the year, chose Earth as the planet of the year in 1988 to underscore the severe problems facing our planet and therefore us. We hear dismal reports everyday about the water shortage, the ozone depletion, and the obscene volume of trash generated by our society. Because the problem is global, many people feel powerless to help. Fortunately, by being environmentally aware, we can take steps to alter what seems inevitable. We can recycle our trash and support politicians and lobbying groups who will work for laws to protect the environment.

Does each paragraph have a topic sentence that provides transition and defines the idea?

Do the paragraphs purposefully support the thesis? Do they have interesting details and examples?

While one day recycling may be mandatory in all states, right now it is voluntary in many communities. Those of us who participate in recycling are amazed by how much material is recycled. For many communities, the blue box recycling program has had an immediate effect. By just recycling glass, aluminum cans, and plastic bottles, we have reduced the volume of disposable trash by one-third, thus extending the useful life of local landfills by over a decade. Imagine the difference if those dramatic results were achieved nationwide. The amount of reusable items we thoughtlessly dispose of is staggering. For example, Americans dispose of enough steel everyday to supply Detroit car manufacturers for three months. Additionally, we dispose of enough aluminum annually to rebuild the nation's air fleet. These statistics, available from the Environmental Protection Agency (EPA) should encourage us to watch what we throw away. Clearly, recycling in our homes and communities directly improves the environment.

Are the paragraphs unified and coherent? Is the material in each paragraph relevant and important?

Moreover, we must be aware of the political issues involved in environmental protection because, unfortunately, the environmental crisis continues despite policies and laws on the books. Enacted in the 1970s, the federal Clean Water Act was intended to clean up polluted waters throughout the nation and to provide safe drinking water for everyone. However, today, with the Water Act still in place, dangerous medical waste has washed onto public beaches in Florida, and recently several people died from the polluted drinking water in Madison, Wisconsin. Additionally, contradictory government policies often work against resource protection. For example, some state welfare agencies give new mothers money only for disposable, not cloth, diapers. In fact, consumer groups found that cloth diapers are cheaper initially and save money over time as we struggle with the crisis of bulging landfills. Clearly, we need consistent government policies and stiffer laws to ensure mandatory enforcement and heavy fines for polluters. We can do this best by electing politicians who will fight for such laws and by voting out those who won't.

We can also work to save our planet by supporting organizations that lobby for meaningful, enforceable legal changes. Most of us do not have time to write letters, send telegrams, or study every issue concerning the environment. We can join several organizations that act as watchdogs for us all. For example, organizations such as Greenpeace, the Cousteau Society, and the Sierra Club all offer memberships for as low as 15 dollars. By supporting these organizations, we ensure that they have the necessary resources to keep working for all of us and do not have to alter their standards because they must accept funding from special interest groups.

Does the conclusion tie the essay together?

Is the essay edited for grammar and mechanical errors?

Clearly, we all must become environmentally aware. Only through increased awareness can we avoid the tragic consequences of living on a dying planet. We must actively support recycling programs and support those who fight to protect our fragile environment.

Analysis: While not every essay needs to be this thorough in order to pass the exam, this essay shows that with a clear thesis and concept in mind, a writer can produce a literate, interesting piece at one sitting. The introduction creates interest in the general topic and leads to a thesis in the last sentence. The reader has a very clear idea of what will be addressed in the essay, and all body paragraphs have topic sentences that relate to the thesis and provide transition.

The numerous supporting details and examples are presented in a sophisticated style that reads easily and is enhanced by a college-level vocabulary and word choice. Transition words and phrases add unity to sentences and paragraphs. Grammar and mechanics areas are correct, so errors don't detract from the fine writing. For all these reasons, this essay is a polished piece of writing deserving of an upper-range score.

XAMonline, INC. 21 Orient Ave. Melrose, MA 02176

Toll Free number 800-509-4128

TO ORDER Fax 781-662-9268 OR www.XAMonline.com

CERTIFICATION EXAMINATION FOR OKLAHOMA EDUCATORS   - CEOE - 2007

P0#   Store/School:

Address 1:

Address 2 (Ship to other):

City, State Zip

Credit card number_____-_____-_____-_____   expiration_____

EMAIL _____

PHONE   **FAX**

13# ISBN 2007	TITLE	Qty	Retail	Total
978-1-58197-781-3	CEOE OSAT Advanced Mathematics Field 11			
978-1-58197-775-2	CEOE OSAT Art Sample Test Field 02			
978-1-58197-780-6	CEOE OSAT Biological Sciences Field 10			
978-1-58197-776-9	CEOE OSAT Chemistry Field 04			
978-1-58197-778-3	CEOE OSAT Earth Science Field 08			
978-1-58197-794-3	CEOE OSAT Elementary Education Fields 50-51			
978-1-58197-795-0	CEOE OSAT Elementary Education Fields 50-51 Sample Questions			
978-1-58197-777-6	CEOE OSAT English Field 07			
978-1-58197-779-0	CEOE OSAT Family and Consumer Sciences Field 09			
978-1-58197-786-8	CEOE OSAT French Sample Test Field 20			
978-1-58197-798-1	CEOE OGET Oklahoma General Education Test 074			
978-1-58197-792-9	CEOE OSAT Library-Media Specialist Field 38			
978-1-58197-787-5	CEOE OSAT Middle Level English Field 24			
978-1-58197-789-9	CEOE OSAT Middle Level Science Field 26			
978-1-58197-790-5	CEOE OSAT Middle Level Social Studies Field 27			
978-1-58197-788-2	CEOE OSAT Middle Level-Intermediate Mathematics Field 25			
978-1-58197-791-2	CEOE OSAT Mild Moderate Disabilities Field 29			
978-1-58197-782-0	CEOE OSAT Physical Education-Health-Safety Field 12			
978-1-58197-783-7	CEOE OSAT Physics Sample Test Field 14			
978-1-58197-793-6	CEOE OSAT Principal Common Core Field 44			
978-1-58197-796-7	CEOE OPTE Oklahoma Professional Teaching Examination Fields 75-76			
978-1-58197-784-4	CEOE OSAT Reading Specialist Field 15			
978-1-58197-785-1	CEOE OSAT Spanish Field 19			
978-1-58197-797-4	CEOE OSAT U.S. & World History Field 17			
			SUBTOTAL	
FOR PRODUCT PRICES GO TO WWW.XAMONLINE.COM			Ship	$8.25
			TOTAL	